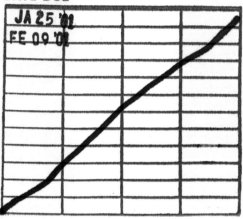

TROUBLED
TEACHERS

TROUBLED TEACHERS

Esther P. Rothman

David McKay Company, Inc.
NEW YORK

Library of Congress Cataloging in Publication Data
Rothman, Esther P
  Troubled teachers.

  1. Classroom management. I. Title.
LB3013.R66   371.1′02   76-54852
ISBN 0-679-50734-5

10 9 8 7 6 5 4 3 2

For Arthur and Amy—again and always—
and to the memory of my mother and father,
Annie Reiner and Max Pomeranz

Contents

Foreword

I became a teacher because I was too cowardly to become anything else. I would have much preferred to be an actress or a journalist, even a saleswoman selling jewelry at Woolworth's, but at age sixteen, even though I could legally have departed from school, I was much too frightened to leave.

At age six, I had much more gumption. I was a truant. I spent first grade with my sister under the rubble of Hell Gate bridge in Queens or in the park adjoining the East River. When the bosomy Mrs. Weeks, the assistant principal, would stalk errant children, we would scatter like cockroaches. Mrs. Weeks never caught us, but the truant officer did, and my sister and I were hauled off to court. My mother, who had no knowledge of our criminal minds, and who indeed had daily packed us off to school, was also summoned. All of us, it seems, had violated the laws of New York State.

My processing had begun! I soon learned that tortured endurance of school was a virtue, that a childhood spent in school was not meant to be a happy one and that education, in order to be profitable, was a serious, doleful and pressured affair.

At age twenty-two, these truths being self-evident, I was fully prepared, qualified and motivated to be a public school teacher.

I succeeded. I was a ghastly teacher and although I convinced myself of my virtue and altruism, looking back at it now, I know that I was a worthy counterpart of Mr. M'Choakumchild,

Dickens's virulent schoolmaster who delighted in acting out his name.

After all, the fault lay with the children; they were mean, they were stupid, they were unmotivated. And I was determined to win—not to win them over, but to win over them. So I went back to college to learn how to conquer the enemy. My victory medal was a master's degree in the education of the handicapped. Somewhere along the way of that master's, however, despite the theory and techniques of educational methodology, I began truly to learn. The children taught me. Within a year, I went back to college for another master's, this time in psychology, and I continued to teach in the public schools—children who were gifted, children who were "adjustment cases," children who were non-English-speaking, children who were disturbed, children who were "all others," our ordinary, human children.

Finally, after seven years of teaching, I landed at the school in Bellevue Psychiatric Hospital, where I taught for nine years. I also got a doctorate in psychology, and later became principal of a special school for angry students.

My book *The Angel Inside Went Sour* grew out of my experiences as principal of the Livingston School for Girls. It tells the story of New York City's most volatile, aggressive and disruptive adolescent girls, who had previously been expelled from the regular schools. It is also my story of learning, and the story of talented teachers who were committed to making the school work.

I wrote *Angel* because I believed in my role. Principal meant principal teacher, and I accepted my mission. The master teacher—the teacher of teachers.

If I sound immodest, it is because I am. I know what I can do well, but I also know what I cannot do. I can teach well. I can write competently, not with the talent for which I crave, but with clarity. I have a great deal I wish to say about children and teachers and teaching.

I became a writer out of compulsion. There is no other valid reason for doing so. I have always written, from my first Christmas poem in second grade to short stories, unpublished novels, many professional articles and two books, *The Disturbed Child* and *Public Education for Disturbed Children in New York City*—both coauthored with Pearl Berkowitz, a very talented teacher and dear friend.

Troubled Teachers grew out of the same matrix. I remember exactly how it began. I was attending a principals' meeting several years ago. The meeting was held in an old elementary school building on Manhattan's Lower East Side. I walked through the main entrance into the inner yard and, as always happens when I enter an old school, the smell and sounds and feel of my own childhood came rushing back.

Two second-grade classes were taking recess. They had formed two circles and were playing a game called Bluebird. It was not a game of my childhood, but it was a game I had taught.

"Bluebird, bluebird, in and out my window," the children sang as they faced each other in their respective circles. "Take a little boy and tap him on the shoulder, take a little boy and tap him on the shoulder, take a little boy . . ." In each circle one little girl was tapping one little boy. Then it would be the boy's turn to tap another girl. It was my favorite recess game. I used to sing off-key and loud. These teachers sang better.

One child sat on a long bench, alone. I noticed her when she suddenly got up to break into one of the charmed chained circles.

"Sally," a long-haired young woman who turned out to be one of the teachers screamed. "Don't you dare play. You are being punished for not studying your arithmetic."

Sally made a face, shrugged one shoulder, laughed and returned to the loneliness of her bench. The children all laughed at her and continued to sing and play.

Sally sang too—from her bench. As if she didn't care. Perhaps she hadn't learned her arithmetic, but I knew for a certainty that what she was learning was how to play the part of a clown. Sally had to survive. This would be her way.

I felt like crying. Nothing seemed to have changed from when I was a child. Oh sure, there was better packaging of the educational merchandise to be sold, but the teachers—the teachers were the same—still doing the same damage by perpetuating the same ignorance.

Didn't that teacher know that no child should be shunned into learning? Couldn't that teacher see that child's pain? Couldn't she reach beyond the outer layers of that child's disdain to see the inner feelings of shame? Couldn't she find another way?

Obviously, she couldn't. At any rate, she didn't. And so I started to write.

Acknowledgments

I am indebted to the thousands of children and their teachers I have known and from whom I have learned. Without them this book obviously could not have been written. I am particularly indebted to the wonderful teachers and students of the Livingston School, of which I am privileged to be principal.

To my own great teachers—Rebecca Wideroff, whom I remember from my Hebrew school days; Wanda Wright, whose death still seems incredible; Florence Halpern; and the late John Rockwell—I shall always be grateful.

For her help in the preparation of this book, I am particularly grateful to Elyse Feldman, who typed and retyped revision after revision at the oddest hours of the day and night, above and beyond the call of friendship. Her comments, suggestions, and questions were important guideposts to me in the development of the book.

I am also extremely grateful to count among my friends Ruth and Sonny Murrain, Arthur Weitzman, Esther Magnus, and Charlie Gray, who read sections of the manuscript and who were always helpful and encouraging. My secretary, Esther Magnus, particularly, put up with all my madness during the writing of the book. I love her dearly.

Adrienne Weil Parks, a dear friend and brilliant newspaper editor, has shared her skills with me. I cannot repay the debt I owe her.

Finally, I wish to thank my daughter, Amy, for her insightful discussions on education and for her patience with me. And to my husband, Arthur, I can only say that he gave me the courage to do many things I did not think I could do. He has been my love and my mentor. His is an incisive and inquiring mind. He always knows the irksome questions that demand to be asked.

TROUBLED
TEACHERS

1

Teachers Need Children More Than Children Need Teachers, or The Art of Self-deception

Teaching has become the art of self-deception. Most teachers have mastered it well. They have convinced themselves of their dedication, altruism, and nobility. Thus, they cover up their true motivations for teaching and live out their delusions in the classroom at the expense of the children.

I have observed the practice of this deception often. As a child, I suffered from it. As an adult, I practiced it. I was taught how to perfect it in college. They called it teacher training.

As teacher, principal, psychologist, part-time college lecturer, and researcher, I have met, talked, and worked with thousands of teachers throughout the country. I have observed hundreds of classes and attended thousands of classes, meetings, seminars, panels, and workshops. And only recently have I begun to realize the full extent of the deceptions behind which many educators hide. They are in the psyches of the vast majority of our teachers—embedded, encrusted, and resolute.

1

Our reasons for becoming teachers are often based on those deceptions. That is why we so often fail.

Teachers come into teaching dewy-eyed and full of ideals. Perhaps years ago, particularly during the depression years, teachers came into teaching less out of idealism and more out of the need for financial security. This is not true today. Other professions pay equally well, if not better, and are equally secure. The young people who are attracted to teaching today are generally motivated by an intellectual conviction. They want to do good. They want to be good. What makes many of them such a potent force for evil is their unawareness of the intellectual and emotional factors that lie behind their conscious motivations to teach.

I watched the evil emerge in the classroom one day when I observed Mrs. Young, a woman of about forty-five. I met her at a conference on special education in Buffalo. When she invited me to spend the day at school with her, I accepted, because she spoke of her children with such fondness and high hopes for their achievement. She was particularly concerned with what she felt was the lack of teaching moral values in the country. She felt very keenly that it was incumbent upon teachers to serve as role models for their students. Mrs. Young talked very convincingly about the need for children to learn about decency, about ethics, about honesty of feelings, and about respect for each other. I agreed with her completely. Children do need to learn the ethics of behavior from adults.

When I watched her in action in her fourth-grade class, I cringed. Her words were beautiful, but her teaching was not reflective of those words. Mrs. Young believed she could teach children the concept of respect without giving that respect to the children she taught. Respect to Mrs. Young meant the ritual of pledging allegiance to the flag each morning. Respect meant choosing one boy and one girl each day to hold the big flag front of the room. Respect meant picking only the cleanest boy and the cleanest girl to hold the big flag in front of the room.

First, she asked for a show of handkerchiefs. The children

held them up for her to see. She magnanimously permitted the substitution of tissues. Second, she asked for a show of hands, palms up. Last, she asked for a show of the left ear, with right arm over head, holding said ear pointed in the teacher's direction so that Mrs. Young could look both fore and aft. Apparently, Mrs. Young assumed that if one ear was clean, so was the other. I suppose she didn't expect a child to be a one-ear washer. But if I were a nine-year-old child in that classroom, I knew I would have been—just to spite her. At nine, I had been an active-passive resister.

I could feel my resistance growing as Mrs. Young walked with firm determination down the aisles, peering at the required part of the body that was currently being exhibited. Suddenly I noted Matilda; her head was tilted down, her hands were trembling slightly. She was neither attractive nor particularly shiny looking. In fact, she seemed drab in her brown cotton dress. Somehow I knew, without knowing how, that there was pain in that child. I leaned over and whispered in her ear. Had she ever been chosen to hold the flag? She shook her head no. It was May. From September to May—that is, for nine months—Matilda had never been deemed attractive enough by her teacher to hold the American flag.

Surges of anger swept over me. It took me back in time to Miss Coolidge's classroom, where I had never been clean enough to hold the flag. Nothing really seemed to have changed in all the years that separated Matilda and me. We were suddenly one.

Inspection over, shoulders arched backward. Heads went skyward, Matilda's highest of all. I could feel myself straining even though I didn't move a muscle. My throat ached as my psychic message went out to Mrs. Young: *Call Matilda.*

She did.

The nondescript face lit up.

The class stood at attention as Matilda and a boy equally chosen for cleanliness marched proudly to the back of the room where the flag was held.

"Take the flag," Mrs. Young ordered. Both children lifted it from its stanchion.

"March forward," Mrs. Young further ordered.

Smiling broadly—I smiled, too—both children held the flag and marched from the back of the room, down the last aisle next to the window, and to the front of the room.

"Face the class," Mrs. Young commanded.

The children faced the class. I almost felt relief flooding me, yet I could not let it come. I experienced an almost sexual sensation of extreme tension, excitement, and fear.

"Salu—" Mrs. Young began to order, and then stopped midway.

I knew . . .

I could hear Miss Coolidge's voice coming at me through the years and classrooms that separated Matilda from me.

"Esther, your shoes are not shined. Sit down."

"Matilda, your elbows are filthy. Go back to your seat."

There was a snicker or two now as there had been then.

We both went back to our seats, to cry inwardly. On Matilda's face there was no expression. I don't know what was showing on mine. I know I have rarely felt such anger. Part of it was directed at myself. I had considered intervening—*but I hadn't*. Why *hadn't* I stopped Mrs. Young? Why had sustaining the image of myself as the well-mannered guest been more important to me than Matilda's pain?

I tried to alleviate my own guilt by talking to Mrs. Young after school. I tried to explain my feelings as a child—Matilda's feelings; I tried to tell Mrs. Young as softly as I could that she must never again so damage a child.

Mrs. Young, however, believed that she had been completely right. A child should be unblemished when she holds the flag. I tried to convince her that the welling emotion of respect has nothing to do with two elbows or two shoes, clean or unclean, and that respect has to be accorded a child in order for that child to learn how to give it, either to an individual or to a country. I tried to point out that respect was more than a mere clicking of imaginary heels in the mind.

"Well, *I* was taught respect," she said coldly. "It didn't hurt *me*."

But of course, something had hurt her. Was she now passing on her pain to Matilda? I talked with her at some length and in depth, and as she talked, I felt her hurt almost as keenly as I had felt mine. It was still sharp, yet interlined with some fuzzy pride.

"I had a teacher once who called me fat in front of the whole class. Now, that was cruel, and he didn't respect my feelings, I suppose. But I tell you, I overcame it. I went on a diet, which I should have done long before that. I *was* too fat. My mother kept trying to get me on a diet and that teacher did it. And so in the long run I guess he was right."

"About what?" I asked.

"I learned something," she insisted tightly, but what she had learned, she couldn't explain.

I suppose she meant she had been taught to overcome hurt, except that she had not really overcome it. I could feel that hurt still in her. She was using the classroom for revenge; she was using the classroom to exorcise her own aggression, to do unto others what had been done to her—all under the guise of teaching Matilda to respect the flag. But she didn't know it.

Mrs. Young is not unique. To pass on her hurt, she needed the children to receive it. She needed them more than they needed her. So do many teachers need the children more than the children need them. The question is why.

Psychoanalyst Erik Erikson approached the explanation when he stated that there are opposites in all our struggles: "Male and Female, Ruler and Rulee, Owner and Owned, Light Skin and Dark." To this dichotomy I would add Teacher and Student, and I would say that many children have failed to learn because many teachers are more concerned with the struggle of assuming and maintaining the "role" of teacher than they are with the learning processes of their students. These teachers have made of themselves the enemy.

Why should it be so?

When I first decided to teach at the Bellevue psychiatric school, after seven years of teaching in the regular schools, my mother asked, "Why do you want to spend your life with crazy people?"

At the time, it seemed like a naive question, but it stuck in my mind nevertheless; and somehow, after thirty years of teaching "crazy" people, not so crazy people, and downright normal people, whatever that means, it still sticks. I am still pondering that question because it seems to go to the heart of teaching. Why did I then and why do I still want to spend the greater part of my life being with other people's children? Why do other adult teachers want to spend their time with children? Why are we not out in the adult world with other adults? Why do we circumscribe ourselves within the confines and boundaries of the school world, which theoretically should be, if in fact it sometimes is not, a child's world? *Why do we imprison ourselves in the world of children?*

Teachers, it seems to me, are essentially no different from prison guards. Our commonality is not that we imprison others but that we imprison ourselves. We become co-victims with our charges—the teachers in the schools, the guards in the prisons. We share the environment with those confined there. And we do so deliberately and voluntarily.

There is no doubt that guards in correctional institutions are as much prisoners of their environment as the prisoners themselves. While they are not criminals, not processed through a court system, not sent against their wills to prison, they nevertheless choose to abide by the same prison routines as those incarcerated. They, of course, have the freedom to leave, and this is an important realistic and psychological difference not to be minimized, but once inside those walls, they are in prison— an environment of despair, frustration, depression, hopelessness, and anger.

The analogy of prison guard to teacher is not as far-fetched as it first may appear. Being in school is compulsory for children, not for teachers. Children are categorized and processed and made to remain in their classes. They are daytime prisoners. If they do not go to school, they are charged with delinquency and are sent to correctional institutions. Thus children are compelled by society to remain in school. But why do teachers? Why, having come of age, do they not join an adult society?

The questions that must be asked of prison guards, if we are to understand their motivations and behavior, should also be asked of teachers. Do guards see themselves in the prisoners they guard? Do they recognize within themselves their own potential for crime? Do teachers see themselves in the children they teach? Do they recognize within themselves the remnants of their own childishness?

Do guards remain in an alien environment to explore, enjoy, and relish their own wickedness, or do they stay to punish themselves for their own hidden desires to be wicked? Do teachers remain in schools to relive and enjoy their own childhood again or to punish themselves and the children before them for their own secret need to be immature and childish? Do both guards and teachers seek in prison and through the classroom a resolution of their own internal conflicts and a gratification of needs that have never been gratified, but should have been?

Are teachers, like guards—in reaction to their own suppressed aggression and their own suppressed needs—dedicating themselves to undo in others what they consider wrong, and to do to others what they consider right? The question is, are teachers, like guards, saints or sadists, idealists or masochists, reformers or conservatives?

It took me a very long time to come to these questions. After thirty years of teaching I am only asking them now. But why weren't these questions asked of me in college? Why aren't they being asked in colleges where teachers are training now? Isn't getting to the heart of this matter part of what colleges are for?

I learned what teaching is from inside me and from the

innards of others. It was painful learning—and it needn't have been. It shouldn't have been. Learning should be exciting and zestful, and if hurt is unavoidably involved, it should not be abruptly inflicted by the teacher, as it often is, but assuaged and molded and made to fit softly by that teacher into the skin, body, shape, and form of the learner—medicinally, therapeutically.

I am now trying to forge some answers to the questions it has taken me so long to formulate. My answers undoubtedly will anger some teachers. It is not my intention to do so. It is my hope that, with learning, insight will replace anger.

I now know that there are two teachers in us all: the outer teacher, who is intellectually and emotionally concerned with children and with teaching, who works, struggles, and often expends great emotion in a process that is called teaching but is not; and the inner teacher, who often scuttles everything the outer teacher is trying to do.

There is a duality in most of living. We can hate the person most whom we love the most. We do our deeds of greatest courage when we are most afraid. There is no one single emotion that exists in isolation or in simplistic purity—not even physical hunger. Emotions are complex. We choose professions out of these complexities. Almost every profession has its stated noble purpose. Underneath the nobility often lies a more human need, one we may even consider ignoble.

It is popular psychological wisdom, for instance, to refer to the brilliant surgeon as one who is meeting his aggressive needs by cutting into flesh. The surgeon and the neighborhood butcher, so the argument goes, are therefore really not dissimilar in the way they choose to gratify their need for aggression. What separates them is money, education, an intervening social structure, and the components of personality that led each to choose his specific path.

There is, of course, no such thing as a single surgeon personality, mother personality, or child personality. Nor is there a single teacher personality. Even the old stereotype of what teachers should look like—prim, bespectacled, starched, and over thirty—has passed into fiction. There is no common teacher appearance. What many teachers do have in common, however, is their need to live out their true feelings of aggression, which they may long have suppressed, and to find expression for their needs for love, youth, and immortality, the full extent of which they may not recognize themselves. In search of who they are, therefore, teachers teach.

I drifted into teaching because I was afraid of doing anything else. I really wanted to be an actress or a newspaper writer, but I was too shy, too inhibited, too frightened to try. I had convinced myself that I was totally unaggressive. I also had persuaded myself that I was not angry at myself for suppressing my aggression. Perhaps if I really had known myself and my own potential for aggression, I would not now be writing this book about teaching, I would now be that actress or journalist.

But I was not then what I am now. The year was 1940—a time when there weren't many professions beckoning to young girls. Certainly my college instructors were not making us aware of them if they did exist, and I most decidedly and definitely did not want to work in my mother's small business—folding shower curtains for commercial packaging, and cleaning used zippers for wholesale resale.

Teaching was safe. It paid well. It was prestigious. Anything was, compared to those zippers.

When I began to teach, however, I also started to learn that teaching offered more than mere personal refuge. I began to discover, too, that there were a multiple of "me's," all of whom I didn't know, and all of whom didn't know what teaching really was and almost didn't care. I survived that first year in the classroom, but I doubt that I taught much.

My second year was much better; at least I cried less. I also changed schools, although I had been asked to stay, and I demoted myself from seventh grade to second grade. In the second grade I began to learn about myself in earnest. I even managed, I think, to learn about children and teach a little.

My primary purpose that year, particularly after the frenzy of my first year of teaching on the junior high school level, panic style, was to show those second-graders that I could handle anything and everything, that I was strong and smart. I wanted them to know I was boss. Not that I didn't love them, I did, passionately. Only I didn't know then that my needs were as compelling as my passion. I needed to be boss. I needed to be boss because I was so afraid of almost everyone around me, other teachers, the principal, the parents—even the sixth-graders who seemed so awesome in the way they swaggered about the school on their way to monitorial duties. Oh, to have had the assurance of those sixth-graders!

When Judith wouldn't stop crying that first day of school after her mother had left her in the classroom, I felt I had to exert my power. The other children, of course, were not really concerned about whether I was powerful or not. They didn't care. But I cared. I had to show them I could make Judith do what I wanted. She needed comfort, but I needed instant obedience. I met my needs, not hers, when I tried to stop her crying by saying loudly and firmly in authoritative teacher style, "Shame on you, a big girl like you."

Judith sobbed herself into eventual silence and conformity. After an irritating moment of personal disquiet, I went back to what I then thought was teaching. Later on in the day, in thinking it over, I decided that I must have been right. After all, Judith had stopped crying and so the end had justified the means. I told myself that I had taught her to act her age.

It didn't take me long to learn how incredibly stupid I had been! Seven is the age for crying. If you can't cry out of emotion and pain at seven, when can you cry? What is so unacceptable, so horrible about crying, anyway?

How hypocritical of me! I had not made her more mature. I had acted out of my own immaturity. By fighting an ignoble battle and beating down a seven-year-old, I had established my authority. What price authority? What was this authority I needed, wanted? How much kinder it would have been if I had held Judith close, soothed her with soft words, given her candy, or simply let her cry a little.

How much wiser, kinder it would have been if I had led her to explore the magic of the classroom—the doll corner, the rocking chair, the paints. That would have been aggressive *teaching*. Instead, *I* became aggressive.

Teaching should not be a series of emotional commands imposed upon children out of personal trauma, bewilderment, or need. Teachers should not demand that children give them instant emotional gratification in the form of obedience. But that is what I had commanded of Judith, all to prove my control over her. In the process of pleasing myself, I had hurt the child.

Yet I was not a conscious villain. Most teachers aren't. What makes villains out of us all is our ignorance of who we really are, what we really need and want. I did not know that I had become a teacher, and that I had inadvertently harmed Judith, because I had the very ordinary and human need to be aggressive, a need I had refused to recognize. If I had been aware of my own need for power, my own feelings of extreme inadequacy when the puny power I had was threatened, and my own need to conquer my inadequacy with a show of strength, I never would have shamed that little girl.

Most young people today are as afraid as I was, but they come to teaching with conscious motivations that are far more exemplary and altruistic than were mine. We live in an era in which it is fashionable to talk a good game of love. Teachers today try to see themselves as dedicated people who teach out of love, nobility, altruism, and commitment. They convince themselves of this concern and then they applaud themselves for having the concern in the first place. They cherish their own humanity. And therein lies the trouble.

Teachers have profound difficulty in dealing with their own humanity because, unfortunately, to them having humanity means possessing only qualities of goodness and compassion. This is an erroneous perception. It is a perception that cripples.

Having humanity merely means belonging to the genus of man, and therefore possessing all the feelings, thoughts, and needs of man and woman. To have humanity merely describes the condition of being human. Being human means thinking, feeling, needing, wanting, even being aggressive.

Aggression is not necessarily bad—it can be a force for good. What teachers do not understand is that there can be no life without aggression. Aggression is movement and movement is life. Even the self is constantly moving. The self is transient even while it is permanent. It consists of the self that was from time past and the self that is in the present. The self changes from one segment of life to another; it also changes in relating from one person to another. No one person is the same person even during the course of a single day. The people one meets, each in turn different, contribute to the making of the self. One is a different person when shopping, making love, teaching, or studying. The self is a thousand selves—always moving as people, time, and perspective change. The self, therefore, even while it maintains a core of permanent personality traits, is also an aggressive self, changing and adapting to each new situation. This is as it should be. One cannot be a principal of a school while cooking dinner at home. How often I have learned that lesson, when my daughter Amy has shouted, "Hey, Ma, come off it, you're not in school now!"

Invariably, she was right. She wanted a mother concerned about rice pudding, not a principal worrying about the struggle to get the school painted in reds and oranges instead of institutional green. Quickly I had to shift emotional gear. This is true of us all. We all shift to meet new situations. If we don't, we're in emotional trouble. We must recognize, therefore, that there is psychological movement as well as physical movement in every daily moment of living. Without psychological movement we would be psychically dead. Without the innate movement of our bodies, the circulation of blood, the neural explosions of our brains, we would be physically dead.

Movement is generated by aggressive impulses. Without

aggression we would be dead. We would not feed ourselves, clothe ourselves, or reproduce. Nor would we feel.

Nevertheless, aggression is a negatively imbued word. It has evil connotations. It is not, however, necessarily evil. Unfortunately, we have been trained into thinking it is. Aggression can be a constructive force as well as a destructive one. An individual can be a scientist or a murderer. Both are aggressive pursuits and demonstrations of personal aggression. Charles Manson was aggressive; so was Madame Curie. One's pursuit was evil; the other's good. It is the individual *pursuit* that may be evil, not the potential *force* inherent in all of us.

Our culture, however, frowns upon the acceptance of aggression or even the recognition of it. Children are taught in all our modern cultures, in all races, in all levels of the social strata, diverse as they may be, that aggression is "bad." They are told to suppress all aggressive impulses, because they don't want to be "bad," do they? A great potential for good is often lost in such suppression, because the positive aspects of aggression are suppressed along with the negative.

Teachers as a group are masters at suppression. They have been suppressed by their own teachers and parents, and they have been trained to suppress themselves. They perpetuate the syndrome by suppressing their students. They demand obeisance and conformity. It seems they have swallowed some half-truths which they have mistakenly gleaned from psychiatry, namely, that they must "tame the wild beast" in themselves and in their students. They interpret the beast to be aggression and sex, and when they see either of these drives in their students, they feel that the students must be molded and bent into a form that they, the teachers—already bent and molded—can accept.

Teachers must learn, however, that there is not a feeling or thought or need or drive that is bad—not even aggressive feelings. They are merely human feelings. They must learn that feelings, needs, desires, thoughts, sensations, are not good or bad, wrong or right, moral or immoral, legal or illegal; that feelings cannot be bad. Neither are there "right" feelings. Feelings just are.

Yet teachers often find it unworthy of themselves to accept the inevitability of their own feelings and needs. They put distance between themselves and their emotions and desires. They do not accept their own humanity, because to do so would make them consciously ashamed.

Many teachers, for instance, cannot admit to ever hating a child. Yet, there is not a person who has taught who at least once hasn't experienced a moment of intense hatred for a particular child. To have experienced such feelings does not make the teacher a lesser person, a "bad" or an inhuman person. The feeling of hatred merely proves that the teacher is a feeling human being. Yet, there are thousands upon thousands of teachers who try to convince themselves that they love all the children they teach, even those children who are completely unlovable.

There are many children who have been so brutalized by their parents or by society that in return they act with brutality in the classroom. Who can love such children *naturally*? We have to teach and train ourselves to carry that burden. Yet there are many teachers who deny that love takes constant work, effort, and self-control. They assume that love comes easily, naturally, and biologically. They assume that teachers love all children as readily as ducks love water.

What a whopping, self-defeating lie!

Teachers tend to talk of love as if to love were easy. It is not. Love requires work, because feelings of hatred, envy, intolerance, and frustration often intervene. These feelings have to be accepted and resolved. Relationships of true love are real only when the participants are able to admit to themselves and to each other the surges of anger and moments of hate that are inherent in love. For instance, who can like, enjoy, or love all children all the time—even our own? There are moments of irritation, annoyance, dislike, and hatred in any long-term relationship, even an adult-child relationship. It is a very rare parent, if one exists at all, who at a time of desperation has not wished fleetingly that a child was unborn. It is a rare teacher who hasn't at one time or another been tempted to slap or hit a child.

Feelings of anger and aggression are human, and the teacher must know they exist. They are not bad feelings, nor does having them make us bad people. What would be bad is the act. To effect the feeling of anger into action, to slap the child, would be an evil act. Slapping children is morally and educationally wrong. All that it does is momentarily relieve the teacher's anger—an anger that is more often than not replaced by guilt. The teacher as well as the child can learn little from this emotional transaction. Both are always damaged by it.

Yet, if the feeling of momentary hatred were accepted, if the teacher said, "Okay, this kid makes me mad," and if the teacher then explored the reason for the anger, he or she would most often find that it has little to do with the child. Most of the time hatred of the child stems from the teacher's *inability to cope with the child's behavior, rather than with the unacceptable behavior itself.* Hatred stems from inadequacy and frustration. Such hatred of a child is often self-hatred. Once the teacher accepts the basis for the hatred, the problem is put into its proper place, and the solution becomes easier. The teacher can begin to deal with the self, as well as with the child, to look into the self as well as into the child. Solutions to difficult classroom situations, particularly with troublesome children, often can be found when the teacher recognizes that part of the solution lies within the teacher and the teacher's own feelings as well as in the behavior of the child.

While I was supervising student teachers in a very good elementary school in a suburban area of New York City, I observed Mary Ann, a six-year-old child whose only purpose in life appeared to be to drive her teacher crazy. Mary Ann was constantly shouting and fighting. Even in play, she bullied the other children and frequently had temper tantrums when the teacher tried to restrain her from hitting another child. Mary

Ann did not listen to Miss Fulton. She did not listen when Miss
Fulton was firm with her. Nor did she listen when Miss Fulton
was lenient with her. Under any conditions, Mary Ann's
behavior was unacceptable in that first-grade classroom, and
Miss Fulton began to hate Mary Ann, not because her behavior
was destructive, but because she could not control her. Miss
Fulton was frustrated at her own inability to control the child,
therefore she was angry at herself.

I liked Miss Fulton. She had the insights to be a really good
teacher, and although my job was to supervise my student
teacher in her classroom, and not Miss Fulton, I found myself
having long conversations with her. One of the results of our
many discussions was Miss Fulton's growing awareness of her
own feelings of powerlessness where Mary Ann was concerned. Only then, when she began to realize that Mary Ann
made her angry at herself, did she begin to deal effectively with
the child, partly by ignoring her in class and partly by giving her
special attention during lunch when she permitted Mary Ann to
eat with her. Mary Ann's inordinate need for attention was met.
Miss Fulton's needs were also met when she recognized that it
was her feelings of impotence that frustrated her, not Mary
Ann's behavior, and that it was not the child with whom she was
angry but herself.

Yet, teachers are not taught to think of their own feelings.
They have been taught to think only of the child. The delusion
that teachers are concerned only with "meeting the needs of the
child" feeds the phony system of altruism that they build. It is
educational brainwashing at its most damaging, because
teachers are conditioned in the schools and colleges they attend
and by society at large to accept their own innate goodness and
to believe that they must have only "good" feelings.

I was speaking at a conference in Milwaukee, Wisconsin,
and, as I usually do when I go to another city, I asked to visit
schools. On one such visit, I met Mr. Wexler, who was teaching
ninth-grade English in a so-called "difficult" school, which

meant a school ghettoed by poverty. Mr. Wexler prided himself on his ability to relate to his children. He especially prided himself on his sophistication.

Yet, the day I visited him, he became extremely angry with a boy who had shouted "motherfucker!" to another boy in the classroom.

Mr. Wexler misinterpreted the direction of the child's remarks.

"Don't you insult my mother," he shouted at the boy.

"I wasn't talkin' to you, Teach," the boy muttered.

"You'd better not be," Mr. Wexler shot back, his face contorted by anger. "Nobody insults my mother."

I wondered why not. Why was Mr. Wexler's mother different from the mother of any other teacher who worked with angry children? What terrible pain was Mr. Wexler bearing so that the gutter language of an upset boy could throw him so easily off balance?

Later, over coffee, we talked about the incident. Mr. Wexler admitted his sensitivity to references about his mother.

"I can't stand that phrase," he admitted with some embarrassment. "I know it's stupid, but it makes me see red."

"But why should a child who doesn't know your mother upset you so?" I asked. "What makes his words so real that you react as if they were real? After all, you don't really fuck your mother, do you?"

I caught him off guard and he began to laugh.

"Well, that's what you become angry about," I explained. "The reference about the relationship between you and your mother. Isn't that right?"

Mr. Wexler immediately denied what I had said, but it was clear that he was uncomfortable with his feelings. He had never verbalized them before, much less faced them. They were not feelings upon which he could place the value of good or bad. The student's words had triggered Mr. Wexler's own conflicts, and in order to smother his feelings, he had dealt less than adequately with the child. Later that day a fight erupted between the same two boys. If Mr. Wexler had intervened at that moment of name-calling instead of only trying to censor his own feelings, perhaps that fight would never have taken place. Unfortunately, Mr. Wexler was trained to believe, as too many of us have been, that our inner feelings, needs, and desires of hatred, anger, envy, and sex are "bad." To have those "bad" feelings makes us "bad" people and above all, we do not want to be "bad." We inhibit, suppress, repress, and deny what conventional wisdom tells us are "bad" feelings, pretend they don't exist, push them back into the sublayers of the unconscious, and try to kill them off.

The trouble is that these feelings, motives, drives, don't remain dead. They seek fulfillment in various and devious ways. Instead of being aired, accepted, understood, and gratified, they are pushed down and back into the area of unawareness, later to emerge distorted and disguised as harmful components of personality, inflicting harm on the self and others. If teachers give way to this process, they become masters at self-deception and teaching becomes the fulfillment of needs, which is in fact a process of self-deception. The deceptions, however, do not make them happy. They are indeed troubled.

In this process there are two victims—the teacher and the child. There is pain in teaching as it is now practiced, for both students and teachers. The unfulfillment of teacher needs, the repressive mechanisms of denial, the self-lies and self-doubts, the illusions, take their terrible toll. Teachers resent and hate themselves because they feel inadequate. They resent and hate their students for making them feel inadequate. Unidentified, unrecognized, and unfulfilled needs lead to tremendous and massive frustration. Frustration carries with it tensions, anxieties, and depression. The teacher's self-concepts become threatened. Something is wrong. Warning signals go up—but what are they warned about? It is intolerable to blame the self, to look inward and find a person one does not know and will not recognize. It is obvious then what the defense must be. Look to the children—find the enemy, focus on the target—fire!

"What's wrong with them?"

"Why won't they listen?"

"Where is the method? There must be a method—"

"Why am I failing—but I'm not failing. It's the children who are failing. There's something wrong with them."

Partial awareness of their internal conflicts and hatreds results in guilt. Teachers do not want to be hating people. Hatred conflicts with their idealized self-image. Feeling weak and vulnerable, suffering from loss of self-esteem, they attempt appraisals. Unfortunately, these most often are surface appraisals, because teacher-training institutions are devoid of self-exploration. They train for the teaching of geography and for "teaching the whole child," a cherished educational cliché. Frankly, I never heard of half a child, but I certainly know many half-teachers. The half that shows is the surface dedication. The hidden half is far from dedicated but very understandably human. This hidden humanity that frightens teachers must be uncovered if education is to change.

Suffering under their repressions, teachers generally are a depressed group of people. This does not mean that they are emotionally disturbed. In the teaching profession there are, of course, emotionally disturbed and mentally ill teachers, because all professions have their share of such people. I am not concerned here, however, with teachers who may be ill. I am concerned with the majority of teachers who have chosen teaching as a career without understanding why they have done so. They are depressed because they are so troubled by their failures and their own mechanisms of deception.

I am also not concerned about teachers who teach only for the money, although they may insist that they do not. They are merely lying. Nor am I concerned about the teachers who work only for the long vacation or a short working day and who are absent on Monday and Friday. These are simply charlatan

teachers, no different from teachers who deliberately raise the reading scores of their children on record cards in order to give the impression they are good teachers.

I once asked a prospective teacher why he wanted to work in my school.

"Because teachers here leave at two-thirty," he said, "and it leaves me so much free time to do other things."

I told him to go home and do other things.

Teachers like these are in the minority. They are what they are. They deceive no one, least of all themselves. Their honesty is unquestionably admirable even if their motives are not. They should not be teachers, certainly not because they are honest but because they don't really care about teaching or children. Let them not teach.

On the other hand, there are thousands of good teachers in this country, teachers who do care about teaching and children. What makes them good is the journey they have made into themselves. They have learned how to accept their own humanity, including what they consider to be their own weaknesses, and they have learned how to differentiate themselves from their students. They have also learned how to use themselves in the classroom as deftly and clearly as they use subject matter. They become the tools by which they teach. Unfortunately, mere thousands aren't enough. Unfortunately, too, other thousands who have the potential to be good have simply given up the struggle to be good.

Yet, there is still hope.

Most teachers can be good teachers, because most people have within them the capacity to find their real selves. What they have not learned is how to find that capacity.

I write of myself as I write of others. I learned very little as a student in school. I learned to read and write at home, and to cheat on arithmetic and geography tests at school. When I began to teach, I began to learn—about myself, about children, even about subject matter. I learned my times tables when I taught fourth grade, and I stopped adding on my fingers when I taught second grade. Sometimes I revert to my original method and still count that way.

I am a part of the system. As much as I abhor it, I am involved in it and I do have an emotional stake in it. Can I look back and say after thirty years of teaching in the school system that it was all a waste? What does it make of me? Can I declare my personal history as a teacher to be ineffectual? Does that make my commitment a lie? I do not know. Certainly, I must have helped one or two children along the way. Just the natural probability of chance leads me to believe I have succeeded with some. But what of those I have failed?

I was once described as compassionate. I was flattered by the word. Now I hate it, because being compassionate sometimes meant that I was simply a coward.

I can be compassionate with a child when I recognize the horrors of that child's life, and I can move with that child toward some reconstruction of a life. My personal beliefs and my training lead me in that direction.

But it was cowardice, not compassion, that prevented me from firing a teacher when I knew that the teacher was a bigot—albeit an unconscious bigot—but a bigot nevertheless.

I knew, for instance, that Mr. Roberts was consciously dedicated to working with the extremely aggressive girls who came to the Livingston School for Girls. I also knew that there were many times when his emotional prejudices broke through his intellectual guard.

"She's very dark skinned," he once said of a student in his class, "but she's pretty."

I asked him what he meant by "but."

There were many such statements. It was clear to me that Mr. Roberts was struggling with himself, trying to overcome his basic prejudices. I told myself that I could feel for his conflicts as I could feel for the conflicts of any child. In defense of my

reluctance to fire anybody, because it is not easy to fire anybody, I took solace from the writings of a social activist, Saul
Alinsky, who said that we must train ourselves to hate a situation or a process, not an individual; that an individual is as much
processed by his own machinations and the system he represents as he is a processor of others; he is to be dealt with kindly
and with understanding.

According to my interpretation of Alinsky, then, I tried to
help that teacher undo his prejudices by endless conversations
centered on his own feelings and values. I may have helped Mr.
Roberts somewhat, although I am inclined to doubt that I did
even that; prejudices are not easily eradicated. There was no
doubt, however, that the children exposed to his subtle prejudices were damaged. Yet, I was reluctant to fire him, under the
guise of "compassion." Instead, I tried in the language of
educators to "work things out."

I now recognize that my therapy of "working it out" was
sheer cowardice, and possibly a prejudice of my own. I also
recognize that I have this terrible messianic fantasy that I
distrust and continually fight, that Saint Esther or Therapist
Rothman will help the teacher to salvation and all will be
salutory in the classroom and in the teacher's life. I, too, am
inclined to self-deception.

In protecting myself from my own particular set of deceptions, I always go back to my childhood for constant reminders
of who I am and what kind of person I want to be—what kind of
person I still struggle to be. I go back to my first day of school. It
was then, although I couldn't possibly have known it, that my
real training to become a teacher began.

I was taken by my mother's hand to a kindergarten class at
P.S. 122, in Queens, New York. I have never forgotten the
child that I was or the chill of the view from the child's side of
the teacher's desk—the imposing assistant principal, the
grimacing children, the strident bells, the adjoining brown
desks linked into a row like one huge snake. I was afraid not

only of my kindergarten teacher but of all the teachers in the school who did not bother to notice that I was special. I was afraid, too, of the alien children who seemed to laugh all the time, and sometimes teased. I was afraid of dying, and afraid that my parents would die.

Looking back, I know now that if I were a child today, it is likely that someone in school, most likely a school psychologist, would diagnose my case as one of school phobia. Possibly so. And while the diagnosis might categorize the reasons for my subsequent truancy in kindergarten and first grade, it could not possibly describe my terror and anguish.

Around the age of eight, I chanced upon a book in our family bookcase, which was made of heavy oak and had glass doors. The books belonged to my father and were written mainly in Hebrew and Yiddish. Other books, the English ones, belonged to my oldest brother, Eli, whom I deeply loved and whose values I tried to absorb emotionally within me. He was thirteen years older than I and he loved to read. I read every book he read, from the works of Gene Stratton Porter to Robert Louis Stevenson to Jack London to the entire Tom Swift series and the adventures of Sherlock Holmes. In school I pretended I couldn't read because I was too afraid to read aloud to the teachers . . . they frightened me. Not admitting my fears, I lied to myself and told myself that I didn't want to be a show-off, that I didn't really want the teachers and the other children to know I could read. Besides, my teachers thought I was dull, and I accepted their verdict. I knew I was dull. What would my reading prove to them, anyway?

One of the sets of books Eli had bought with his own money, which was not easy for him to earn, was entitled *The World's Littlest Books*. There were about six of them, each measuring about two inches high. Eli had sheltered them in a homemade cardboard cradle. In one of the books I found my philosophical home. It was a poem written by James Oppenheim. It went something like this:

After years of living I found myself a lie.
The self I had built up for the world
Did not wear well
And the other self
Came tearing through like a rapier.
Or a blade of burning steel.

My memory may be somewhat faulty and the words may not be entirely accurate, but from the moment I read that poem it shot out at me. I was its target. It struck. At eight.

Perhaps it was then, although I have no conscious memory of such a revelation, that I first became aware that I was already living a lie. Or perhaps, too, it was then that I first became aware of the illusions and lies with which people try to shelter themselves. At any rate, somehow I knew that the poem would guide my life.

That poem is still with me, and now as I conceptualize my pain, the pain of teachers who struggle against themselves, and the pain of children I see daily—the pain of children in school— I know that self-deception is the basis of poor living and poor teaching.

I know that most teachers come to their jobs not lovingly, not as artisans to a craft, but out of other less laudatory motives. Certainly, these teachers do not understand such motives. What they should be they are not—introspective, perfectly clear why they are compelled toward teaching, and aware that underneath their dedication and love there is always aggression and a need for power.

I know that the solutions to our poor education lie mainly within the teacher, not within our institutional systems, for the teacher makes up the system and the system nurtures the teacher. Together, the system and teachers have seen to it that two-thirds of entering college freshmen throughout the nation have reading disabilities, that only 25 to 35 percent of students who graduate from high school have employable skills, and that eight million students have dropped out of high school.

These are hard facts that teachers cannot deny. Therefore, they must try to explain them. The explanation has become their mythology—a defense of themselves and the system.

2

The Mythology of Teaching

Every system develops its own fables. Our educational system and the teachers within it are no exception. The mythology serves to perpetuate the self-delusions upon which poor teaching is unfortunately based and to exonerate teachers from their failures. The mythology starts with a simple statement of faith, which means that the statement need never and can never be proved. Faith is *beyond* proof.

Myth Number One—Teaching Is a Mystique

The process of teaching is complex, mysterious, awesome, wonderful, difficult, heartrending, heartwarming, indefinable, impossible.

To make certain that teaching is indeed impossible, educators proceed to make it uncommunicable, even to each other. Toward this end, they develop their own ritualistic language, which often goes like the following quote from one educational journal:

"A concept seems to be a quorum of properties which, in combination, leads to the assigning of a particular definition. . . . The resultant suggestion is that the concept of 'concept' implies observable behaviors, which are categorized."

26

Educators, like the emperor, are indeed naked, but everyone is afraid to point the finger of honesty. Pleased with their own aura, they parade before the public the most vicious of all myths:

Myth Number Two—It's Never the Teacher's Fault When Children Don't Learn

This myth is a terrible indictment of children. It also serves to absolve educators of any culpability. Its inherent premise is that some children can't learn and some children won't learn. It is always the child's problem when learning does not take place, never the teacher's. Of course, there are moments of teacher self-truth when flashes of insight sometimes strike. There are times when teachers bare their intellectual breasts and blame themselves. These moments are rare, however. When genuine, they are quickly repressed. Sometimes, out of such genuine insight, teachers leave their jobs, or they become what they were meant to be—teachers who can honestly accept their own feelings and who therefore can accept children. But most often, the self-analysis and the self-blame are superficial, and part of the self-denial.

Teachers, for instance, convince themselves that children fail to learn because they are too slow or unmotivated or unruly or disturbed or maladjusted or alienated or culturally deprived or bored—or *something*. Teachers will always find a reason. It doesn't have to be valid or even make sense.

Books are one such reason—too few or too many.

"Do you have books in your home, Mrs. Peters?" asked one first-grade teacher. "You know, some children don't begin to read because they haven't been exposed to books, they don't see books around."

Mrs. Peters looked at her in astonishment.

"I thought Wendy might have told you," Mrs. Peters answered. "My husband is a television writer, and if there's one thing we have too much of in our house, it's books. Wendy has been exposed to a lot of reading. That's why we're concerned, because she should be beginning to read, but she's not.''

''Oh, well, that must explain it then,'' said the teacher. ''You have too many books. Wendy's rebelling against you and therefore resisting reading.''

With this kind of Alice-in-Wonderland reasoning, parents can't win. More important, neither can their children. I sat in on one parent-teacher conference while I was visiting a school in New Jersey.

''Your son resents your working,'' Mrs. Merrill, the teacher, stated in unctuous tones. ''That's why he seems to be having trouble obeying rules in school.''

The parent, Mrs. Clayston, was visibly shaken.

''But I'm not running around having a good time,'' she explained. ''I'm working because I have to work. His father and I are divorced, you know. . . .''

Her words trailed off. The minute Mrs. Clayston had said the word *divorce*, she knew she had given Mrs. Merrill a weapon to use against her son. The fact that her divorce had been amicable, that her son saw his father regularly, and that many mothers worked whether they were divorced or not seemed to be irrelevant to Mrs. Merrill's preconceptions. Mrs. Merrill had heard two words, *divorced* and *working*, and she knew without further question why Jonathan was restless in school. Never for one moment had Mrs. Merrill considered it ironic that she was a working mother herself.

No doubt, there are often home factors that may interfere with a child's ability to function at optimum in school, but to close in on these factors, to determine that they are the *sole* determinants for a child's discomfort, is a dishonest defense. Teachers must stop looking for scapegoats upon which to cast their own inadequacies.

Psychologist Rollo May has said that there are no untreatable patients. Untreatable refers ''not to a state of a patient but to the limitations of an individual psychotherapist's methods.'' I hold the same to be true of children. *There are no unteachable children*, only the professional limitations of teachers, and I do not minimize the savagery of which children are capable when, out of fear of anticipated failure and psychic hurt, they shield themselves with weapons and barriers of impenetrability.

Yet, despite their armor, despite their angers, despite their apparent refusals to learn, *all children want to learn. They want the prestige of learning and the power of knowledge*. They want to think of themselves as students and to be recognized as students.

I have never met a child who did not want to learn, did not want to be smart, did not want to achieve.

I have worked with the go-to-bed-at-nine-and-get-up-at-seven children who go to school early, come home at three, and are in every way "normal" and "good"—the "our" children of the majority—and they want to learn.

I have worked with retarded children, truants, delinquents, disturbed, and neglected children, and each child I have ever known wanted to learn.

I learned this lesson when I was teaching a CRMD class. The initials stand for Children with Retarded Mental Development. It was one of the beginnings of my teaching career.

Willie's IQ was 72 as measured by the school psychologist on a standardized test of intelligence. According to standard psychological theory, therefore, Willie was a moron. He was also black, fifteen, 5 feet 11 inches, 160 pounds, a nonreader, and very, very angry. Only I did not know about his anger because Willie played a fearsome clown.

"Teach," he once told me, "never fight when the weight's on the other side."

It was hardly a moronic remark! Out of self-protection I took his advice. I didn't fight him because he ruled that class. He grimaced, teased, snickered, laughed, pummeled, pushed, jumped, poked, insulted, snorted, fought, and threatened his way through the school day. Not one of those seventeen retarded children was Willie's match. Neither was I. Sporadically, out of benevolence to me, he permitted me to play my role and try to teach.

Then one day, Willie just seemed to crumble. I didn't know why or how it happened, and looking back, I still don't know why or how, but the fighting clown in Willie collapsed. Tears came streaming down his cheeks, books were hurled, desks were overturned, pencils were thrown, glass was broken, and Willie screamed at me, "Teach, don't ya know I *wanta* learn?"

I hadn't. And not knowing it, I had tolerated him as he seemed to be because I had feared him. I had accepted him as he presented himself, rather than finding out that underneath that protective act he really was a deeply troubled boy, crying out to me for help. In the process of my so-called tolerance, I had taught him what he had already suspected, that he was stupid.

Obviously, he was not. Looking back at it now, I know that Willie didn't belong in that class of retarded children. He was there because he had tested retarded. It was not a true test of his basic ability. Willie never let anyone know, not even himself, of what heights he was capable. On the other hand, no one bothered to find out.

I never had a chance to prove to Willie that he could learn, that even if he were intellectually, organically retarded, which he was not, he could learn, because retarded children can and do learn.

Willie left school right after his self-betrayal and never came back. He became one of thousands of names on a register, a name to be discharged automatically at age seventeen—named, untaught, and a burden on my conscience. He is still there.

There is a Willie in us all, a potential learner or a potential failure. Which we become depends largely upon our teachers. There is a drive in us all that impels us toward learning; and even though that drive becomes obfuscated, rusted over, and hidden from view, it is inside us nonetheless. Learning is a condition of health and we all want to be healthy. The drive toward health is innate.

Anthropologist Margaret Mead taught us that a child's function in society is set for him by his culture. Our culture determines that it is a child's work to go to school. It then follows that a successful child must be a successful learner. In other words, the child's business in our adult world is to attend school. Thus, the child's drive toward health is centered upon successful learning. If he learns, he has achieved. Achievement leads to gratification, gratification leads to self-fulfillment, and self-fulfillment to self-esteem and to feelings of *me*-ness. The child establishes his own significance, first to himself, and later to others. He becomes a person who has a defined ego. He has incorporated certain knowledge and skills into his own personality structure and he develops controls over his own emotions and intellect. He knows where he is going in life. He has power.

In our classrooms today, teachers are afraid of that power. They are fearful of children who wish to express themselves freely, who demand the right to make their own determinations, who see education as a partnership between teachers and children rather than as a dictatorship by teachers over children. Teachers therefore try to keep children powerless. It is not hard. The most effective way to keep children powerless is to sell parents the idea that their children are too immature to make correct decisions. Many parents, grappling with their own need to be powerful over their own children, embrace this idea enthusiastically.

"Ma, let me cook the broccoli," my friend Carol's ten-year-old daughter asked one evening when I had been invited to dinner. I had arrived early and was in the kitchen helping with the salad.

"You better not," Carol answered. "It's hard to clean."

"Really, Mother," Ruthie protested, and I knew that whenever Carol was called *Mother*, Ruthie was annoyed. "It's no big decision to decide which leaves go in the pot and which go in the garbage."

Carol and I had to laugh, because Ruthie was right. Carol, like many parents, was infantilizing Ruthie without realizing it.

Parents who help keep their children immature feed into the

power structure of the schools. They make it easier for the teachers to maintain power. Thus, the next most effective way for teachers to keep children powerless is to tell the children themselves that they are incapable of making decisions. Children are taught to believe that they are stupid, and they are never permitted to feel their own strength. They are not taught to see the relationships between action and consequences, to weigh and judge alternative actions. They are not given the opportunity to make decisions for themselves. For instance, children are still taught that old fallacy that they must "think before they speak." They are not taught that speaking very often *is* thinking; that speaking generates and stimulates thought; that speaking, even without preconceived thought, is learning. Following the adage they are taught, children are not even given the choice of deciding whether or not they will speak. They have to ask and then be permitted. If they are not permitted, they do not speak. Yet, what is the worst thing that could happen if they spoke without asking? They would learn that everyone could not be heard. Isn't that an important lesson to learn?

"If you are hungry, you may eat or you may continue to be hungry."

This is a simple fact of everyday life, but we do not make this proposal to children. We do not let them see, learn, feel, understand the mechanism of decision making. We simply tell them *when* to eat, *when* to speak. Yet, the single most important skill we can teach is how to make decisions. Throughout life, the single most important skill we have to exercise many times in the course of a day is to make decisions. Where shall I eat tonight? What work will I do? When will I marry? Or should I marry? Shall I smoke? Should I enlist?

John Dewey, the seminal educator, said that "learning begins at the forked road." It is toward *this* kind of learning that teaching must be geared.

"Makes me no mind," said fourteen-year-old Kim, "if I get arrested, it's gonna happen anyway."

"Yes," I agreed, "if you continue to smash bulbs in the

subway trains and hold the subway doors open so the trains can't start. Sooner or later, you'll get caught and be arrested.''

"Makes me no mind," she repeated.

"Well, if you want to get arrested," I repeated, "then break the law. If you don't want to get arrested, all you have to do is stop. The decision is yours."

"But I'm only playin'," she explained.

"Then you have to decide whether playing is more important to you than not playing," I answered, "because smashing lights in a subway train may be playing to you, but it's also against the law. So decide if it's more important to have fun, break the law, maybe get arrested, or if it's better not to play, not to break the law, and not to get arrested."

At several points in our conversation Kim held on to her thesis that no matter what she did or didn't do, she would be arrested anyway, because life was like that.

"Look, Kim," I said, "do you believe that every policeman in New York City will get up one morning and say, 'Let's arrest Kim today'? "

"Not if I don't do nothin', " she said, "they better not."

"Exactly," I replied. "So whose decision is it if you get arrested?"

"Don't give me none of that old dry talk," she said.

"Well, whose decision is it?" I persisted.

"Mines," she said finally.

At no point did I tell her what to do. My telling wouldn't have helped, anyway. She had to understand for herself the consequences of her behavior. She had to decide for herself the life she wanted.

Kim decided. She began to realize—and realization is learning—that she could be responsible for her own actions. She was the one who walked in her own shoes.

Teaching the decision making process also applies to teaching subject matter. Children must be involved in deciding what they want to learn, when they want to learn it, and if they want to learn it. The teacher's role is to guide, to help children see the potential consequences of their decisions, to show alternatives.

"If you really don't want to learn to be a good reader, June, I can't help you," said Mrs. Gray, the assistant principal at Livingston, "but being a bad reader means people will think you're stupid. But what is more important is that you will *feel* stupid and you might even end up *being* stupid, because then there will be many things you will not know. Is that what you want?"

June didn't want that.

Mrs. Gray then went on to discuss with June what she wanted to read, and when she would read it. At no point did Mrs. Gray insist that she read at all.

How different from the seventh-grade teacher in a very expensive prestigious private school who insisted everyone read *Ivanhoe*.

"But I hate *Ivanhoe*, I loathe *Ivanhoe*, I despise *Ivanhoe*, I shall kill myself if I have to read *Ivanhoe*," lamented Beth. Beth was given to hyperbole.

"Everyone has to read *Ivanhoe*," said her teacher. "After all, this is an advanced class in English. You students are supposed to be superior students."

"Can't I read *Catcher in the Rye* instead?" begged Beth.

The *no* was flat, absolute, deafening.

"*Ivanhoe!*"

What a way to kill the love of reading. Why should the decision of what to read be mandated by the teacher? Why couldn't the teacher suggest to children books they might enjoy? Why couldn't the class discuss different styles of writing, different literary forms? And why did every child have to read the same book? Perhaps, because the teacher had prepared a lesson four years earlier, or fourteen, or twenty-four, and it was convenient? Reading is and should be a personal and private matter. The whole point of reading, in this advanced class, was to open up literature to the children, not to seal the grave.

Naturally, Beth didn't read *Ivanhoe*. She struck it lucky

however, discovered it was being performed on *The Late Show* on TV, and wrote her paper from that, instead.

The teacher, of course, thought Beth had studied the book, especially when Beth's paper on *Ivanhoe* was read as one of the best in the class.

The teacher was smug. "See," she exulted to Beth, "you liked it after all. I was right."

Beth merely smiled. But she knew who had won. She had made her own decision; she had chosen to lie. She had learned, in effect, how to be corrupt and how to get away with it. This is not what teachers should be teaching. If that teacher had permitted Beth to read *Catcher in the Rye*, Beth's paper would have been written out of enjoyment and intellectual conviction, and Beth would have had the satisfaction of deciding for herself what she wanted to enjoy.

Beth's seventh-grade teacher, however, will never know what she really taught Beth. All she will know, if she thinks of it at all, is that children must be told what to read because teachers know what is good for them to read.

Self-determination, self-power for children, is frightening to teachers because they are a dependent group of people, themselves powerless. They do not make their own decisions easily. They were not taught how to do so when they were students. Subjected throughout their own school lives to learning the "correct" or "right" method of approaching or doing a problem, they do not know the skills involved in learning how to make a decision or in teaching how to make a decision. Myth Number Three, therefore, develops.

Myth Number Three—Teachers Know Best

There is one "correct" approach to life. There are no alternatives. Nor should there be. There are "right" answers and "wrong" ones. The right or correct way is the Teacher's Way. Children must be told what to do.

Teachers are for telling, lecturing, showing, proving, ordaining, correcting, and ordering. It is no wonder, then, that teachers have to talk of education as a "process of preparing children *for* living." This is not what education should be. Education should be a process *of* living. Children in the classroom should be able to make real decisions about themselves and their learning. Millions of children roam the streets in this country and all over the world. They are homeless, school-less, and yet they survive by their wits. I am not suggesting that we throw our children in the streets. I am suggesting that we help children to see school as lovingly as they see the street.

Perhaps they love the street so much because they are given a cafeteria style of learning. Everything is displayed so enticingly—mostly their own independence—they can choose what they want. Unfortunately, their choices are often poor and damaging ones. But need they be? Cannot teachers learn from the environment of the streets? Cannot teachers make the school an environment of enticing choices? Cannot children be given the opportunity that is offered in the streets—to live by their minds, that is, to make decisions about what they will learn, about who shall teach them, and about all else that is pertinent to them? In that way, the best of the street values could be brought into school. Education as it now exists has little value for children who love the streets, who love play, who love fun, who love making up their own minds about what they will do.

Teachers, however, do not recognize that education is life. They insist that education should be a preparation for life.

When I first began teaching, in 1943, the Activity Program was the approved method of "preparation." It was conceived of John Dewey's brilliant ideology of education. Dewey was generally right, but we did everything wrong. Let children believe they were learning about banking by collecting milk money, or tell them they were learning about our social system by starting orange-crate post offices and "mailing" letters to each other.

There came into being in those days a lot of teachers who

hoarded a lot of orange crates, and a lot of gimmicky teaching that convinced teachers they were dealing with reality when in fact they were merely deluding themselves that they were teaching. I was one of these orange-crate teachers. When I taught third grade I collected more orange crates than any other single teacher in the school, and I convinced myself that I was successfully teaching "Conversation Skills and Language Arts." We ran a classroom and later a schoolwide post office. I taught the form of a friendly letter as distinct from a business letter, and we licked our homemade stamps and we sent each other notes. Sometimes we contrived situations, like "pretend Johnny is sick so you can write him a get-well card."

"But, Teach, I can tell him on the telephone."

To myself, "Cunning kid." Aloud, "Yes, but let's write a get-well letter, shall we?"

Fake—all of it. But I had fun. I enjoyed it more than the children, because to me it was play. I was playing. To them it wasn't genuine play. They were being used. I was shoving education down their throats and making them pretend it was fun.

Fun and play are essential in a classroom. I didn't know that then—or we would have just flung paint around a little.

"Let's write a letter to your mothers inviting them to open school week."

"Why? I can just tell her."

The Activity Program is in disrepute now, as it should be. Yet, the Society School (everyone, it seems, likes that word *society*) is the bastard offspring that does not acknowledge or recognize its own parent. The Society School attempts to emulate society. Children are given fake money, they are told they have fake purchasing power, and they are sold the notion that they run their school as if it were their country.

This is a totally dishonest idea, because children do not run their own classrooms any more than they run their own country. Yet teachers lie to them and lie to themselves. They let the children pretend they are making their own decisions when in fact it is the teacher who makes the decisions that the children are coerced into following. Teachers have a word for the coercion. They call it motivation. Teachers delude themselves into believing that the children really want to learn what the teachers have been ordered to teach. The fact is, teachers no more make their own decisions about what to teach than do children make their own decisions about what to learn. They just think they do. It seems that teachers and children are at the beck and call of the curriculum makers, or superteachers. After all, superteachers really are the ones who know best.

I watched Mrs. Anderson "motivating" her fifth-grade class to study about Indians, because that's what the superteachers who had set up the curriculum decided she had to teach—and everyone knew that the curriculum was the law of the school. Mrs. Anderson obeyed the law. So did the children. Her motivating lesson therefore became one perfunctory question to which everyone knew the answer before it was ever asked.

"Children, wouldn't you"—not even "would you?"—"wouldn't you like to learn about American Indians this term?"

"Yes, Mrs. Anderson," the children replied in unison.

The sad part of that very sad lesson was that some children obviously meant it. They had been conditioned by the motivations of previous students.

"Oh, wait until you do wigwams," I had heard an Anderson graduate say to an incoming Anderson student, "you'll love wigwams."

But what did wigwams have to do with understanding Indians and their problems *today*? Weren't the children being cheated?

Yet Mrs. Anderson was considered a good teacher. She had lesson plans piled upon lesson plans upon lesson plans. The trouble was they were geared to another time and yesterday's children. Mrs. Anderson had taught fifth grade for as long as anyone could remember. And for as long as she had taught fifth grade, she had taught Indians—the wigwam way. There seemed to be some prestige in studying about Mrs. Anderson's wigwams.

Mrs. Anderson's so-called motivation and Mrs. Anderson's simplistic teaching are reflective of many school systems. Holland, for instance, is a traditional third-grade country. And in the fourth grade, Jamestown was founded in 1607. But what is Jamestown to me or I to Jamestown that I should discover it at this precise time in my life?

The idea that children must be motivated to learn and that teachers know best about what to teach is really an absurd concept. Children want to learn. They want to learn when it is they who decide what it is they want to learn. Teachers, however, kill these yearnings with their spurious motivations.

Last Christmas Elyse Feldman, a teacher at Livingston, and I went to the main branch of the New York Post Office to pick up some letters that children had addressed to Santa Claus, North Pole. The post office personnel save this mail and distribute the letters before Christmas to anyone who wants to play Santa. Elyse always does. She collects letters and invites her friends to a pre-Christmas party, where the price of an invitation is a toy. Toys are matched to letters and there are some surprised children in New York City on Christmas Day.

It's a wonderful idea and I very enthusiastically went to the post office with her. One of the pieces of mail that I picked up was a large, brown manila envelope addressed to Santa Claus at the New York Post Office. I knew that no child had sent it. Obviously it had to be someone more sophisticated. When I looked at the return address, it had the name of a school in Brooklyn. I opened the envelope. In it were thirty-two letters to Santa Claus, all saying exactly the same thing.

Dear Santa:
I am in class 3-2. I do my work and I behave well. I learn math, handwriting and reading. I do my homework. For

Xmas I want ——————. I hope you can give me what
I ask for. Merry Xmas to you.

                              Your friend, ——————

Each child obviously had copied the letter from the blackboard, including the line! Above the line, each child had written
a specific request for a toy, often misspelled. Moreover, each
letter was stapled to the left side of a large sheet of drawing
paper, and on the right side of the paper, each child had drawn a
Christmas tree. The drawings were almost identical. It was
obvious that they, too, were copied. Trees, letters, and teacher
all seemed stunted to me.

Some children copied so poorly that their papers were one
undifferentiated mass of malformed letters. It was clear that
they could not read—much less write.

Some children copied well. It was equally clear that if they
had been given the chance, they could have written more
spontaneous letters on their own.

I suddenly remembered Bobby. He was a seven-year-old in
my second-grade class who wrote his Santa letter in September—to be first on the list. And he didn't even believe in Santa!
He was having a private joke that I was privileged to share with
him. He wanted to write that letter and he made the decision for
himself. Bobby learned the form of a friendly letter, but he
learned it because he had decided he needed to know it. I was
happy to teach it to him.

Remembering Bobby and remembering in his letter his
promise to leave a peanut butter and jelly sandwich and a glass
of milk for Santa at the bottom of the chimney he didn't have, I
almost wept for class 3-2; and in a very un-ho ho ho, un-
Santaish way, I wanted to murder that teacher for murdering
Christmas for those children.

Why did she have the children write to Santa Claus, knowing
it was not likely that the letters would be answered? Why
disappoint the children? Or did she not believe that the children
would be disappointed? Did she know that the children really

did not believe in Santa Claus? If she did, then why have the children write at all? Or, did she believe that she was conditioning the children to reality? "Now children, see, I've proved it—there is no Santa Claus." On the other hand, if the children truly believed and the teacher really wanted Santa to answer, why didn't she play Santa herself?

The point, of course, is that this teacher undoubtedly thought of herself as a good teacher. She was teaching her class the "correct way" to write a letter. The words were "correct." The form was "correct." The drawings were "correct." But she was all wrong.

Teachers have a penchant for correctness, including correctness in behavior. Behavior is viewed as right or wrong, like spelling or an arithmetic problem. There is no recognition of the fact that even spelling changes, as do mathematical concepts. It is possible, for instance, to get two different answers to a mathematical problem following two different routes of reasoning. Yet teachers seem to believe that there is a correct way to respond to every situation. The teacher always knows the correct way to respond to any particular situation and the children must follow. When the children don't obey the correct way—the teachers' way—teachers deem their behavior inappropriate, disorganized, or meaningless. Teachers never seem to understand that there are many routes to travel to a given point, that behavior is never random or unreasonable. There is always a reason behind it; it is merely the teacher-viewer, seeing only the correct solution, to whom the behavior seems unreasonable. To the child, it may be perfectly clear.

"What kind of a bird are you if you can't fly?" chirped the bird.

"What kind of a bird are you if you can't swim?" replied the duck.

Teachers have not learned this lesson from *Peter and the Wolf*; they continue to try to understand the child by developing their own explanatory theories about the child, rather than by viewing the world from the child's own point of view.

A psychiatrist once interviewed a child in my classroom when I taught at Bellevue Psychiatric Hospital.

"Do you ever hear voices when you're alone in a room?" he asked sagely.

"Yes," said the child.

The psychiatrist was pleased. The child obviously had proven to the psychiatrist that his diagnosis of schizophrenia was correct.

The child continued to talk to me after the psychiatrist had left. "When I'm alone in the room and the television is on, I hear voices."

I was tempted to let the psychiatrist choke on his own preconceived and predigested diagnosis, but of course I didn't, and I searched him out to tell him the rest of the conversation.

That psychiatrist never spoke to me again.

Myth Number Four—Children Must Never Be Wiser Than Their Psychiatrists or Teachers

To keep children in their places—that is to say, in their places *below* us—we group them. We group them by achievement, by intelligence, sometimes even by sex. Polarize. Make one group the enemy of the other.

We organize schools as primary or elementary, middle or junior high school, and high school. Depending upon individual educational idiosyncrasies, elementary schools may be inclusive of kindergarten to fourth, sixth, or eighth grade; middle schools may start at grades five or seven; high schools at the seventh, eighth, or tenth grade. And within each group, we subgroup on the basis of age and levels of achievement—as if in this world, we live on our blocks segregated by age and reading scores.

"Sorry, Madam," states the real estate agent, "I can't lease that apartment to you. All the people in that house can read on the eleventh-grade level."

Yet, quite absurdly, children are supposedly preparing for life, instead of living it, by being forced in their classrooms to associate only with people of their own ages and their own achievement levels. A child can become unhealthily inflated when he is placed in a class in which everyone is openly labeled smart. And what about the children who are covertly labeled stupid?

"Hey, Teach, we're the dopes," I was once told as I came to substitute in a class euphemistically called adjustment. "We can't learn nothin'. "

Homogeneous grouping on the basis of achievement isn't healthy or realistic. It is, however, certainly easier for the teacher, because ten or twenty children are fused into the concept of one, and one roundly amorphous child is less trouble than ten sharply differentiated ones.

In one school, the principal was very proud of his reading program, as were all the teachers, because not only were children grouped according to their inability to read, but they were also grouped according to their levels of poor behavior. The entire school used the same basal readers. The reason, according to the principal: "Because the teacher's guide manual is simply written and easy to follow."

Schools are generally run for the convenience of teachers. If they were really run for the learning of children, if schools were really representative of life, as they should be, students of all ages from the very young to the very old would be grouped together within the same school and class environments. Cannot a grandparent learn art alongside and in the same classroom as his grandchild? Why must adult education be separate and distinct from child education? Wide age-range grouping might even manage serendipitously to bring closer understanding between generations.

Teachers won't generally admit, however, that the rationale for homogeneous grouping and subgrouping is really for teacher convenience. Instead, they excuse themselves with such comments as "Children have to keep up with each other," or "It's not fair to keep a whole class waiting for one child to catch up," or "It's not right for the dull child, he'll find it harder than ever."

They completely negate the concept of individualized instruction and individual progress, in which a child need only compete with himself. Why can't a good reader be in the same class with a child poor in reading? The answer is simple: They can be together if teaching is individualized. But no, grouping by age, ability, and grade makes it easier for the teacher. Therefore, faced with group instruction, it is the teachers who decide what is to be taught and when. That is, they don't really decide. It is decided for them by the so-called superteacher curriculum experts, who have given wide circulation to the next myth.

Myth Number Five—Learning Is Sequential

This myth states that learning takes place in developmental and therefore sequential stages. In plain English, it means that educators ritualize learning by insisting that no child can acquire a difficult skill or concept before he has learned the preceding simpler skill or concept. Thus, a child cannot grasp the concept of infinity unless he first knows numbers, a child cannot learn to read hard words before he knows easy ones. Nonsense! Learning is not sequential—learning occurs unpredictably and often, seemingly spontaneously. Frequently, it is a "happening." A child may speak in a simple sentence without first uttering a single word. Similarly, one can learn to type on an electric typewriter without ever using a manual one.

I remember the look of astonishment on the face of one official from the Olympian heights of The Board of Education when I requested electric typewriters.

He insisted that the students first learn on manual ones. "Why?" I argued. "We're teaching these girls office skills.

All offices have electric typewriters now. The simpler skill is obsolete. It's wasted effort and it's useless.''

He wouldn't be convinced until Bill McMahon, a teacher at Livingston, asked him, "If you were teaching your wife to drive, would you teach her on a stick shift?''

We received the electric typewriters—which proves there is hope that educators can learn. The point I am making is that a child learns not on the basis of grasping the simple before the complex but on the basis of what he is interested in learning at the time he is interested in learning it. Whether something is hard or easy is almost irrelevant. *Thus, it is just as important for teachers to learn when to teach as it is what to teach. Timing in education, as in sex, can produce new life.* But to do so, the student must be involved in making the decision about what to learn and how to learn it—and it need not be in English. This brings us to:

Myth Number Six—All Teaching Must Be in English

Instruction should be and must be in English. Immediately, teachers belittle five million children, or a little over 8 percent of our school population, for not speaking English as their native language. The children may speak Spanish or Cree or Navaho or Polish or Italian or Romany or Russian, but they definitely do not speak English.

Think of it—the incredible stupidity and cruelty of it—over three million Spanish-speaking children sitting in front of teachers who literally do not understand them. Is it surprising that the Indian dropout rate is almost 90 percent and that over 90 percent of Indian adults never graduate from elementary school? Is it shocking that the heave-ho rate for Spanish-speaking children is estimated at 85 percent, and that 80 percent of Chicanos never graduate from our schools?

Five million children are being sacrificed to the needs of

teachers who cannot, or who are not willing, or who are not interested in learning the language of the children they teach and who do not teach in that language.

To teach concepts of mathematics in Chinese to Chinese students would be educational heresy, not because Chinese-speaking teachers couldn't be found, but because we must teach in English. To teach Spanish-speaking children to read Spanish would be equally heretical—because teaching in English is the "American way of life" of learning. Knowledge gained through any other language must be suspect. The pernicious thought is perpetuated that if we don't learn in English, we are unpatriotic—certainly un-American—or we are stupid, and probably both.

Like ostriches, we dig our heads deeper in the sand, frustrating ourselves. At best we ignore, at worst damage, our Indian, Mexican, Spanish, and Chinese children and variations upon variations of racial and religious and cultural mixes.

So in most cities, New York is an exception, we continue to teach in English and we apply Band-Aid methods to our bleeding students. In 1967, for instance, the Federal Bilingual Education Act provided financial assistance for bilingual educational programs. The federal guidelines and procedures were so comprehensive, elaborate, and misguiding (it takes a special staff of pedagoguese-speaking professionals to abide by any educational statute) that only eighty-eight thousand pupils nationally were enrolled in bilingual programs for which the federal government stood part of the cost. As educational budgets come and go, even though the statute remains on the books, most of these allotments went. Using lack of federal funds as an excuse, very few communities provided or now provide such programs. If an educational law that is not in the best interests of teachers can be scuttled, it will be scuttled. As it was largely interpreted, therefore, bilingual programs became programs in which non-English-speaking children were not taught mathematics and reading and social history in their *own* languages, but bilingual teachers were hired to teach the children *English*.

Now certainly, I am not averse to teaching English to children. It is, after all, an essential knowledge in our country. I am, however, averse to teaching mathematics and science in English to Navaho- or Chinese- or Spanish-speaking children, whose primary language is not English. Math, after all, is math, is math, is math. It can be taught in Spanish, Italian, or Chinese. English can be introduced as a second language *at the time that the child can absorb a second language*. For some children it will be in the first grade, for other children later on.

English should be taught as a second language to children who do not speak it natively, much as English-speaking children on the border of Mexico should be taught Spanish, and children on the eastern border of Quebec, Canada, should be taught French. American children, however, learning Spanish, don't learn mathematics or science in Spanish. Why shouldn't our Indian children learn basic skills and knowledges in their own language of competency?

But no, as it is now, we insist on English right from the start. In effect, we are telling our non-English-speaking first-, second-, and third-graders that their own language is not acceptable. It is never acceptable, not in elementary schools, not in high schools. We are telling them that the language of their parents is not acceptable. We let them know that both they and their parents are inferior to us. We teach them to be ashamed of themselves and their parents because we are ashamed of their language. We create our own terrible culture conflicts. What price melting pot!

Is it not time we let that pot boil down and out and be charred to the ground? No, we are not meltable! To melt down is to be crippled. Isn't it time that we stopped melting down our children and resculpting them in our image? Isn't that what God forbade—the creation and worship of false idols—ourselves in our children? Yet, we stubbornly cling to the delusion that we are a monolithic society, teaching the monolithic child who turns out to be in our middle-class ideal image—Protestant, white, middle-class suburban.

There is some method to our madness. It is called prejudice. It is a prejudice that is based on economic self-interest. If we enlist minority-group teachers into the teaching ranks, if we permit Indians to teach in the Indian languages and Puerto Rican and Mexican teachers to teach in Spanish, how many thousands of English-speaking teachers will be without jobs? Thousands. Unions and teacher groups are waging battles on just that issue—only they dare not speak the ugly truth of the matter. Instead, they imply that we are lowering our teacher standards if we accept those who speak English with a foreign accent. It is not surprising, then, that in many cities very competent teachers cannot get jobs because they speak with a foreign intonation. I guess those little accents do contaminate! I wonder how they affect those children who attend the United Nations International School in New York City, or in Geneva, where all teachers speak some language other than their own with an accent; or if the students who were subjected to Albert Einstein's accent at Princeton were damaged.

Myth Number Seven—Reading Is the Only Avenue to Learning

Perhaps it used to be that way. It isn't any longer. Or hasn't anyone looked at TV lately? Now, while I certainly approve of reading and think that children should learn to read, I strongly insist that there are avenues to learning other than through the visual system of reading. Blind people learn to read tactually. They also learn orally. We have not begun to tap the oral and tactual ways in which people learn. Assuredly, the way children can rattle off commercials and the way they can remember lyric after lyric of a popular song would indicate that learning is not limited to the visual presentation of material.

Children can and do learn by total experience, by listening, by touching, by play. Adults can and do learn by tapes, by lectures, by pictures, rather than just by words. A new type of cookbook has just been published. It is a tape; the cook follows directions given orally. Is it not conceivable that what we do for the cook we could do for children?

But no. One corrective reading teacher stated, "In my class, if a child is not learning to read as he should I contact the parent and together we squeeze the kid."

Squeezing children even when done out of so-called love, and I doubt that it ever is, hurts children. Yet teachers do it all the time, not always meaning to hurt, but not realizing the consequences of the squeezing. For instance, I talked with one music teacher who was extremely unhappy. She loved music and she wanted to teach it well, but she felt she couldn't, not in the junior high school in which she taught.

"Well, why can't you teach it well?" I asked.

"Because I have too many children, at least fifty in a music appreciation class, and they can't read the text. It causes all kinds of problems."

I could see where it would. Fifty children in a group can't be taught. They can be contained—maybe. I suggested that she accept the idea that she wasn't teaching, only baby sitting, and that the sooner she wanted to teach, the sooner she discuss with her principal the impossibility of teaching under such conditions.

She agreed.

"As for the text," I asked, "why must they read a text? Music is to be listened to, appreciated, sung, discussed, felt. Why must it be read about—particularly when the kids can't read?"

"Because there is some information they should have," she insisted, "even about listening. They should know something about the composers, so they have to read."

"Why can't *you* tell them what you want them to know then?"

"Well, how will they learn to read then?" she asked.

"Are you the reading teacher?" I asked.

She became exasperated. "No, of course not, I teach music, I told you."

"Do you want them to love music?" I asked.

"Of course I do."

"Then don't teach them reading. Teach them music through records, through listening, through singing, through films. Music is a performer's art. Let them hear. Don't take a subject they hate because they are failures in it and make them read about music. Let them feel music. Don't make them hate music because they can't read. Don't keep them rooted to failure so that they'll end up hating both music *and* reading."

I am advocating a very simple idea. Why do teachers find it so hard to understand? A music teacher can teach music without ever using a book. A science teacher can teach science without ever using a book. An art teacher can teach art without ever using a book. Even a reading teacher need not necessarily use a book. Reading can be taught by games and by perceptual training.

Certainly, books should be used if children can read, and certainly it is preferable that children do read, but if children have difficulty in reading, why make them hate other subjects—and ensure their failure in them—by making them read about them? Emphasizing reading very often only increases the gaps in learning. It does not fill them in.

When will we learn to concentrate on children's successes and interests rather than on their failures? Not while reading is oversold as a prerequisite for all learning. Yet, keeping children dependent upon reading as if reading were the only way of learning keeps the money pouring into our schools for remedial reading programs. Teaching becomes holding on to jobs and power by holding on to nonreaders and poor readers. Is this more methodical madness?

Wait—our madness increases.

Reading is not only oversold and overplayed as a prerequisite for learning, but it becomes enthroned as a subject unto itself, separate and distinct from others. Myth Number Eight is born.

Myth Number Eight—Reading Is a Book; Mathematics Is Numbers

This myth states that there is little or no contextual relationship between mathematics and music, psychology and literature, literature and history, art and music, language and science, etc., etc., etc. If relationships are recognized at all, they are tangential. Schools, particularly high schools, plot courses by subject matter, and subject matter must be kept separate at all costs. Content is squared off, boxed, and pigeonholed.

But isn't a rose also a flower?

I observed a third-grade class during recess in the gym. They were marching around in a circle, then hopping, then skipping, responding to the teacher's command. They were getting ready for an assembly presentation. One little boy appeared to be having difficulty differentiating between his right and left foot. The teacher did not take the time to teach him the difference. Instead, the teacher removed the child from the circle so that her teaching demonstration would be flawless. The child, of course, cried.

The ignorance and cruelty of one individual teacher is not so isolated as one would hope.

Later, I talked with that teacher.

"Oh, Paulie," she said, "he's impossible—he can't do anything right—no matter how I try."

I didn't think she had tried very hard, but I didn't tell her that then.

"He's a very poor reader," she confided. "Has a lot of trouble with phonics. Poor child."

I know that pseudosympathetic "poor child" syndrome so well. It always seems to come from inadequate teachers who exploit their supposed compassion with words.

Her compassion, however, had not been for Paulie. He had already learned he was a class misfit. His teacher had taught him that he didn't belong in that magic circle of achievers.

Paulie's teacher, sensing my disapproval, found it necessary to explain her behavior. She reversed her diagnosis of "poor child."

"He's no angel, you know," she said.

I wondered how much of a devil a seven-year-old could be.

I tried to help Paulie.

I suggested to her that she could correlate her physical activity program with reading. I pointed out what optometrists, psychologists, and neurologists already know—that there is a great correlation between body coordination, visual perception, and reading; that is, the better a child is coordinated, the better that child will read.

By the vacant way she looked at me, I knew she was unhearing and uncaring. I also knew that to her, a reader was a pair of eyes (not necessarily focused), buttocks rooted in a seat, and a mechanism for obedience that more than occasionally goes out of whack. She felt it incumbent upon herself to put the whack into place.

I tried again. I told her that she had missed an opportunity to teach Paulie the difference between left and right. After all, we read from left to right, and this kind of discrimination is essential to reading.

"Oh, yes," she finally muttered, as if to get me off her back, "we'll do that in reading."

She had missed my point. The preparatory skills of coordination necessary for reading can take place during recess—in games, in dances, in play. It can take place anywhere. It doesn't even have to be called reading to be reading. But in education, subject matter is discrete, disparate, and separate, and never shall the subjects meet in thought.

Thinking is not often done in school. Obeying is. Yet, despite what education should be, despite the need for us to know how to make effective personal decisions, teachers develop and stress the dogmatism of Myth Number Nine.

Myth Number Nine—"You Have To"

"You have to" is a powerful and favorite stronghold of teachers. There are many themes of "you have to," some major, some minor. They are determined by time, place, and idiosyncratic whim. They are infinite in number.

"You have to show respect."
"You have to be quiet."
"You have to walk in line."
"You have to learn to read."
"You have to attend school."
"You have to be polite."

"You have to learn" is number one of the "you have to's." The fact that teachers say it doesn't make it true. One can decide to be ignorant if one chooses.

"You have to learn to read," I once very stupidly said to a girl in my school, "or you won't be able to get a job."

"Go get a job and test for toilet paper," was the answer I received. "I don't hafta learn and I don't hafta work, honey."

The student was right. No student "has to do" anything. No person "has to do" anything—learn or work. If we have not had the good sense to be born into wealth, we can always apply for government aid. The point is, no, we definitely do not have to work if we choose not to work. People can choose alternatives, drastic as those alternatives may be, including the alternative of the street. In another day and time, such alternatives were heretic if not illegal.

The "have to" period in our culture is over. Revolts are occurring in government, in churches, in schools, in families, and in our styles of living. When before did a sixteen-year-old go to live in an American commune, or a homosexual get married by a minister to another homosexual, or a fourteen-year-old girl receive a legal abortion without consent of parents?

I am not particularly pleased with what is happening in the world today; I do not like what I see, I do not approve of violence or sexual promiscuity. I do not think children—or adults, for that matter—should feel it a necessity to protect themselves with weapons, but whether I like it or not, I do have to accept the fact that these things are happening. We cannot lie to children, offer mealy-mouthed moral treatises, or pretend that young people are not using drugs; that political corruption doesn't exist at high levels of government, that marriage is the only true bond between a man and a woman, or that if one works hard, one will achieve.

We can achieve nefariously as well as legally; our wars are real whether they are legal or not; men and women live together whether or not they are married, and work does not always lead to riches.

There is very little we have to do. Survival is possible without having to do anything but breathe.

Audrey, the girl who suggested I work for the paper industry, was very wise. She didn't have to read to get a job. She might not be able to get a *good* job without the ability to read, but she could get a job. She also told me, "I don't hafta do nothin' but die."

But I, circumscribed as I am by my own inhibitions and the upbringing of a period past, by my own particular set of values, find that particular philosophy very hard to accept.

I struggle with the truth, as I suspect others must struggle with it also, knowing that Audrey was right: We don't have to do anything but die.

In my past struggles, during my first few months of being principal of Livingston, I stupidly wrote the following notice and had it posted in each classroom of the school:

LIVINGSTON SCHOOL FOR GIRLS
29 KING STREET
NEW YORK, N. Y.

EXECUTIVE NOTICE

Post prominently:

The Board of Education regulations state that girls *must follow* their daily programs without exception.

Therefore, no girl is to be permitted to deviate from her daily program.

The official heading and the word *executive*, I felt, would show them I meant business. It did. The girls told me to mind my own.

Learning cannot be mandated.

I am always amused at the shock teachers register when the "have to" approach to learning simply does not work. Children do not learn because teachers say they have to. In fact, the "have to" command draws rebellion. In reaction against the "have to" philosophies of their teachers, many high school students are dropping out, doing nothing, using drugs, running away, or becoming revolutionaries against our value system of society and government. Our "have to's" are lies. The students know it.

When I asked Mr. Graham why he refused permission for Yolanda to come to the art room, he replied, "I told her she couldn't go unless she keeps her appointments with the remedial reading teacher."

"But why?" I persisted. "Yolanda is extremely gifted in art. You told me so yourself."

"That's the point," he answered smugly. "She has to learn to read, and I felt if I didn't let her come to art unless she went to reading, she'd go to reading."

"Instead, she didn't come to school at all," I replied. "She truanted. You see, she didn't have to do what you wanted her to. Yolanda knew that."

"Well, that's the risk," he answered.

"There should be no risk at all," I replied. "You don't deprive a girl of a successful experience in order to make her go to an unsuccessful one, Mr. Graham. You don't deprive a girl of something she likes, and is good at, to make her go to something she is not good at and therefore hates. We must build on strengths, not on weaknesses. With enough success in art, Yolanda might be willing to go to reading. Feeling successful in one subject might give her the ego to tackle something she's not good in. Of one thing I'm certain, you can't face people with their own failures all the time and deprive them of their only chances at success."

The point I was making was that Yolanda knew she did not have to learn to read just because Mr. Graham said so any more than Marivel had to stop cursing just because I said so.

"But Marivel," I explained, and the minute I said it I knew I was wrong, "you can't talk that way in society."

"Who's gonna stop me?" she demanded. "You?"

I admitted I couldn't.

"Well, all right then," Marivel agreed, "only I can stop myself from cursing, right?"

"But Marivel," I said, "we're not helping you if we let you talk that way."

"Why not?" she answered. "When I hurt, I scream. When I'm angry, I curse. That's reality, man. I know cursing won't get me nowhere. I'll stop when I'm ready."

"Well, are you ready now?" I asked.

"Shit—yeah," she laughed.

A visitor to the school who had heard Marivel's string of expletives and who had listened to our exchange was most critical of me.

"You're not helping her if you let her talk that way."

He missed the point entirely. I wasn't letting her talk that way. I could not stop her. Far better that I accept her language and communicate with her than suspend her from school. What would be accomplished then? Aggression should be dealt with and worked with. It cannot always be repressed. Nor should it be.

The "have to" approach in learning, however, is based on suppression. Teachers have not learned that suppression is a very damaging force—far more dangerous than the aggression they so fear. Unfortunately, teachers have not yet learned to explore within themselves their potential for the positive uses of aggression. Instead, they stifle it within themselves and then blame the system for their impotence and frustrations. It is but another mechanism of self-deception.

3

The Power of the System and Self-entrapment

Teachers are both the power and the powerless as it serves their purpose. One of the prime reasons teachers come to teaching, whether they are aware of it or not, is to wield power. What is more powerful than standing in front of a room and presenting the façade of omniscience to children? What is more powerful than being able to demand, and usually get, obedience from a room full of students? What is more powerful than having the right to pass momentous judgments on others, rewarding the learner with the ritual of passing grades, diplomas, awards, and honors, and punishing the nonlearner by failure, unemployability, and, therefore, poverty?

The power of judgment is an awesome power because it is almost absolute. Teachers proclaim who is stupid or smart, who goes to college or drops out, and who, in effect, lives the good or the poor life in America.

Yet, while teachers seek the power of control over children, they are fearful of such power. Their own aggression frightens them, so they deny their aggression and their need for power, and in turn become powerless children themselves. They permit themselves to be entrapped by the system and to be dominated by the powers above them.

One way to assume powerlessness is to blame the failures of the schools on conditions of massive social injustices, political corruption, economic and political inequalities, moral disintegration, and lack of money. All of these factors, of course, play

58

a very important part, and in no way do I mean to minimize them. They must be widely attacked. However, teachers have excused their own failures too long by pointing to the larger failures of society.

The other way to assume powerlessness is to take the opposite stance—to deny the existence of social disequilibrium, poverty, and illness as diseases that occupy those classroom seats as openly as do the children. These teachers who deny the reality of ugliness see their failures only in terms of the children and the schools. They overlook the negative influences of a complex and often unfair society.

Both groups of teachers, those who blame all failure on society, and those who blame only the children and the schools for their failures, victimize themselves through their immobilization. They simply accept the conditions of their failures, and no matter how loud they may cry for educational change, they do not accept their own power to effect change.

Change generates emotional reactions. Change generates feelings. Thus, teachers who fear their own feelings, who have long suppressed or denied those feelings, resent and rebel against change. In this way, they maintain their own emotional status quo and the status quo of the schools.

One of the purposes of education for teachers as well as for children should be to learn *how to feel, how to cope with feelings*, and how to effect change in an imperfect society, as well as how to read and write and calculate. Otherwise, teachers are no more than professional corpses, and the children whom they teach will follow them to their emotional graves.

For both teachers and pupils, education should be a process of looking inward upon the self, with a view toward self-expansion and a commitment toward society. Yet many teachers are too fearful of themselves to make the hegira.

I once sat through a junior high school teachers' meeting in a private school in New York City in which the group decided after much debate that the bombing of black children in a Birmingham church should not be discussed in their school's classes, as some students had proposed, because it would be too upsetting to the majority of students, who were predominantly white, middle class, and educationally privileged.

One impassioned teacher, who dissented and wanted the event discussed by all the children in every classroom, made the point that it had happened, and that it couldn't be denied, much as one wanted to deny it. The rest of the group, however, voted to keep the crime out of the classroom. No discussion!

The fact that all the students knew about it, were horrified by it, and would have benefited by discussing it, was overlooked. The teachers preferred to blot out the sordid reality of the bombing by maintaining the fantasy that education means reading, writing, and arithmetic only. Their blindness stultified them, making them emotionally smaller and psychologically impoverished. What the teachers suppressed and failed to recognize was the emotional necessity for both themselves and the children to discuss, understand, and feel the horror of the situation and, in so doing, to absorb the pain of that particular reality.

The world should not be shut out of the classroom under the guise that it is too upsetting to students, and besides, what can students do about the world, anyway? Perhaps students may not be able to do a thing, I don't know. Yet, I am not at all convinced of their impotence—look at the effective warfare of gangs and the fear they generate in adults. If that organization and energy could be channeled constructively, children might be able to do a great deal. At any rate, teachers who shut the world out also shut themselves in—away from involvement, away from action, away from their own access to power.

It is a provocative phenomenon that while many teachers have an inordinate need for personal power, they do not exercise it *within the power structure of their schools or the system*, where it should and could be a force for good. Instead, they take their silent places within the system, even though they may openly decry that system, and exercise their power only in relation to their entrapped students.

Everything that is bad in education, they may say, is the fault of the system. Yet, they defend their inactivity and sometimes their self-immolation by saying they had no choice, they could do nothing, they had no power. They have not accepted the idea that they cannot become victims unless they are willing to be victims. Our public school systems are not in a totalitarian state, where most of the victims have no choice.

Teachers do have the choice and they can make the choice not to victimize themselves, and thereby not to victimize the children.

I was leading a workshop on reading problems at a national conference for teachers when I met Mr. Laurence. He taught in the Midwest in an elementary school. We were discussing the program at his school over my perennial cup of coffee.

"In our school *every* classroom teacher has reading from nine to ten every morning," Mr. Laurence explained.

"Why?" I asked.

"So the children know how important it is and realize that the whole school emphasizes reading skills. It sets the tone for the importance of reading. At our monthly conferences we discuss our reading methods. There is continuity through the grades because we're all using more or less the same phonic approaches. Anyway, that's the way the principal wants it." Even though he spoke about his school in the most laudatory way, something in the shift of his tone when he spoke about reading made me ask whether this system really worked the way he wanted it to.

"I don't know," he answered, "it sounds right and I guess it works, at least no one says it doesn't, but in my class the poor readers manage to come in later and later each day, and sometimes miss reading altogether."

"Did you ever raise that point with other teachers?" I asked.

"Yes, with some of my friends at the school," he answered. "But you know, it's really a good school and I think our principal is doing a good job. He runs a tight ship."

I have heard teachers use that phrase frequently. It always

annoys me, because I don't think schools should be run like ships, with tightness.

"Tight ship or not," I asked, "can't you ask him what to do about the latecomers?"

"Well, I did, but he seems to believe that they need to be punished, have their parents come in and all that!"

"And you don't?" I asked.

"I don't know," he finally admitted. "I'm confused. How can you punish kids for hating reading when they're not good at it? I hate doing repairs on my house because I'm bad at it, so I guess I know how the kids feel. We're not making them want to read, this way. We're making it a punishment for lots of them. The ones who really want to read will read any time, so what are we gaining by everyone reading at the same time? We're keeping the nonreaders away from school."

"What do you do about the repairs in your house?" I asked. "Do you end up doing them?"

"Not if I can help it," he said, "and that raises other problems with my wife." He laughed ruefully. "Sometimes I hire help. And finally, when I have to, I eventually make do."

"Won't that work with reading too?" I asked. "If they have to, they will." I said it, but I didn't believe it.

"I don't know," he said quietly. "Some will, but many won't, but is that what teaching should be? Can't we *make* them want to?"

"Those are the questions," I said, "that you should raise at your school. Just because your principal sets a policy doesn't make it right. Just because teachers don't question it openly doesn't mean they, too, are not questioning it to themselves. Why don't you raise that question openly at a meeting, or see a few teachers alone, or better still, talk to the principal? The point is, why remain silent?"

"I don't know." He said the words in a tone of surprise at himself. "I guess I'm just used to being a Yo-Yo."

"Must you be?" I asked.

"No." He started to laugh at his sudden awareness of how he

truly felt. "You know something, I really feel it stinks to have an entire school reading at one time. What for? It even makes the teachers tense. We expect the principal to march in at any moment, and what if we're not doing reading and it's five to ten?"

"Does he?" I asked.

"No, he's not that kind of guy, but that isn't even the point—"

I agreed it wasn't.

"There's something wrong," he continued. "Teachers and kids should plan their own time for reading, or for doing anything else for that matter. Maybe if we did more of that, we wouldn't have kids hating reading so much."

I agreed with him wholeheartedly.

"So what about the Yo-Yo?" I asked. "Must you go up and down on a string at someone's whim?"

He left that conference ready for the battle of questions to be asked.

The truth is, that Mr. Laurence, like many teachers both experienced and inexperienced, had not looked hard enough within himself for the power that is there—the power of a question to be asked, *the power of discussion, of dissent, of thinking for oneself.*

In order to use their personal power, teachers must first learn to have the courage to look at themselves and at the inherently powerful forces within them. Second, they must learn to look at their potential for collective power. Third, they have to look at the system itself, because the system assumes an identity, a personality of its own. It becomes a palpable, almost living organism. And like any living organism, it can die.

The organism that is an educational system is part of a larger system. It is part of the political community in which it thrives. The purpose of education in any country, from dictatorship to democracy, is not only to teach skills of literacy to children but to transmit the culture of the country as well. All countries want to preserve and perpetuate their own form of government, no matter what it may be. No government wants a school system to teach revolution. No government wants to be put out of business.

Neither do teachers. They pledge allegiance to the structure. Change may make them obsolete. It is an unspoken fear. The hidden agenda in many schools is therefore to resist change.

A school system is beholden to its governing forces—locally and nationally, politically, economically, socially, and culturally. Teachers are part of the culture they perpetuate; and even while culture, politics, economics, and social conditions may change in an evolutionary sense, the educational system and teachers, by their very function of nurturing the status quo, lag behind their own time, and behind the change. A school system has built into it, by its very structure, a resistance to change— even change that is not geared toward revolution politically, educationally, or culturally. Therein lies the problem. Teachers seem always to dress for yesterday's weather. But the world and the weather are *now*.

Teachers are a nostalgic breed, looking to the time past of their own childhoods, looking for their childhood securities. The system represents that security. It is stable. Teachers know their place in it. They are the middle rung of the ladder. Supervisors, boards of education are above them; children below them. Boards of education control their superintendents, the superintendents control their supervisors, the supervisors control their teachers, and the teachers victimize the children.

When a child cries out and sometimes retaliates with a bad word or an aggressive act, it is the child who is squashed. The total sum of the aggressive energy of every member of that group on that totem pole goes downward. The child is entirely powerless. Even if the child were to turn aggressively upon the teacher, which of course does happen, the teacher has to absorb the attack or retaliate. The teacher cannot afford economically or psychologically to turn the aggression upward and attack the supervisory staff directly.

Economically, aggression personally expressed to a supervisor might result in the loss of a job. Psychologically, the teacher is a product of someone else's need for power and so the hard boot of a supervisor is accepted as part of the system. The teacher is both the suppressed and the suppressor, the victim and the victimizer. Why do teachers remain in this vise? To protest to one's supervisor, to be aggressive to one's supervisor, threatens the teacher's own sense of security. Teachers fear aggression, especially their own, because they have been taught that it is ignoble to be aggressive.

Teachers lie to themselves when they cry out for change, since they refuse to take the first steps toward that change. They only partially explain their inaction when they talk of the need for financial security and job tenure. Certainly, their concerns are real. Teachers require and should have the right to redress a wrong or search for educational justice without the fear of being fired. Yet this is not the prime reason they do not speak out, even when they feel and know they should. The prime reason for their silence is their firm belief in the structures of power, and the structures of power call for allegiance to that power.

Going contrary to the wishes of a supervisor or a system of course bears certain risks, the most important of which is the risk of being fired. A teacher who defies a supervisor or the system must be willing to take that risk.

How brave is brave, however, is an individual assessment. Some teachers have the psychological strength to act in contradiction to a policy or to question that policy. Others have not that strength or maturity. In the last analysis, therefore, a teacher must be able to act upon the principles of decision making, to look at the possible consequences of a decision, to weigh alternatives, and to decide, knowing that some decisions will end in failure. A teacher may decide to defy a supervisor and risk being fired. A teacher may decide to organize a collective action by enlisting the aid of other teachers, thus minimizing the risk of being fired. After all, a principal can't fire an entire department. A teacher may decide to do nothing and have no risk of being fired. If the decision is not to act at all, not to change, not to defy, not to try, not to be able to fail, then the not deciding becomes a decision to let things be. It is a powerful decision. It is rooted in fear. Shaking the power structure shakes the individual's own psychological security and belief in self-power. In giving obedience to the system, therefore, teachers feel that the system owes them obedience in return. This means the children.

There is emotional security in a hierarchy of positions. Teachers feel safe knowing who steps on them and on whom they can step. Change represents instability. They fear it. Thus, no matter how much educators talk reform, they continue to do the same old deeds. Too often, when they want to seem to be doing something new, they simply alter a program cosmetically rather than fundamentally. The word becomes the deed. Call it right, do it wrong, and no one will be the wiser.

For instance, the open classroom concept can be an excellent environment for learning; it merely means that children move from one center of learning to another, easily and at their own need and pace, without waiting for a group, or indeed, without waiting for a mandate from a teacher. Openness refers to the room setting and to the program. Children are not made to conform to the teacher's preordained schedule. It is the teacher, instead, who follows the child. Naturally, the teacher must know each child well. The teacher must help the child choose alternatives, make decisions, guide the child into meaningful areas of work.

The open classroom is a good program for most children. It gives them the opportunity to learn to make decisions. That is the way it should be. It is not the way it generally is.

In one New York City elementary school, for instance, teachers chose splendid isolation and remained in the classroom while they shoved children into the corridors with the instructions to go and learn. The children, of course, did no such thing. They roamed and screamed and banged and fought. The teachers sighed and called the program a failure. It wasn't the program, however, that was at fault. They were. They had completely abdicated their roles as teachers by refusing to point the way to learning. Certainly, they did nothing to teach children the skills of decision making.

Teachers look to many panaceas. If the open classroom doesn't work, they try small classes, as if smallness with a rotten teacher is any better than bigness with a rotten teacher. In fact, often it is worse. A child with thirty-five other children in a classroom can often become somewhat lost, particularly in a high school. With twenty children, that child is more visible and more stigmatized. The teacher gives "more attention." The fact is that the child may not need "more" of the same decay but a whole new way of educational life.

When smallness alone does not work, carpets are put on those classroom floors to dull the noise, as if noise were not a healthy condition of play and learning, and a requisite most times for a healthy classroom environment. When carpets do not work, team teaching is discovered, and rediscovered, and when there are teams there are coordinators of those teams, and when there are coordinators there are endless meetings, not after school, heaven forbid, but on school time, of course. There are planned meetings, evaluation meetings, reevaluation meetings, review meetings, task force meetings, and preparation-for-pre-sentation-of-reports meetings. Naturally, the children that the teams should be teaching are shunted into someone else's classroom, often for something vaguely called enrichment.

What enrichment is often depends on which art or music teacher is available that particular period on that particular day to do the "enriching," which really translates into merely covering the class.

One art teacher whose turn it was to cover a group of children she really didn't know and had never taught asked each child in the first seat of each row to draw a line on a sheet of drawing paper. She then asked that the child pass the paper to the child behind, who added a line to the first line. Thus, each child in a row passed the paper to a child behind and each child added a line. The last child in each row held up the completed design, to be met by varying levels of indifference on the part of most of the children.

The teacher called it the add-a-line game. And it was just that—a game to occupy time, a game that had no relevance. Hit-and-run teaching.

Is this kind of teaching really enriching the lives of children? And even more important, shouldn't art and music be relevant essentials of education rather than superfluities known as enrichment? Shouldn't all education be enriching? Isn't it a woeful commentary on the inadequacies of our educators, our times, and our society that the definition of education as the process of "nourishing and nurturing," which is the process of enriching, is now obsolete? As it is now, art, music, and drama are of secondary significance in our schools. They should not be. They are as essential as mathematics and reading because they are expressive areas that develop the self, and because they can and do lead to the academic skills of reading and mathematics if we would but follow them there.

If that art teacher had worked with those children regularly, if she had been permitted to provide continuity, to relate art to other areas of knowledge and expression, that very same lesson that had been merely a game could have developed into enrichment, indeed. It could have been an experiment in artistic form and design. It could have led to discussion of the physics of movement. It could have been a starting point for mathematics and the concept of linear measurement or infinity; it could have been poetry or philosophy or history. A line, like the wheel, is an exciting idea, and ideas are the stuff of which education should be made—but too often isn't.

Our alternative schools, and nobody knows exactly what manner of educational breed they are, are built on the idea that students need alternative approaches to learning, because obviously the old approaches have not worked. The idea is a worthy one. But how do we put it into practice? By corrupting it.

First, we precede the word *school* with such words as *mini, storefront, street, youth diversion*, or *satellite*. Then, we go through the motions of being casual. This means that teachers are prone to imitate the kids in dress and speech. Both are affectations, of course, and extremely inappropriate. It takes more to be a teacher than an adult pretending to be a child.

I asked one fifty-year-old renegade male teacher who had long hair tied by a ribbon flowing down his back, dirty toes pointing out of torn sandals, dirty white smock over soiled blue jeans, why he was teaching in an alternative school, which inauspiciously was merely a classroom segregated on the top floor of the regular high school. He replied happily, "Because my principal doesn't like me, I guess."

I believed him. But why couldn't the principal merely fire him?

I knew why, of course. Union. The principal wasn't going to go that route. So, not knowing what else to do with him, the principal undoubtedly took the smart way out. He resolved all his problems at once by choosing two other teachers with whom he also was having difficulties, taking sixty kids who also wore dirty jeans, sandals, and a defiant air, and putting them all on the top floor of his school. An "alternative" was born. It should have been aborted.

That goes for most experiments in education. They usually are hatched out of the brains of supervisors, college instructors, sociologists, and government officials—people far removed from where the action is. Rarely are classroom teachers consulted. They are merely ordered to comply without preparation, without understanding, without consultation, without involvement. Moreover, experiments are often not experiments at all. The fact that the experiment is not new and was done previously in some other place at some other time is considered unimportant. No one bothers to find out what happened before, anyway. It might influence the current research. Besides, everyone has to discover individually that the world is round and research designs are conceived out of equal shares of financial self-interest and fear of knowledge. Knowledge, after all, leads to new insights, to change, to action. The last thing educators want is to make a *modus operandi* obsolete. Old jobs may be lost and new ones created, for which the old teachers and the old system are not competent. I have come to believe, therefore, that experiments are often almost deliberately based on concepts and experiments that have already failed.

The National Science Foundation, the *Wall Street Journal* reports, "pumped over the years some $68 million into modern math curriculum development and teacher training projects." The federal government has also allotted colossal sums to improve mathematics skills. For instance, the Comprehensive School Mathematics Program is a $6 million federal project. The University of Wisconsin Math Curriculum Development Project alone cost $2.5 million. The Madison Project in Math at Illinois cost $2.5 million. The result of all this experimentation? Mathematics skills have decreased dramatically throughout the country. Shall we spend more money in mathematics "experiments"?

Reading, anybody?

Nonreaders and poor readers make millions of dollars yearly for educators, colleges, learning cooperatives, learning corporations, learning centers, multimedia centers, and just plain publishers. There are thousands of "reading kits," "reading packets," "reading programs," "reading games"—all "experimental," all essentially the same. True, sometimes the pictures in the primers change. Instead of a cow there may be a car, our concession to the city child. And instead of a white child there may be a black child or a brown one, our recognition of integration. The arguments persist, however—"Looksees," or memory, vs. phonics; or the International Teaching Alphabet vs. videotaped closed circuit TV; or workbooks, talking typewriters, talking computers, and electric tapes hanging down from the ceilings of classrooms into which children plug and unplug themselves. Literally.

In order to rationalize their researches and experiments into failure, educators circulate the myth that more research is needed. One newspaper, for instance, reporting on the poor health of the state of reading in New York City schools, noted, "There is no formalized approach to diagnose each pupil's weaknesses in specific reading skills and to provide individualized corrective measures."

Nonsense.

Prescriptive reading is one such formalized approach. In prescriptive reading, a neatly turned out phrase based on the language of doctors and designed to impress, every child who is having trouble in reading receives a battery of tests to determine what it is that the child actually doesn't know, what little cog is keeping that brain from really working, what little prescription must be provided to uncog that brain. So in a truly distinctive procedure known only to educators, we provide both the disease and the cure. We don't change the system for those children who can't learn to read in it, we create the pathology, diagnose the children, and then provide a prescription.

I visited a diagnostic and remedial reading center in one "experimental" program in New York City. The room was an ordinary schoolroom in an ordinary old building. Both the building and room were bare and painted "school green." What made that particular room a reading center was the presence of one filmstrip machine and one tape recorder, each partitioned by a homemade cubbyhole. In front of the room, there were a dozen brown envelopes, each clearly marked with such words as *Phonograms, Initial Consonants, Final Consonants,* and *Vowels*.

Upon admission to the program—and admission depended upon failure to read adequately in the classroom—each child was dissected, analyzed, verbally scrubbed down to his every vowel, consonant, and phonogram, and thereby thoroughly innoculated against the germ of reading.

I watched one child's first exposure to this new "experimental" reading program. The teacher presented him with a mimeographed list of sounds.

"Read," said the teacher, as she pointed to the list of unfamiliar, truly puzzling nonwords:

1. weh   zup
2. yup   fas
3. hib   derf
4. mih   lur
5. jeb
6. zin

The child didn't say "ugh," but he should have, as he struggled and clearly could make no sense of the list. Instead he made a valiant effort. I cringed at his defeat. What a way to teach reading to a child who was already defeated.

Yet, the teacher felt justified.

"I have to know which sounds he doesn't know," she explained.

"Why?" I asked. "He's here because he can't read. Can't you start him off with success, instead of immediately confronting him with his failures? If you work with him with a book he likes to read you'll find out what sounds he doesn't know. Besides, if he begins to like you he'll probably tell you himself."

But enjoyment and success were not part of this "experimental" reading program.

Yolanda, a girl who graduated from Livingston and is now attending college, could have taught that child to read without prescription but with fun. I remembered her wonderful sense of humor. "If I don't know a word, I try to sound it out, and if I don't get it, I figure the word don't want me to know it."

With such creative reasoning and such joy in learning, there weren't many words Yolanda didn't know.

Educators could learn a great deal from listening to students like Yolanda. They don't. Instead, they listen to themselves not even to each other.

For instance, the University of Chicago has finally discovered, in research sponsored by the government, that vision and hearing are important to success in school. New York City, however, never having heard about Chicago, is planning a new study to examine the "factors influencing reading skills."

Alexsandr Solzhenitsyn, in accepting the Nobel Prize for literature, said, "That which some nations have already experienced, considered, and rejected is suddenly discovered by others to be the latest word." He might well have been speaking of educators.

Educators, it seems, discover, research, and study endlessly without learning very much, not because they can't learn, but because they won't. Patterns of failure keep them in business and keep teachers in their jobs.

It is no accident that inner-city children in our big cities test below national norms. This, by the way, does not necessarily mean that they are poorer readers. It merely means they are poor readers on the basis of *the tests used*, and all of the tests are irrelevant to city children. Many of the tests, for instance, don't measure reading ability at all. They may test for spelling in English or English usage or even a wide variety of cultural experiences at the middle-class level—but they do not necessarily test for *reading*. One reading test, for instance, asks children to define the word *mallard*. Not many inner-city children may know that a mallard is a duck. It is just not within their circumference of experiences, and why should they necessarily know that particular word? On the other hand, how many test makers would know that a *face to face* is an official hearing? Ask them to take a vocabulary test of the ghetto and see how they would score—possibly as functional illiterates.

I am not implying that all inner-city children are crusading readers, rushing onward to conquer all texts. They are not. I am implying, however, that it behooves teachers, schools, colleges, and universities to produce poor readers. The tests used produce poor readers because they are invalid and test for factors other than reading without regard for cultural experiences. On the basis of these tests, money for remedial work is allocated to school districts by the government. Of course, the more money the district obtains, the greater the power of those running the district becomes.

There is no doubt about it, there is money in education—a good deal of it misspent. Not long ago, for instance, teachers throughout the country were paid as much as one hundred dollars a week to attend summer session graduate courses. The government, under the National Defense Education Act, paid them to learn. What they learned was the usual pedagoguese they had been taught in undergraduate courses. The government, by the way, also paid the universities to offer the courses. Apparently, it never occurred to anyone to take that same money, which amounted to millions of dollars, and simply *pay the children to learn*. Skip the middleman!

I am not being facetious. Children should be paid to learn. Learning is their business, just as working is an adult's. Paying children who increase their reading grades is certainly one of the best ways I know to motivate them to begin to learn. Upon experiencing pleasure in the skill, once they had acquired it, children would read solely for the pleasure of reading.

To be sure, paying children to learn makes more sense than the Federal Right to Read Program, initiated by President Nixon in 1970 and operated out of the Office of Education. In 1972 Representative Edith Green revealed that 60 percent of its first year's budget was misspent in unauthorized architectural and office decorating expenses, public relations, and salaries. Representative Green asked, ''What is the need for a center that after two years and three millions of dollars has produced a stack of press releases and reports 18 inches high; two national surveys on the extent of illiteracy; one thousand people who are supposed to train a corps of volunteer reading tutors; and one and a half million milk cartons carrying messages designed to encourage children to read?''

Further examples of the big money to be made in education range from $25-a-day private workshops in such courses as ''Teaching Reading the Sue Foster Way,'' to a $162 million request to Congress by the National Institute of Education for more research projects to be allocated to public schools and colleges throughout the country.

One other way to make money and accumulate power in the educational establishment is by performance contracting. For instance, the city of Gary, Indiana, contracted with a private educational service company to operate one of its elementary schools on a money-back guaranteed performance basis. Either the kids would learn, via teaching machines, programmed learning, and multimedia gimmicky drill, or the city would get its money back. The city got its money back. The reading performances of those children did not improve any more than those of the children who attended the nonparticipating schools.

It is obvious that the answer to improved teaching is not through expensive equipment and the pressurized approach of big business. Teachers constantly need to be reminded that in teaching *the presence of the teacher is what is important*, and what kind of person the teacher is. Yet research is not oriented in this direction.

Research is geared toward proving the value of research. For instance, evaluating experimental educational programs is an exercise in keeping the power where the power is. Evaluators do not really have to evaluate. They do not necessarily have to be efficient in research. They do not have to prove themselves. Anybody can be an evaluator. All an evaluator has to do is set up a business. After that, all he or she has to say is that the programs being evaluated are good. The reason is very simple. Educational evaluators thrive on government subsidies.

That is, anybody applying for a research grant in education must provide in the proposal for an evaluation of the research being proposed. This is fair enough. Why should the government, or a private foundation, for that matter, put money into schools unless that funding agency is assured through relevant research that the program being funded is an effective one? The trouble with the system, however, is that the government does not decide who is doing the evaluation; *the grantee does*. For example, if any board of education in any city wants to seek funds for an experimental program, it must award a contract to someone to evaluate its program. That evaluator, of course, gets paid *only after the grantee gets the funds*. Now, obviously, the city wants to continue receiving federal funds. So does the evaluator. How else will they survive? Ergo, all evaluations report great success. God forbid that honesty should intervene, bad programs not be funded, and the money used elsewhere to a better purpose.

A friend of mine worked for an evaluation firm. She began to suspect that a program she was evaluating was not good, and she wanted to say so. She was fired.

Unhappily, I am becoming more and more firmly convinced, and I have struggled against believing it, that many educators and some high-level people in our federal government really do not want our children to learn. There is some evidence. The educational establishment's emphasis on the need to read, and the way that the business and civil service establishments follow up by requiring a high school diploma for jobs that do not really rely upon reading, combine to keep large numbers of people from earning decent salaries. An additional result of this combination is a high demand for reading teachers.

It is also true that a really educated, well-versed population could be disastrous to our continuing embracement of the national hypocrisies with which we are being daily faced.

How easy it is to say, after we pour some millions of dollars into educating our minorities, ''See, no matter what we do for them, they can't learn, they're stupid, they're black or Chicano or Indian or Puerto Rican.''

I have heard words like these—said and implied—from educators and from political figures, and I do firmly believe that it benefits those in power to keep our populace uneducated, to keep our minorities ''in place,'' to maintain a quota of unteachables. First, it proves that our minorities are indeed intellectually inferior, and it keeps the majority in power. Second, it keeps the money pouring into the universities and school systems, into the cities and the states. Federal money goes to schools where there are underachievers, not where children are achieving! It goes where pupils are stupid, not smart. A lot of smart kids go to private schools in the upper grades, anyway, either on scholarship or at their families' expense.

Teacher-training institutions, teaching staffs, and school systems flourish when children don't learn. When children do learn, teachers are fired, programs are dropped. The money is withdrawn. We do not need it. No one will pay to keep us healthy, to keep our children learning. When our children don't learn, however, the economics of teaching flourish. We have built a vast teaching empire based on the rearing of stupid children.

The vested interests work toward the benefit of the vested. Everyone takes his place in the arrangement. Everyone plays his own role in the conspiracy of "Let's research, let's fail, and then let's research some more as to why."

John Holt, an educational reformer, has an answer to these irrelevancies: Do away with school, school is meaningless anyway; let the children learn directly from the city. Why aren't there teachers throughout the city wearing badges that say READING TEACHER, and when a child wants to know a word, he merely asks a roaming teacher. Lovely sentiment, John, but totally impractical.

Compulsory education may have partially outlived its usefulness, in that recent studies seem to indicate that there is little relationship between achievement and length of time students spend in school.

During the 1960s, for instance, the International Association for the Evaluation of Educational Achievement launched a massive survey of school effectiveness in at least twelve countries. Its studies suggested that the length of time spent in a school system was irrelevant to achievement.

Another factor to be considered in questioning the advisability of compulsory education to age sixteen or seventeen is our process of overtraining. We call it education but the fact is that we are keeping students in school longer than is necessary for them to learn the skills that are a prerequisite for some jobs. Very often, we overtrain so much that by the time students are ready to leave school the jobs for which we have overtrained them have become obsolete and unavailable. It is apparent that we are keeping our children in school longer than is really necessary because they cannot be absorbed in the adult job market as that market is now controlled by unions, industry, and professions.

It is also true that we are keeping them in school longer because our teaching jobs are dependent upon the children's staying in school. Thus, the more the teachers are needed in schools to attend to those students who are enforced and often reluctant to attend school, the more teaching jobs are created.

Moreover, we uphold compulsory education without considering that there are some viable arguments against it. For one thing, it obviously is not working well. Also, it may be in violation of children's rights. Does not a child have the right *not* to attend school? Is not compulsory attendance a violation of a basic constitutional right of freedom of choice? Adults do not go into involuntary servitude. Even our standing army is primarily a volunteer one. Why should children be forced to attend school?

Teachers, of course, uphold compulsory education. Not only do they want more education for everyone, but longer periods of education. Keep the kids in school until they are no longer kids but young adults. Keep them in school all year. But talk of a longer school year for teachers, or shorter vacation periods, and their personal needs come before their professed concerns for children. They will give up nothing—not unless they get handsomely paid.

Yet, to do away with compulsory education, as John Holt and

Ivan Illich suggest, is really a disservice to so-called liberalism and to the children. Cannot we educate our children without overtraining? Cannot we educate for the full exploration of a child's potential?

As I stated previously, most educators are not revolutionaries. Our society will not be economically or politically saner because of us. We follow the crowd, not lead it. We know that the children of the poor will remain poor and the children of the rich will continue to be rich, while our political and economic institutions remain essentially the same. Education, we have learned, does not necessarily lead to upward economic mobility.

Yet, for teachers to accept the condition of powerlessness and the consequent presumption that they cannot teach children unless and until there is a more egalitarian society and until there is a major social and economic upheaval, is a catastrophic and defeating philosophy. It keeps teachers in a constant state of hypocrisy.

They cannot teach because—and there are a million becauses.

They want to teach but—and there are a million buts.

An angry graduate student asked me how I could continue to teach in the "totality of the whole rotten racist system." She was disquieted because I wasn't a revolutionary.

My answer to her was simple. There are many kinds of revolutions. The bombs we throw may not be at our institutions but at ourselves—and they can be just as incendiary. If teaching for self-exploration, self-determination, and self-power does not lead to a remaking of society, what will? Who will?

To cry for political or economic revolution and settle for nothing less is self-defeating to teachers and destructive to students. Teachers who openly decry the cruelties of the system, the ineffectiveness of their students, and their own ineffectiveness—but who nevertheless cling to the system—are cheating their students of their own potential for wisdom. They are also cheating themselves. They have not yet found freedom, the joys of self-understanding and real commitment, the joys of interaction with students, and that rarity, real teaching. Until their inner selves are released, aired, accepted, and understood, the system will remain what it is—a ceremonial totem pole— and the teachers will remain what they are—suppressed and secretly angry.

4

Power Games Teachers Play with Students

In pursuit of personal power, teachers play many games. They use the classroom as a checkerboard stage on which they move children like pawns in order to play out their fantasies and release their suppressions, inhibitions, angers, and aggressions.

In the playing of these games of the subconscious, the children are always expendable. They become the unsuspecting and unwilling participating members of the audience, who do not know the rules of the games and who, therefore, are crushed to failure. Thus, children are sacrificed to nourish the neurotic development of their teachers.

The most flagrant of all the games that generate false power is The Game of Omniscience. It is based on the need of teachers to be all-knowing and to fantasize that the sum total of knowledge rests in the self. Knowledge, after all, is power. What eludes the game's players, however, is the fact that true knowledge is knowing that one can't know everything. Teachers who can admit that they do not know everything and that they need not know everything have real knowledge and thus they have real power. They are not ashamed to admit to fallibility in their classrooms and thus to demonstrate their strengths. Teachers who do not have such knowledge must pretend to know everything. They maintain their façade of powerful omniscience by refusing to admit to ignorance or to error. Thus, they play the Game of Omniscience and act like fools.

Elyse Feldman told me of the time she was a high school

student and dared disagree with her English teacher. The class was discussing *Silas Marner* and she felt that the teacher's evaluation of the main character was inaccurate and unfair. She had loved the miserly Silas. The teacher hadn't. She tried to convince the class that the teacher was wrong. When she had finished, there was an acute and embarrassed silence. She realized her mistake even before her teacher spoke.

"Miss Feldman," he said, "you know, don't you, that you've just failed this course." She remembered that his lips hardly moved, but that his mustache, which she had always equated with that of an Oxford scholar, seemed to bob up and down.

She sat down, flustered and angry. English, the subject she loved the most, became a subject of endurance for her. She did not concentrate on learning. She concentrated on agreeing. She needed to pass in order to graduate. What she learned was to stifle her own creativity.

When she told me the story, and her anger had not abated even after twelve years, I remembered the time I had played the same game. I was lucky, however. I had lost.

Michael was a very gifted sixteen-year-old boy who liked holding forth in the very first high school English class I ever taught. It seemed Michael had read everything I had ever read, knew everything I had ever known, and more. Michael unnerved me. My concept of teaching English was to dictate concepts, but how could I when Michael questioned everything I said?

We were beginning to read *A Midsummer Night's Dream*, bored child by bored child. I was bored, too, but it had been the way I had been taught Shakespeare, and what had been hateful enough for me was good enough for them. Intermittently, as my teacher had done, I interrupted a droning voice to clarify vocabulary or ask a question. Suddenly, Michael raised his hand. I pretended not to see. Michael kept his hand raised. I cringed and recognized him.

"Do you agree that there are elements of Norse mythology in

the sources," he said, "as Goldstein wrote in his studies of Shakespeare?"

Goldstein? Who the hell was Goldstein? Norse mythology? All I knew about Norse mythology was that a helmet with horns was part of it.

I hurriedly agreed with Michael and pointed to a hapless girl to continue reading.

There was giggling in the back of the room and a lot of whispering. I knew I shouldn't ask the question but I couldn't stop myself either. My guilt about my pretense at knowledge and my guilt about a real ignorance of Shakespearean sources propelled me toward finding my own punishment.

"Something funny?" I asked.

More giggling.

"Well, is there?" I demanded angrily.

Finally, a loud whisper that reverberated, "Michael just made that up."

I went on as if I hadn't heard, but my pathetic stab at omniscience had been fully exposed. Michael, Goldstein, horned helmet and all, had just gored me.

I didn't think it was funny at the time. Now I can laugh at my stupidity. Certainly, Michael was testing me. Why did I fail his test? Because, already feeling inadequate, I could not admit to further ignorance. If I had done so, had asked who Goldstein was, had said I did not know much about Norse mythology, I would have gained Michael's trust. I also would have found out that Chicken Little was wrong. The sky would not have fallen down.

The words "I don't know" are three of the hardest words for a teacher to say. The next two hardest are "I'm sorry." The first implies that the teacher is ignorant, the second that the teacher was wrong. Both admissions are signs of "losing face," which is symptomatic of loss of control and loss of power.

Teachers always lose when they are concerned with losing face, as if the face lost were really the inner self instead of a masked defense. Teachers should unmask themselves, admit into consciousness the idea that one does not need to know everything there is to know and one does not have to pretend to know everything there is to know. It is not necessary to be omniscient to be a teacher. It is not necessary to play the game.

The teacher's mask of omniscience, unreal as it is, pushes children away. Children often want to confide in their teachers, want to talk of hate or love, jealousy, anger, or sadness. Between teacher and child, the sharing of an emotion brings closeness. Yet, teachers, not knowing what to do with the emotion expressed, refuse to listen. This denial keeps their omniscience intact. They do not have to admit to quandary.

I observed an individual lesson in remedial mathematics. John, the tutor, was an undergraduate student in one of my college classes. He had been tutoring a ninth-grade student weekly. I observed John and his student through a one-way screen. They couldn't see me, but I could see them. John, of course, knew I was there.

John had been tutoring the boy for several months and, according to him, the boy seemed to like him. In addition to math, they spent some time talking about baseball, which both liked.

That day, however, it was obvious the boy didn't want to do mathematics or even talk. When John asked what the matter was, the boy explained that he had a headache.

"Aw, come on," John urged, "you're here for your math lesson."

"I know, but my head aches."

"Did you take an aspirin?"

"Don't have any—"

"Well, I don't either," John answered. "Let's try these examples, maybe you'll feel better."

"I won't—" the boy muttered.

There was a silence.

"I feel bad about somethin'," the boy suddenly whispered.

"Yeah—what?"

I don't know what John was expecting to hear, but it certainly wasn't what he got.

"Well—I can't—can I tell you something private?"

"Sure—" John was very cavalier.

"Can you make a girl pregnant the first time it happens?"

John's shock could almost be felt. It was so palpable I could almost touch it.

After a long pause, John evaded a direct answer, looked embarrassed, and merely grunted, "Uh—not likely."

The boy reacted to the teacher's obvious discomfort by immediately withdrawing his attempt at closeness.

"Well, I suppose we could do the math if you want," he said.

They went on for a few minutes and did some perfunctory examples but it was obvious to both of them that learning could not take place that day. John ended the lesson and the boy scooted out. The boy had dared present him with a problem he couldn't handle, much less solve. John suddenly felt extremely unknowing and therefore vulnerable, incompetent, and totally inadequate. He was unprepared for failure. He thrust his anger upon the boy.

"After all," he said to me later, "I'm a math teacher, not a social worker."

But John needn't have been a social worker just to listen to the boy's anguish. He needn't have been a social worker just to make himself feel what the boy was feeling, to put himself back in time to his own first sexual experience and his own anxieties. He needn't have been a social worker to let the boy know he cared about him and to suggest that he talk to someone, perhaps a counselor, who could help him with his feelings.

In defense of his inadequacy, however, John had suddenly switched games. He was now playing the game of Professionalism. He was protecting himself from acknowledging his own inadequacies and from his own feelings by staying within the circumscribed circle of subject matter known as teaching.

Professionalism is a defensive armor. By keeping disciplines separate, teachers shield themselves from the emotional needs of the children. Teachers teach facts, social workers talk to parents, guidance counselors counsel, psychologists test, and psychiatrists consult. Where are understanding and relationships in all of this?

It is this kind of professionalism that keeps teachers emotionally distant from their students and therefore protected from feelings. Teachers who may occasionally have the urge to bridge that distance, perhaps when a particular child touches them and enriches their lives, are often afraid of becoming involved with the child—afraid of becoming involved with their own emotions. How ironic that when teachers are emotionally involved with their students they often feel guilty about it. They have been taught that it is wrong to feel.

I once heard a professor tell his class of would-be teachers, "Professionalism means protecting your own feelings. Teachers must be concerned about their pupils, of course, but they must not get emotionally involved."

One principal of a large urban high school took one step further back from accepting emotions when he wrote in a manual that he presented to the new teachers in his school, "Don't be friendly with your pupils. Remember—keep this a professional relationship."

He then went on to tell the teachers that it might be wise if they tried to remember all their pupils' names.

It would seem that teachers are not only being told that they cannot be caring and professional at the same time, but that they cannot even be friendly.

Teachers who are truly professional, however, *are* concerned, *are* friendly, *are* caring. They know that professionalism calls for the doctor never getting used to a patient's dying, the teacher never getting used to a child's pain. They know that professionalism does not call for becoming hard-hearted with experience but becoming more receptive to the human condition. The true professional, therefore, does not call for a denial of anguish but a greater acceptance of anguish, for anguish must be heeded.

The teachers I have known who have been true professionals have been able with each year they have taught to accept more hostility, more negative behavior, more anger from their students without being devastated by it, because they have learned to absorb and appreciate the meaning of pain.

Other teachers, however, fearing this kind of professionalism, hide from feelings and look for facts. Teaching for them becomes the dispensing of facts. They depend upon facts and they therefore lean upon the security of tests and the knowledge of case histories. They cripple themselves by needing a timetable and chronology of past events for each child before they can react humanly to that child in the present. They want a history of each child's past and a blueprint for future action. Dealing with situations piecemeal, responding to a child spontaneously without knowing everything there is to know about that child, is a skill teachers are not taught.

"Geraldine told me she was getting married," one teacher reported at a high school faculty conference that I attended, "but I didn't know if it was true or not, so I didn't say anything."

"Why not?" asked the guidance counselor.

"Well, I didn't know—" said the teacher, "she lies so much."

"You could have congratulated her," the counselor insisted. "Isn't that what you would have done with a friend?"

"Well, yes," the teacher insisted, "but she lies so much."

The point was the teacher didn't have to know. She simply could have reacted spontaneously with an expression of congratulations, or she could have said, "Are you putting me on again?" So what if Geraldine had lied? The lie, too, could be handled. The teacher did neither, and contact with another human being was lost. Whether Geraldine was lying or not was irrelevant. The teacher lost the moment to relate—to find out what Geraldine really meant and was trying to tell her—to help Geraldine if, in fact, she was a pathological liar, or to congratulate her if she was telling the truth.

Either way, lie or truth, what Geraldine expected from her teacher was an interaction of feeling. What she got was stony silence. Communication was broken. What teaching could take place after that?

It is not necessary to know everything about a child before one can react. People relate to each other on all levels of life without knowing everything there is to know about one another. People meet, talk, and learn from each other at parties, in classes, in the supermarket, in taxicabs. It is possible to relate positively and for such a relationship to have meaning even if it is temporary and tangential. It is also possible to have deep, satisfying relationships that are permanent, even if those relationships are based strictly on the present, without reference to the past or to a case history.

Chess players can share such moments. So can two strangers who suddenly confide in each other in a park and never see each other again. So can teachers and children. They are valid relationships, deep and personal and meaningful. Learning takes place. One need not know anything about another person before one can receive great emotional satisfaction from the relationship.

Now, I certainly am not adverse to knowledge. I am not opposed to teachers knowing about the personal lives of the children they teach; often such knowledge gives us insight and greater understanding.

Mr. Nevinsky, for instance, knew that Charlene's father was dying of cancer. Knowing it, Mr. Nevinsky understood Charlene's sudden spurts of anger at other students. Charlene was angry at her father for dying, for deserting her. Mr. Nevinsky, of course, did not interpret Charlene's anger to her. In fact, he never discussed her father at all. Charlene spoke at great length to her guidance counselor, who in turn had discussed Charlene's anger and sadness with Mr. Nevinsky. Just knowing about Charlene, however, made a difference in the way Mr. Nevinsky related to her. When Charlene did not do her homework, Mr. Nevinsky did not scold her. He knew she couldn't concentrate. He gave her a way out by permitting her to do extra class projects at her own time. When Charlene was irrationally angry at other students, he gave her time to cool off outside the classroom. Perhaps if Mr. Nevinsky were not aware of the tragedy with which Charlene lived, he would have made more demands upon her and dealt more harshly with her.

Mr. Nevinsky did not need to know Charlene's case history, but he certainly needed to know that she lived with a dying parent.

Knowing the factual history of a child's life is not necessarily synonymous with understanding that child. Such knowledge sometimes adds nothing to the relationship between a teacher and a child. Sometimes it detracts. Some teachers, "knowing" that a child has been in a mental hospital, for instance, often fear that child and withdraw from a relationship. Such knowledge is damaging when the teacher, out of ignorance of mental illness and fear of personal inadequacy in dealing with a so-called sick child, withdraws emotionally from the child. The child is then deprived of the strong relationship that she or he may desperately need.

There are some things, however, that should not be part of a child's record, because they are not always understood and work to the disadvantage of the child. For instance, it is not always necessary to know that a child was born out of wedlock, that a parent has syphilis, that a grandparent is in jail. Such knowledge is necessary only when *not* knowing it is detrimental to the child. The teacher can relate, can teach, can help that child without knowing something that should be, if it is not, confidential.

Confidentiality, unfortunately, is another game of power. The staffs of social agencies and clinical staffs within schools, including social workers and psychologists as well as principals and other supervisory personnel, are particularly prone to this power grab bag. Sometimes they refuse to give helpful information if it is classified by them as confidential. Often, though, it is information a teacher or guidance counselor should have if that teacher or guidance counselor is to work effectively with that child.

I remember battling with a social worker because she didn't tell the guidance counselor that a girl who was attending Livingston was three months' pregnant.

"Well, how does that help the girl," I angrily demanded, "keeping the information confidential? The guidance counselor and the teachers are planning for next term's work. This girl will need medical attention, and certainly her educational program might need to be changed. How does not telling us help her?"

"But she told it to me in confidence," the social worker wailed.

"And you couldn't get her to tell her counselor or teachers?" I asked. "You couldn't be professionally skilled enough to suggest to her that either you or she tell us? After all, how does it help her to keep her pregnancy a secret? How does she begin to feel about her baby—to have to reject it by denying its existence even before it's born?"

"It was confidential," she repeated.

"Pregnancy can't be confidential forever," I insisted. "But the point is, it is either your lack of skill which prevented you from suggesting to her that she tell us, or you didn't want her to tell us because you became the important professional person in her life. You were competing with her teachers."

That social worker became angry with me. Yet, I knew she was playing tug of war with me. We had become adversaries over who was more significant in that girl's life. The social worker definitely needed to feel her importance. I know that she was also concerned about the girl, because she was not an uncaring person, but her own unconscious feelings overrode her concern for the student. She convinced herself that confidentiality was the real issue. It was not. Of course, what happened was that the girl told her teacher anyway, and plans were made for her to continue her education in a special school and to return to Livingston after her baby was born.

The matter was settled and the girl was happy. The social worker was not. It was as if the sharing of the confidential knowledge became the sharing of the child, and the keeper of the information became the keeper of the child. Power battles between school personnel and clinicians often are fought on the basis of who knows more about whom. In most cases, the teacher loses—the child always does.

The purpose of all the games of power is to make ignoble losers of the children. None is more easily played by the teacher than the games of Competition and Testing. They proceed in tandem. They are played very simply. The results are always devastating to the children.

Children are tested weekly or as frequently as possible. Friday is a favorite test day, possibly to ensure that the children will have a worrisome weekend. Teachers fail as many children as possible by making the test too hard or the passing grade too high. Those children who don't fail are told that "you can do better," or that "you are not living up to your potential."

Other teachers read out individual test grades to the entire class in much the same way as they take attendance, so that every student in the class will know who is smarter than who— according to a particular test, that is—and who is dumber than who. One teacher I know, in one of the most prestigious private high schools in the world, passed the teacher rating form around the class so that every student could clearly learn who was failing and who was passing. Moreover, he rated each student not only on work but on attitude. It was not surprising that students who received a D in attitude also received a D in work. They were therefore double failures.

The course was a special one for students gifted in writing. What a way to destroy the sensitivities of any child; what a way to inhibit writing, as if creativity can be graded, as if the internal experiences of a writer can be translated into attitude. Are we still throwing our Shelleys out of Oxford?

Teachers, however, often rationalize this procedure of demoralization by pointing allegorically to the window and crying in stentorian tones: "But it is rough out there."

They call it teaching for reality.

I watched Cecilia Johnson, a young black teacher who was in her first year of teaching in a school in California, "prepare children for reality" as she returned spelling tests to her class. She called Amanda to the front of the room. Amanda's eyes opened wide and she smiled as she glanced at the paper Miss Johnson handed her. It was obvious she was pleased. Her smile disappeared quickly enough, however, as Miss Johnson muttered, not in an unfriendly tone, which somehow made it worse, "You can do better, Amanda."

"But I got ninety-four," Amanda pleaded.

"You can get a hundred," Miss Johnson stated. "Josephine got a hundred. That's because she studied."

"But I studied too," Amanda protested.

"Obviously not enough," Miss Johnson replied.

What had been an expression of delight faded to a slight frown on Amanda's face. If Miss Johnson's object was to create a neurotic student, she was succeeding admirably. I had no doubt that before her next test, Amanda would study even harder, and would become agitated and nervous. In the classroom she would become more competitive and be displeased with her performance unless it was absolutely perfect. Her price of achieving six points higher on a test would be pervasive anxiety.

After school that day, I asked Miss Johnson where she had gotten the list of spelling words that she had required her class to memorize. I was particularly interested, because the words seemed so totally unrelated to anything the children had been learning about. She told me they were from an eighth-grade speller. When I asked her what relevancy such words as *pariah, unctuous*, and *uxorious* could have to those eighth graders, she explained that they were literary.

Miss Johnson should have known that the time to teach those words was when the children came across them in their reading in some other aspects of learning, because I could not imagine by what set of circumstances one eighth-grade student would have occasion to say to another, "Hey man, that unctuous man is a pariah because he's uxorious."

"Huh—you nuts or somethin'!"

My ephemeral fantasy over, I asked Miss Johnson if she thought it had helped Amanda to know that her friend Josephine had received one hundred.

"The sooner the children learn that there are a lot of people in the world smarter than they are, the better off they will be," she replied primly. "That's reality."

"Sure there are people smarter," I agreed, "but that doesn't mean we have to compete with them, does it? Competition should be with the self, not with others."

"Well, that's what I was encouraging," she explained.

I had the feeling she was agreeing with me only to get rid of me, because it was not what she had been doing and she probably knew it. If she had indeed known it, she would have praised Amanda for what she had accomplished instead of mildly criticizing her for what she had not accomplished. Amanda would then have tried harder, because she had been successful. Or perhaps Amanda had done the best she could at that time. Do we all perform at the height of our potential all the time? Can we? Should we?

When I asked Miss Johnson these questions, it was obvious she had not given them any thought. She reiterated that competition was facing reality. Then, rather proudly, she told me that 80 percent of the students in that class thought that 80 percent of the other students in the class were smarter than they. "And that's good," she went on. "Satisfaction leads to smugness. No, you must always be dissatisfied with your own accomplishments; that makes you want to learn more."

Miss Johnson was dead wrong.

What makes children want to learn is interest in what they are learning, and in satisfaction and success with what they have learned, not competition that is falsely created in the classroom for the sake of competition.

If those spelling words had had any real meaning for those children, they would have learned them without a test. As it was, the class studied to pass a test—not because they wanted to learn. And as happens under these conditions, learning that is motivated only to pass a test is quickly forgotten. The transitory knowledge gained becomes as meaningless as the test has been. Good teachers can help children learn more by giving them successful experiences at learning, and by making learning essential, than by testing to find out what they don't know or how they "deviate from the norm."

As a matter of fact, good teachers know when children are learning; they don't need to test. When they do test, it is to find out what the children have not learned, in order to reteach. The test is for the teacher, rather than for the child. Tests for such purposes need not even be marked or returned to children.

Competition in school under the pretense of preparing children to face reality is a cruel exercise in power. We know that there will always be people who can achieve more than we can, be smarter or more talented or richer, just as we know that there are people who will achieve less. Education should give us the strengths to deal with these differences. We gain strength not by learning how inadequate we are but by learning how adequate we can be. Why do we think that in order to prepare for starvation we must not eat? Isn't it better to be healthy? We can approach adversity better when we feel good about ourselves, just as we can fight off disease when we are strong.

There is nothing wrong with self-satisfaction when it is based on achievement and realistic expectations of oneself. Why are we so fearful of appearing happy and fulfilled? Why must we make children feel like failures from the time they start school to the time they finish—all under the guise of facing the reality of competition? Why must we produce chronic dissatisfaction within children and within ourselves, as if there were some special merit or honor in unhappiness, or as if gratification were immoral?

Now, I am certainly not advocating a state in which self-satisfaction is so extreme that learning stops. I am not suggesting that enjoyment in learning and with the self should be allowed to degenerate into smugness, complacency, or the refusal to increase one's learning. Nor am I saying that the work of students must never be criticized. Of course, it must. I am saying that criticism is an important tool of the teacher. I am saying that the art of criticism is the art of helping each student achieve self-evaluation.

Criticism should not be the blow of humiliation it too often is. Criticism that is directed at the integrity and the core of the student rather than at the work of the student crushes the human spirit. Criticism, however, that is oriented toward the student's own self-evaluation is an uplifting, insightful learning experience and leads toward constructive learning. It leads to satisfaction as motivation, pleasure as motivation, excitement as motivation, and zest as activation to learning. Learning under these healthy and happy conditions does not decrease; it increases. Competition becomes competition with the self, not with others.

We can't all be Rembrandts. Why must we try to be? Why can't we learn to appreciate the artists we are instead of trying to be like the artists we can't be? There is a sensitivity and a creativity in each of us that is crying out to be heard, to be released.

Yet, my daughter Amy's teacher said to me at one parent-teacher conference, "Amy writes well, but she can't write to time."

I didn't know what she meant. She explained that on a test, Amy's analysis of Hamlet was not as good as it should have been, because she was unable to write well under the pressure of time.

But why should an analysis of Hamlet be timed in the first place? Was Amy being tested on her ability to write fast or on her understanding of Hamlet?

"Testing for time" should have no place within a school system. Tests should be used for an evaluation of self-growth, and as such they need not necessarily be made part of a child's record. Tests, as they now are, are little more than barriers. They keep some people in, and keep some people out. Children are placed in smart classes or stupid ones. Tests measure very little except the ability to take a test. They do not measure an individual's real knowledge. They measure whatever a tester has decided is a basis of knowledge. As long as tests are used to place people in their place on a continuum, they really have no value for teachers or for the children themselves, except as statistics, and statistics are important not to the individual taking the test but to the organization using the tests.

A failing mark does not necessarily mean a student knows little. It may simply mean that failure was determined by the number of people needed to fulfill a certain function. If two thousand high school applicants took a test for entrance to a college having only two hundred student vacancies, it is obvious that the failing mark has to be placed very high. Failing marks, therefore, are arbitrary devices set at the whim of the test givers to fit a particular set of circumstances. Failing marks do not necessarily eliminate incompetent people.

How many students have been hindered in making their contributions to society because they have not been able to take tests well? How many surgeons have we lost? On the other hand, how many people have passed tests who were not competent at all?

I was one.

I remember the first teaching test I ever took. One question asked on that test was, "Which is the only animal to sleep standing up?" I knew the answer. Horse. I knew it only because I had studied for the test by looking at old examinations, and questions are often repeated.

I passed that test and was stamped a teacher. I should not have been. I was a terrible teacher. What did the test prove? That I had assembled some intellectual bric-a-brac that was rattling around in my brain somewhere.

I believe that I am a good teacher now. I became one after I began to teach—not because I passed a teaching test, but because I made myself learn from the children, and because I was willing to learn from some very good teachers who also were willing to listen to the children.

Being a good teacher today, I doubt that I could pass a teaching test now. I no longer walk around in command of trivia and educational clichés. I do not know, for instance, what a grammatical ''retained object'' is, or what musical time signature ''America'' is written in. Furthermore, I could not write a lesson plan that would fit the prescription of the curriculum makers. I no longer know what has to be taught at what grade. It seems to me that there are a lot of children these days in all grades who are wiser and more knowledgeable than their teachers, and it is they who know what it is they need to know.

No, I doubt that I could pass a teaching test now—I have forgotten what an oxymoron is and I have since learned from watching old cowboy movies on *The Late Show* that the horse also sleeps lying down. Does that mean my original answer was incorrect or does it mean that a horse sleeps both ways, but that no other animal can sleep while standing? I do not know. All I know is that the knowledge I once had of the sleeping patterns of horses, a knowledge that I thought so absolute, is scanty indeed.

When, then, is a fact a fact?

I am not always certain. Reality shifts in many ways, depending on the perspective of time and place. Is not one country's spy another country's traitor? Cannot one person's lie be another's truth?

Unfortunately, educators do not often raise these issues. A fact is a fact is a fact makes teaching easier. And so it is indeed a fact that students must pass Regent examinations. Thus, I must reluctantly assume that students should either be made immune to tests, which is unfortunately not likely, or to be taught how to take them. And there is no doubt about it, test taking *is* a skill. Students can be taught how to guess, keeping the risk of casualties to a minimum. They can be taught how to organize an answer. Such skills do not necessarily test for mastery of a subject but mastery of how to take a test. They are not the same thing. When we test, therefore, let us at least recognize that we often are testing our memory and our skill in taking a test, not our knowledge. Memory is not knowledge. Neither is the skill of test taking.

If only performance were the measure of competency as it should be, tests would not be necessary at all, and the game of competition and testing would not keep thousands of good people down in their economic places and out of unions, colleges, and employment.

The games of Competition and Testing support the thesis that teachers are superior to their students. They lead directly to the next game, in which teachers' superiority goes unchallenged. It is the Game of Unchallenge.

The purpose of the Game of Unchallenge is not only to make the students feel inadequate but to ensure that they will *be* inadequate. The game is based on the hypothesis that if students are not given the challenge to think, they will not think.

"I don't want anyone to read past the first act," I heard one high school teacher command her class in English when she gave the assignment to read a Galsworthy play. It was on one of my visits to California.

I was stunned. What if a student wanted to read the whole play? Shouldn't that student be permitted to? What a way to stifle both reading and thinking! The teacher, however, was interested in keeping everybody in the class at the same place at the same time. Perhaps she hadn't read past Act One herself. At any rate, she made certain no one would run with an idea that was ahead of her contrived lesson plan. Most of the students appeared grateful for her barricade. In her class, at least, they had already given up their right to curiosity. I had no doubt, however, that a few students would brook her displeasure and read ahead of her instructions, though they would be fearful of letting on that they had done so. In either case, whether or not they followed her instructions to curb their reading, their learning was leashed.

It is this kind of teaching that often makes it impossible for students to spread their wings. Teachers give assignments that are so limited or so easy that children do not have to think. As a result, children never begin to tap their own abilities and rarely do they believe in their own potential for wisdom. It is easy, therefore, for teachers to play their next game of power—the Game of Privilege. It is a game they play even while they talk of the inherent right of Americans to equal opportunity and equal rights.

Teachers talk a good game of democracy, but the last thing they want in a classroom is equality with their students. Teachers don't want equal rights. They want greater rights.

Equality of rights, however, cannot easily be philosophically denied in democracy, although in fact these rights are often denied in reality. There have been violations of students' rights throughout the country. Students have been denied freedom of speech in some cases, freedom of press in others. When lawsuits have been waged and won, and when students have won their rights, teachers have hypocritically agreed with the decision and blamed the system for suppression. Righteously, most of them finally agreed that male students have the right to wear long hair. Earlier, however, they had decried that right.

"It leads to discipline problems," they had said. "How can we teach when a kid's hair is so long?"

"Easy," I answered, "by holding on to it and pinning them down to their seats with it. Hair doesn't bruise, so it won't show."

They didn't think I was funny.

Students may have civil rights, teachers finally concede, but teachers have privilege. Privilege is inherent in the teacher's role. One privilege is suppressing student rights. The referee blows the whistle and the Game of Privilege is on.

Teachers can smoke. Students can't. Teachers can eat in the classroom. Students can't.

I used to believe in the shibboleth of privilege. I no longer do.

A school rule is a school law. If a law applies to one, it should apply to all. A No Jaywalking sign in front of a school building is a No Jaywalking sign for all. If rules are necessary for the common good—and that's why rules are made—then they must be upheld by everyone. Otherwise, where is the concept of the common good? And if it is not necessary to uphold a rule or law, then why have it at all? It should be abolished.

When the fire bell rings, everyone should leave the building, including all teachers who are not at the moment teaching, and who may be on a "free period." How often have I seen teachers stay behind because they didn't want to walk the stairs. Let a child do that? Suspension!

I cannot find one single act that a teacher should be permitted to do in a school building that a child should not be equally permitted to do, including smoking in an elementary school. Smoking regulations are fire regulations. If a law applies to one, it should apply to all. A No Smoking sign in a public school is a No Smoking sign for all. If smoking is permitted in designated areas, then it should be permitted for all. Let us not be two-faced and say children should not be permitted to smoke and then smoke in front of them. Let us not tell them we are concerned for their health, while we inhale the smoke in our own lungs. If we are smoking ourselves to death, we cannot tell them not to smoke. They have the same right to kill themselves that we have.

I am not a believer in smoking. I do not smoke. I don't think children or adults should smoke. But let's not play the Game of Privilege, smoke in front of them, and tell them not to.

The Game of Privilege smacks of royal superiority or totalitarianism. It smacks of the benign ruler, and sometimes it is hard to differentiate between this game and the Game of the Missionary Spirit. In this game, the power wielder, the teacher, forgives everything "bad" in a child without trying to understand the child or relate to the child. Forgiveness, where the student does not want it or ask for it, is potent indeed. The child is made to feel like a sinner.

"Your stomach is full of unspilled piss," Lavinia, a student at Livingston, screamed at her teacher when he insisted she could not bang on the typewriter.

The teacher knew Lavinia had struggled valiantly to learn how to type, but she had been born with a disfigurement of some fingers and she became easily frustrated at her inability to put pressure on her little finger. Instead of letting her know he understood her frustration and her feelings of defeat, and instead of giving her other typing exercises with which she could have more success, because she needed more success, he merely said, "I forgive you, Lavinia, for what you just said. You didn't mean it."

He had made a cardinal error. Not only had he forgiven her when she had not asked for forgiveness, but he had argued with her feelings, and feelings cannot be argued with. They just are.

"Who the hell are you to forgive me?" she cried. "I speak English, are your ears Italian?" She stalked out of the room.

Because he was a very good teacher, he recognized his mistake and went after her. He found her sobbing in the hall.

"I'm sorry, Lavinia," he said. "I really didn't understand how upset you were."

"That's okay," she said. Then she began to laugh. "I guess I shot off my mouth. I'm sorry."

They went back to the typing room at the teacher's suggestion. Both felt better.

Later when we were discussing the incident, which I had witnessed, the teacher laughed at himself. "Every once in a while I get the great urge to be a messiah."

I knew exactly how he felt. We all want to be messiahs— occasionally. The important thing is to be aware of it.

The games we play are damaging because we play them so subtly. The Game of Silent Sitting, for instance, is an easy game to play. Nevertheless, it produces backaches and conformity.

My first week of teaching I developed two major illnesses, a complete and overwhelming case of laryngitis and the sorest feet in the school. I learned two things: to shut up and sit down. Too many teachers, however, continue to talk and continue to stand all day. They deny both activities to children.

Teachers in search of power demand silence. They never penetrate the mechanisms of silence—that it acts as a barrier to communication, relationships, enjoyment, learning. Even obscenities are communication, but these teachers pretend that our movies, television programs, and even our parties are not permeated with verbal indelicacies. Ignoring our own culture, teachers repeatedly demand that children be silent until they have raised their hands, their right hands at that, and have been given the nod of approval to speak. The irony of this system, and the way teachers really prove to themselves that they are in control, is that many times teachers deliberately refuse to recognize some children whose hands are raised all the time. The teachers feel such children are "smart alecky," or that they demand too much attention emotionally; they withhold that attention. The child remains seated and silent.

Children who need attention from the teacher and who don't get it are emotionally hungry. You can spot them by the way they react. They either talk out; act out and become "discipline cases"; or they retreat, give up, and become silent. For these children, whatever form their reaction takes, the excitement of learning dims.

On the other hand, there are those children who do not want to talk out at all and so they do not raise their hands to be recognized. They may be too shy to talk in a group even if they know the answer. Or they may not know the answer and do not want to reveal their inadequacy. Yet, there are many power-playing teachers who call upon these children under the guise of seeing "who is paying attention." They succeed only in making public the failure of a child who does not know the answer, or in embarrassing the child who does know the answer but who is fearful of talking in a group.

The teacher who insists upon hand-raising primarily to ignore it is proving who is boss in that classroom.

Cannot the children and the teacher regulate discussion without hand-raising? Assuredly, they can. When teaching is not dictatorial and autocratic, when teaching is individualized or in small groups, when teaching is centered on human relationships, hand-raising becomes totally unnecessary. Naturally, in large assemblies, where parliamentary procedures should be taught, hand-raising is essential. Classrooms, however, should be intimate, hand-raising unnecessary, and there should be movement.

The show-of-strength stratagem of silence and sitting bears no relationship to learning or teaching, and it should have no place in a school. Unfortunately, the show-of-strength play is very prevalent in most schools.

"Don't you curse at me!"

"Fuck you—whatya gonna do about it?"

What indeed? Wash his mouth with soap?

Incredible as it sounds, some teachers still do. They act out of anger and frustration. Their power has seemingly been diminished, and in fact it *has* been diminished if they *feel* it has been diminished. The teacher who sees cursing as an expression of the child's discomfort and need will not feel threatened by it, and will not turn it into an expression against him- or herself.

Only then can the teacher deal effectively with it. Only then can the teacher help the child. After all, cursing is generally not acceptable in adult society and teachers cannot condone it, even while they may have to accept it.

"Charlene," Diana Greenthal, a teacher at Livingston, said, "I know you're angry, but I'm not cursing at you and I don't like it when you curse at me. Can you tell me in a way I can listen to why you are angry?"

What Mrs. Greenthal did was recognize the child's right to be angry. Thus, she recognized and accepted the child even though she did not accept the cursing. However, she did not cut off communication. She did not say, "Stop cursing." This would have been a foolhardy command. Such commands are rarely obeyed. When they are, they often lead only to suppressed anger on the part of the student.

One of the tools of education is communication. It must be kept open at all times. When words seem unacceptable it is sometimes better to ignore them than to fight a battle over them and lose the substance of what the child is trying to say.

Teachers who are fearful of words, fearful of aggression either in themselves or in the children, act autocratically out of suppression of their own fears.

They rely on the show-of-strength stratagems. They demand constant attention. All eyes on teacher. All ears listening to teacher. Teacher is on!

The power game of Routine and Procedure is a game in which the teacher is in autocratic control—such teachers depend upon the mechanisms of routine to establish their own form of dictatorship.

I watched Mr. Abbate, a fifth-grade teacher, take his class to assembly.

"Boys in pairs in front of the line, girls in pairs at the back," he ordered.

"But can't I walk with Jaime?" Elvira asked.

"No."

"Why not?"

"Because I said so."

"I said so" becomes the raison d'être, and a mechanism of repression. I heard him order his class not to chew gum. When I asked why, he really couldn't give a reasonable answer.

"Because we never do," he stated. "It's precedent."

"And precedent should never be questioned?" I asked.

He agreed it should.

"Well, what do you think I should do?" he asked.

"Well," I answered, "if there's really no reason not to chew, except that it's a time-honored law of schools for no apparent reason, then let them chew."

When I saw him again, he was less than enchanted with me.

"I gave them a chewing period," he said stoically. "I announced it a day before and look what happened."

"What happened?" I asked.

"They stuffed the keyholes with gum."

I tried not to laugh. Whoever heard of a chewing-gum period? Why hadn't he just permitted a child to chew gum casually whenever that child felt like it? Why make it a special period at his command? The children were merely getting even with his autocratic manner.

I told him that the only successful chewing lesson I had ever heard of was given by a friend of mine, Pearl Berkowitz, when she first began teaching in the Bellevue psychiatric school. Her class consisted of twelve angry adolescent boys. They wanted no part of school or of her. One day she brought in a pound of bubble gum and announced a contest to see who could chew the biggest and smoothest wad of gum in the class. Those boys chewed for an entire morning. She still laughs when she says it was the quietest day of her entire teaching career. But it was a fun day also and fun is not to be minimized—neither the teacher's nor the children's. It is an essential ingredient in every classroom. That gum-chewing day had a purpose—to establish a relationship between a group of hostile, aggressive boys and their teacher—to show them she could play their games with them, because, naturally, she chewed too.

Mr. Abbate's period of chewing was gum of another flavor. He had merely noblessed and obliged and expected fealty in return. The children, however, did not want serfdom. They rebelled. I felt it was the healthiest thing they could have done. I told him so.

"I guess so," he admitted glumly, and then he saw the humor

and began to smile. I knew he would be all right. He was ready to learn.

Mr. Sanderson was not. He stuck to autocracy as if to the manner born. I watched him teach a science lesson.

"Class, folders out!"

Forty folders came out.

"Pencils ready."

Forty pencils were readied.

"Write: The aim of today's lesson is scientific measuring. We will measure water."

The children wrote as the teacher pointed to the words that he had previously written on the blackboard. Writing the aim of the lesson on the blackboard is standard teacher-training procedure. Mr. Sanderson followed all the "right" things he had been taught at college.

As they wrote, the children did not utter a word. It was clear they were terrified of their teacher. Mr. Sanderson called it respect. Of course, fear and respect are not the same. The children did not respect him. How could they?

When it came time to do the actual measuring, each child sitting at the end of each science table, which seated six, was designated the "measurer." The measurer, on command, walked to the front of the room, made a right turn, and then walked to the back of the room to the water faucet. It didn't matter that some children were sitting closer to the water fountain than others. One child was only a few feet away. Like an automaton, walk front, right turn, walk back, draw water, return directly to seat.

Mr. Sanderson's teaching was solely for the sake of power. It was as autocratic as measuring water without reason. Couldn't measurement have a meaning? Couldn't water be measured to make soda, or milk be measured to make ice cream? Why water with no meaning? Because Mr. Sanderson had convinced himself that he was teaching the methodology of science. "Do what you're told in the way you are told."

Mr. Sanderson did not know that he was teaching the exact

antithesis of what science really is—a questioning approach to life.

Yet Mr. Sanderson considered himself a good teacher. He based his judgment on the fact that he spent hours correcting papers or writing lesson plans. He even kept his classes in after three, assuring the class he was punishing himself as well as the children. In this self-immolation he proved his dedication and/or martyrdom. Yet his punishment was self-inflicted; it was also more time in control, as well as proof of his control.

Another teacher, who truly felt his own power, did not need to flaunt his position of control. So he didn't need to play the Game of Routine and Procedure. In the same science program, this second teacher brought in feathers and pebbles, and asked the children which was heavier—one-half pound of feathers or one-half pound of pebbles. The children argued their particular viewpoints. Feathers flew in the classroom and undoubtedly some pebbles got surreptitiously thrown, but those children measured, felt, and totally experienced those feathers and pebbles, and when the lesson was over they had zestfully absorbed some important concepts of measurement. Even though there were moments of laughter, squabbling, and general movement that at times seemed chaotic, but weren't, this teacher always was in control because he felt his power. He was able to teach aggressively because he permitted the children to utilize the power of their own aggression. Learning not only took place, it really couldn't be avoided.

The avoidance of learning at all costs, however, often has a high priority, as many teachers convince themselves that form is more important than function, appearance is more important than substance.

Miss Nerest, for instance, was such a teacher. She held on to her own power and played the Game of Routine and Procedure by investing all her energies in seeing to it that students filled out job application forms correctly. She then assigned them to school jobs, for which they were paid a stipend. She was also the school librarian.

When I visited the library it was empty of children but filled with books. No class was scheduled. I asked her if she permitted children to take the books home.

"Home?" she exclaimed ferociously, figuratively hugging each book to her ample bosom. "Why, they don't ever leave this room. See, I'll show you," and she went through an elaborate procedure of explaining how every book was counted, shelf by shelf, at the beginning and end of every library period. The children spent ten minutes at the beginning of each period and ten minutes at the end counting. During the counting there had to be absolute silence, naturally. Otherwise, they'd have to start from one—all over again.

"I have never lost a book," she proclaimed proudly.

But many a potential reader.

"When do they read?" I asked.

"Oh, they can read any book they want while they're in the school library."

"Here?" I asked. "What if they don't finish it in a period?"

"They take it again next week. They have one library period a week."

"At that rate it would take a child three years to read *Les Miserables*," I remarked, knowing full well that children don't read *Les Miserables* very much. I was simply angry.

"Oh, they don't read that," she answered smugly.

"How about *Sounder*?" I asked, "or *Down These Mean Streets*? Children read those, don't they?"

"Not really," she answered. "They can't finish them in a period."

She had not realized how circuitously she had argued. I let the discussion drop and asked her how she allotted jobs to the students. Surely she must have more students than she had jobs.

She assured me she did.

"How do you decide who is to get the jobs?" I asked.

She told me how. Applications had to be filled out perfectly by the students. If the application forms weren't perfect, with each *i* dotted, then the student wasn't permitted to work in the school. There were no second chances to fill out the form. The irony of the situation was that no one else saw the forms; they weren't sent to Washington, or to the State Capitol, or to an employment office. They were simply kept in the bottom drawer of Miss Nerest's file cabinet, to be destroyed at the end of the year. Because of Miss Nerest's compulsion to prove her authority to herself, many students were kept jobless. These were the very students who needed the jobs most, the ones with the poorest skills, the ones who therefore had the most difficulty in filling out the forms. It was not the purpose of the job program to keep poor children poor. But that, in effect, is what she did.

"I have standards, you know," she said tightly.

The Game of Standards is yet another bastion of teacher power. The object of the game is to let children know that the expression of overt achievement is more important than the process of learning. In this way, greater value is put on standards, on accomplishments, rather than on the children themselves and their mechanisms or processes of learning.

I saw this phenomenon quite clearly, when as a member of an educational research team studying the feasibility of establishing educational parks in urban areas, I visited schools throughout the country.

In one school in the South I met Miss Crawford, who was pointed out by Dr. Dempsey, the principal of the elementary school in which she taught, as being an excellent first-grade teacher. She had been teaching for many years and it was obvious that Dr. Dempsey was proud of her and her dedication to the school. By that he meant that he relied heavily on her to get the children to paint and draw decorations for the school corridors. All the time that Dr. Dempsey was escorting me down a long corridor to her room, he deplored the fact that because he did not have enough teaching positions in the school, he could not release her entirely from her first-grade class so that she could become the art teacher for the school. He pointed to paintings and drawings hung on the wall. I thought

that they looked teacher-inspired rather than childlike, because
they seemed so perfect, but I didn't say so.

As Dr. Dempsey opened Miss Crawford's room, ten leftover
turkeys from Thanksgiving seemed to fly at me from the upper
rim of the blackboard, where they were posted. On that same
board, pinned to each other downward so that the drawings
covered a large part of the blackboard, were ten Columbuses,
ten Pilgrims, ten sheaves of wheat, ten witches, and ten orange
pumpkins. I could see the full scope of the traditional fall term
holiday season in groups of ten. What struck me immediately
was that all the drawings were alike, except for minor devia-
tions in coloring. It was obvious, and later Miss Crawford
verified my initial impression, that her way of teaching art was
to select a picture generally from a teacher's magazine, draw it
on the board, and ask the children to copy it. Or, occasionally,
she made stencils and asked the children to use them. The day I
was visiting, the children were using Santa Claus stencils—five
stencils for about thirty-two children. The children waited their
turn. Even the stencils were exactly alike, so that the children
didn't even have the choice of picking one stencil out of five.

As we entered, Miss Crawford was leaning over a child. The
gravel in her voice could not be misinterpreted. It was irritation.
I reacted to it with an almost physical pulling back.

"Why can't you cut on a straight line, Jessica?" she complained. "You're so sloppy. I can't put your Santa Claus on the
blackboard looking like that."

Tiny Jessica grappled with the scissors that were too big for
her, and tried even harder, but her small fingers kept slipping.

"Oh, here, let me do it for you." Miss Crawford's exasperation was now total, and she grabbed both the scissors and the
stenciled Santa Claus from Jessica and cut it out for her. The
artist in Jessica died.

Then Miss Crawford saw us and smiled, oblivious to the
emotional assault she had just inflicted on that child.

Later, she explained to me about her standards for displaying
a drawing. She did not permit a picture to hang on that back

blackboard if the coloring was smudged or boundaries were crossed.

"One has to have standards," she stated. I could hear Miss Nerest all over again. Even the intonation was the same.

When I asked about Jessica, because nothing of hers was displayed, she replied, "Oh, poor child, Jessica is a bit uncoordinated."

She dismissed Jessica easily and went on to explain how she loved to keep her room looking lovely, with the children's best work on the walls and boards.

Dr. Dempsey agreed with Miss Crawford that only the best work should be exhibited, apparently not considering the feelings of children whose work would never be deemed best no matter how hard they tried.

What Miss Crawford and Dr. Dempsey didn't know was the damage she was doing. Miss Crawford's judgments of esthetics were not the children's; a stenciled Santa Claus was the teacher's expression, not the child's; and six-year-old children might have difficulty in cutting on straight lines, because this is the nature of six-year-old biological coordination. They are expected to have difficulty. That is why they come to school— to learn. There was nothing wrong with Jessica's cutting of that Santa Claus line that aging couldn't cure. Jessica needed time and practice. Miss Crawford wouldn't give to her what was her psychological, educational, and biological right—time to grow.

When I spoke to Dr. Dempsey about Jessica, he assured me that she was going to be a difficult child.

"Resistant, you know," he smiled. "It often shows even at such an early age."

I could see him three years from then playing a favored game of supervisors. It is a game that is played only after teachers have failed at suppressing the children. Somehow, the children have managed, in reaction to all the games the teachers have played, to thumb their noses literally and figuratively at them. Yvonne, a thirteen-year-old girl who attended Livingston, was a case in point. When she was asked by her teacher to write a poem on friendship, she drew:

"Do you know what that means? If you want a poem, write it yourself."

Yvonne had just come to Livingston and she was still fighting back. She could not yet give up her battle against teachers and the school system. It was easy to see why. On her record card her second-grade teacher had written, "Yvonne does not like to be yelled at." I wonder if anyone had asked that teacher, "Who does?" Her seventh-grade teacher had written in criticism of her that "she was a sour young lady who used foul language and was antagonistic to unfair treatment." Who isn't? Her ninth-grade teacher had given her a grade of one for a term in English, not because she was stupid, but because she had dared to talk out. One? How angry the teacher must have been to be so demeaning to a girl who read on a twelfth-grade level and who wrote poetry.

Yvonne was a heavy contender for power in a classroom, and her teachers had to call on the higher echelons in the school as back-up players—the dean, the behavior counselor (a misnomer if ever there was one), the assistant principal, the principal. All played the Game of Interviewed and Reprimanded. On her record, it read :

ANECDOTAL RECORD: Yvonne ─────────

9-29-72   Disturbing class and teacher—constantly talking, cracking and chewing gum, sassy. Interviewed and reprimanded. Letter sent home.

10-6-72   Drinking soda in class—refused to stop. Interviewed and reprimanded.

10-10-72   Uncooperative, insolent. Refuses to hang up coat in French. Interviewed and reprimanded.

11-3-72   Reading novel instead of textbook. Interviewed and reprimanded.

11-3-72   Disruptive and insolent behavior during full-period exam. Making noise with pen. Insolent to teacher. Refuses to follow instructions or answer questions. Interviewed and reprimanded. Warned. Called home. Mother to come to school, 11/3.

11-10-72   Talking during a test. When reprimanded responded in a surly manner. Interviewed and reprimanded.

11-15-72   Chewing gum in class after being told every day not to. Interviewed and reprimanded.

Many teachers are reluctant to play the game, not necessarily because they are concerned for the child, but because it may appear to make them weak in the eyes of their principals.

One booklet tells teachers how to control the children without sending them to the principal's office. The foreword reads:

> But before you call in the principal, or send a student to the principal's office, stop a minute and consider: Is this trip really necessary?

> It means that someone OUTSIDE your classroom is being

asked to discipline a student for behavior INSIDE your classroom.

The best policy, whenever possible, is to "skin your own skunks."*

The message is loud, clear, and smelly.

Contempt has no place in education, yet teachers often express it carelessly under the pretense of wit. The Game of Wit is an unconscionable game.

"What have you learned all year? Do you know the difference between a triangle and a horse?" Mr. Banes, the geometry teacher, asked.

The class laughed. So did Mr. Banes. The victim never forgot.

Sarcasm under the guise of wit is crude and cruel. Many teachers abhor it, even those who are equally cruel, equally belittling, but without knowing it. Under the guise of altruism they can cut deep into a child.

"I'm glad you're failing with a mark of fifty-five. I thought you would never even come close to passing. You used to get twenties. It shows you're really trying."

This teacher would have been shocked had she been told that she was sarcastic and cruel. Yet even her grade book was reflective of her pleasure at failure.

There was a list of names, and next to each name a series of red marks interspersed with a few black ones.

"The reds are failing marks on tests," she whispered.

I wondered what was wrong with her teaching if almost everybody seemed to fail every test.

"And why do you test so often?" I whispered back, not knowing why I was whispering.

"Well, I have to know what they are *not* learning," she answered.

From her own records, they seemed not to be learning a lot. I couldn't blame them.

*John and Lavono Dunworth and Emery Stoops, *Discipline* (Fairfield, N.J.: The Economics Press, 1972).

"Jonathan, do sit down," she exclaimed with a laugh, "both of you."

Jonathan was a very oversized boy.

Teachers who delight in sarcasm and play its game are proving their own wit, and therefore their own power. Perhaps they may even produce students who learn the subject they teach, but on the other hand, they are also producing students who learn to hate that subject. What price learning!

Learning should not arise out of fears of ridicule or the pain of the experience. Fear and pain have no place in a classroom. Yet, the teacher demanding to maintain personal control uses painful wit as motivation, claiming that pain increases learning.

In some cases, this may be so. An individual may never forget an incident that was painful. The memory may remain for life. On the other hand, pain often causes amnesia. People tend to forget that which is destructive of the self. Nevertheless, teachers rely on dissatisfaction and pain as a motivation for learning.

The utilization of pain is the basis of the last power game teachers play. It is the most dangerous game of all. It is the Game of Behavior Modification, and it is a game educators have taken close to their bosoms. They choose to ignore the contention of B. F. Skinner, the proponent of behaviorist psychology, that "Behaviorism is not the science of human behavior; it is the philosophy of that science," and they act as if behaviorist theory is proven practice and an answer to their prayers of what to do with the errant child.

In the Game of Behavior Modification, which educators so misguidedly play, failure is deemed so unacceptable that it is experienced as pain. Failure is to be avoided at all costs. The Game of Behavior Modification therefore perpetuates our American dream and myth, that achievement must be rewarded, failure must be denigrated. Good people achieve. Bad people fail. The constructive aspects of failure are never utilized. What the players don't realize is that failure and pain need not be synonymous. Pain has no place in a classroom, but failure has. Through failure we learn.

Hundreds of behavior modification programs are sweeping the country. Some are rigorously planned, others are haphazardly casual. Called conditioning or operant conditioning or behavior modification, all are rooted in one basic concept—behavior can be changed or modified and thereby controlled by rewarding success and inflicting psychic pain for failure—physical pain will also suffice. In one learning program, for instance, a small electric shock was administered when children responded incorrectly. Naturally, the children learned to respond correctly.

All behavior modification programs are power enforcers. All stress the teacher's power over the subject and minimize the force of power inherent in the self. Thus, insight and self-knowledge and introspection as a source of power are never utilized.

"That child spelled a word right—stick a lollipop into his mouth."

"Elise got a 100 percent on her spelling. Give her a token to be redeemed at the end of the day for a star."

"Johnny sat in his seat and raised his hand, instead of calling out. He gets five points. When he gets one hundred twenty-five, he can take a trip to the zoo."

"Mary Ellen reported she went to church on Sunday. Give her scrip that she can exchange at the school store for soda."

Evidently Mary Ellen's teacher wanted her to go to church on Sunday. I wondered, however, whatever happened to the idea of separation of church from school.

The Conditioners, the power wielders, reward success. They give tokens or scrip that a child may exchange for a prize, or they give candy or stars or red pencils. A deliberate verbal phrase such as "That's very good" is a reward. Rewards are mechanized, even the verbal ones. They cannot vary or the experiment will be invalid. Rewards are given, not because the giver wants to give, not out of love, concern, or human feeling, but out of planned reaction.

Power wielders do not tolerate failure. Rewarding failure, they feel, is "reinforcing negative behavior." With this scientific phrase that they have coined, they then proceed to eliminate the human experience from teaching and learning.

"If you reward failure," I was told, "the reward will be so pleasant that the child will fail again just to get the reward." This is what reinforcing negative behavior means. I disagree with it entirely.

One essential ingredient is always missing; that in human relationships, of which learning is one, human comfort and reward are needed at times of failure *even more* than at times of success. Success brings its own intrinsic rewards. Failure needs human compassion and the support to try again.

The times we are the most unsuccessful or the most unreasonable, and knowing that we are unsuccessful or unreasonable, but unable to stop ourselves in the destructive process, are those times when we want and need someone to say, "I believe in you. I care." Failure needs a rewarding human experience to counteract the failure. Moreover, by failure we learn.

Education should be geared not only to success but to the reconstruction of failure. It is tragic that we are all success-oriented, that we are ashamed of failure, and that we reward only success. Learning how to utilize failure should be one of the most significant skills we could teach.

I once saw an abstract watercolor exhibited in a museum. It was covered with a glass that had shattered but had not broken. The impact of that painting was dynamic. It leapt out of that frame. The glass picked up and radiated those colors in different prismatic effects. The legend stated that in carting the painting from one museum to another, someone had broken the glass. The artist had decided that the broken glass added to the depth of the painting and so it was exhibited in just that way.

Yet, I remember the hundreds of children I have known who start a drawing or a letter or a composition or an example or a typing exercise or an experiment, make a mistake, and crush it out, throw it away, destroy it. They are learning that they are failures. If only teachers would recapture those drawings and letters and compositions, and reconstruct them, the children would be learning how to build on their mistakes. Failure must be utilized.

I observed a first-grade teacher instructing several seven-year-olds in mathematics. Her teaching was based on punishing failure.

The teacher sat on one side of a three-foot desk, the children on the other. On the desk was a glass globe and a slide. Each time a trigger was pulled by the teacher, a small nugget of candy would come out of that globe and down the slide to where the child was sitting.

The teacher held up a card with an arithmetic example. If a child responded correctly to 3 plus 5, the teacher triggered the lever, the candy emerged from the globe and slid down the slide to the child. If the child did not answer correctly, no trigger, no globe, no slide, no candy. I thought at the time that the child didn't even have the pleasure of slamming that lever. Even that little bit of aggressive fun was denied, permitted only to the teacher.

One child cried during the entire lesson because he never answered the problem correctly. No candy.

Later, in discussing it with the director of the program, a professor of education at one of the leading midwestern universities, I asked what happened when the child consistently failed. "Wouldn't he ever get candy?"

"No," was the answer. "He'll eventually do arithmetic, though, because he wants the candy."

"What would happen," I asked, "if the teacher just gave the children the candy? Why the machine, the distance between them, the mechanization of the process?" It was the most sterile reward system, the most aseptic candy, I ever have seen.

He admitted it was an experiment and they didn't want it colored by human involvement.

"It is an arithmetic program," he stressed, "professionally designed."

"But the child who cries?" I pursued the point. "Doesn't he ever get comfort?"

"Well, eventually he learns his numbers," was the answer. "That should be comfort enough."

Except—is it? And is it even true that one can learn arithmetic under such pain and duress, and is it true that even if one *can* learn under such duress, that it is worth it?

I can only reiterate that pain does not belong in a classroom, and that a child who is pained needs human contact and warmth, not mechanization. A child who cries needs an arm around him, not isolation. Even a child who is most unreasonable, who is having a temper tantrum, who defies the extended arm, needs to know that someone is concerned, cares, and is willing to listen. If nothing more, he needs a presence and a soothing voice.

Conditioning is a very dangerous doctrine—far more dangerous than our political structures or educational ones are willing to admit. It does not allow for emotional growth. There is no place in it for insights, and insight, after all, is learning. For instance, in one program success was judged as an increase in the number of times children raised their hands instead of calling out. These children were judged to be better adjusted in the classroom. They were "modified."

In another program, adolescents in a treatment center were taught arithmetic by a machine. Each time they pressed the button that gave a correct answer, a token, later to be exchanged for cigarettes or soda, slid out of the machine. They learned arithmetic, all right. They also learned to respond to a machine. They became, as a group, more emotionally withdrawn.

I am certain that some children do learn through such programs, but then it must be remembered that some children will learn under any conditions, even standing on their heads, because the drive toward learning is innate.

Many teachers approve of conditioning or behavior modification, whichever they prefer to call it, because it is concrete. It has a handle that they can hold. In a sense it relieves immediate frustrations, although in the long run it adds to frustrations. Only they don't know it. They lend themselves, as easily as they lend the children, to the process.

It makes their job easier for the moment. For instance, in a booklet written for teachers the following luxury for teachers is advocated. The children, of course, are not permitted the luxury of feelings.*

> *Objective*: To alert the children to the teacher's mood as a potential "danger zone."
>
> *Procedure*: The teacher should have a means of communicating to the children when she is nervous or irritable. These can be referred to as "Red Flag" situations, and may appropriately be designated by displaying a red flag on the bulletin board or other conspicuous place. During the "Red Flag" time the children are aware that they may be sent to the time out booth (a place where a child is sent for misbehavior) for any behavior that increases the teacher's irritability, whether or not it is on the official list (a list of behavior that irritates the teacher).

So now a child can be conditioned not to irritate a teacher. The teacher's feelings must be salvaged and soothed at all costs. Never mind the child.

The most frightening aspect of behavior modification is that teachers are so accepting of it. As they lend themselves to the process, as they see their job becoming easier in that it becomes more mechanical and less involved, they in turn are becoming conditioned by their apparent successes.

---

*Carl M. Anderson and Walter B. Barbe, *Classroom Activities for Modifying Behavior in Children* (New York: Center for Applied Research in Education, 1974).

Once more, teachers give evidence of being both the product and the enforcer of authoritarianism. Once more, teachers are both the subject and the power, the victim and the victimizer, the controlled and the controller.

Only a few teachers stop to ask some essential questions. Who is to do the conditioning? Who is to decide who needs to be conditioned? Who is to decide whose behavior needs modifying? Where is the ultimate power? Where does it start and where can it end?

5
Violent Teachers

Fact and truth are not the same.

Fact: Violence exists in our schools.

Truth: Why does violence exist in our schools?

Violence exists in our schools because teachers, like all people, have the capacity for violence in them. Violence exists because the power games that teachers play with students ultimately and justifiably fail. Violence exists because, out of frustration and fear, teachers lash out in anger. Violence exists because teachers rationalize and excuse it.

Power games are psychological assaults. Physical assaults start where the psychological assaults no longer work effectively as controlling mechanisms. When children won't take tests, when children won't conform to orders or regulations that make little sense, when children won't obey mindlessly or tolerate their own modification, when children rebel against standards and procedures, physical violence starts—the violence of teachers, as well as students. Physical violence is hair-pulling, ear-yanking, mouth-washing. It is making children sit with arms on head until backs break. It is pinching, shaking, punching, twisting, paddling, and beating.

Physical violence is neither rare nor the turbulent reaction of only "sick" teachers. It is far more menacing than that, because it has become the mechanism by which thousands of teachers seek a treacherous stability.

Fact: In Dallas, Texas, there were 335 reported cases of

children being spanked in January of 1971. In January of the next year, there were 2,147 reported cases of children being spanked. The total number of children being spanked from October 1970 to June 1971 was 5,358. Many children were spanked with paddles made from baseball bats. Imagine the numbers not reported.

Fact: In 1973, 135 teachers in selected school districts in Ohio admitted to having used corporal punishment 687 times. More than 400 of these punishments were on elementary school children.

Fact: In 1969, in a survey conducted by the National Education Association, 65 percent of the elementary school teachers polled and 55 percent of the secondary school teachers said they favored "judicious use" of violent bodily punishment.

Fact: In California during 1973 and 1974, there were approximately 40,000 cases of corporal punishment on school records.

Teacher violence sets the model from which children learn that violence is sanctioned. The final irony, of course, is that when teachers become violent, they give approval to violence under the guise of maintaining discipline and fighting violence. They therefore become what they say they abhor, and they provide the very role models that they decry.

In New York City, a city that prohibits corporal punishment, a teacher wrote to his prin:

Dear Mr. K.

Following is my statement on Shirley J., class 7-410, with whom I have had great difficulty after exploring every avenue that was possible to reach her and bring her into the mainstream of activity of the 7th grade.

On the above date Shirley walked into the office (307) at 10:15. I told her to "Go to your class Shirley and do your work. I spoke to your father and assured him that I would see to it that you attended classes." She said, "My class is in the library and that's where I'm going." I said, "Your class is in 315 (room 315) and that's where you are going.'' As I walked from behind the desk she ran down the hall. I went after her and followed her from the first floor to the second floor and into the library. I told her to get her books and come upstairs with me to her Social Studies class. She said, "You're not my fucken father, you big-eyed bastard, I'll go when I'm ready." I then said, "O.K., Shirley, that's enough cursing." She said, "I'll go when I'm ready." I then told her to pick up her book bag and come with me. She reluctantly did so, and I escorted her to class and sat her down. I asked Mr. R., her Social Studies teacher, to let me know if she got out of her seat. As I was walking toward the door she said, "You big-eyed bastard, after you leave I'll walk out of the room." I left the room and went back to my office to attend to some other students who were waiting for me.

As I was speaking to another student, a monitor came from Mr. R.'s class and told me that Mr. R. wanted me. I went to the room and he said, "Mr. W., Shirley hit me and threw my pencils and pens on the floor." I then told her to go with me to the office. She said, "You black fuck, you make me sick, I'm not going anywhere." I then took her to my office (holding her by both arms). When we got to the office I told her to sit down on the couch while I called her mother. While I was dialing her mother she got off the couch and ran out of the room. I caught her and spanked her on her bottom. (This action was done with the knowledge of both parents via telephone conversations and written correspondence.)

When I brought her back to the office, she said, "You big-eyed bastard, I'll get my brother after you." I told her to be quiet and to stay seated. She said, "I'll get up if I want to," and proceeded to remove herself from the couch. In the meantime I managed to get her aunt on the telephone, who works with her mother. I asked her if I might speak to Mrs. J. She told me that Mrs. J. was taking inventory but she would take the message. I told her what had happened and she said that she would have Mrs. J. call me back as soon as possible. When I hung the telephone up she jumped out of the seat and started to run. I went after her and tried to sit her down without using too much force. As I was doing so, she took her foot and kicked me in the testicle. When I bent down, she got up and ran downstairs to the principal's office. In the meantime, Mr. J. called me and I was informing him of the situation between Shirley and myself.

During our conversation Mr. K., the principal, called me on the phone and asked me what the problem was. I told him that I was speaking to Mr. J. and to pick up his telephone and join the conversation.

He informed Mr. J. that he would appreciate his coming to school so that we might find out what we could do to help Shirley and to alleviate the problem which seems to confront her.

I have tried to use every form of human behavior to reach this young lady but it has been to no avail. I have written to her doctor to find out what we could do at school to help her so that our efforts would be correlated. I was hoping to receive some kind of response before a situation such as this could arise, but to date I have received no written communication.

I hope that somewhere, somehow, this young lady can be reached so that she might continue her education and to grow mentally and physically into a responsible adult and to share in the great abyss of opportunities that the society in which she lives has to offer her.

Sincerely,
A. W.
Dean, 7th Grade

Mr. W. was so right. The school was offering Shirley a "great abyss of opportunities." No opportunity could sink any lower.

No one in that school ever mentioned the fact that Shirley, disturbed as she was, was treated violently.

Didn't it occur to anyone in that school to ask Shirley why she didn't want to go to her scheduled class, why she wanted to go to the library instead? Did it not occur to anyone to speak rationally to Shirley, to try and understand her reasons? Just maybe, she had reasons, and just maybe she could not express those reasons except by anger and cursing. And why is a scheduled class so sacrosanct, anyway? Cannot children learn at their own time and place? Cannot schedules be rescheduled?

We painstakingly sculpture the situations that propel children into violence. Then, in reaction to their violence, we rationalize our own.

A very young graduate student of mine came to me in desperation.

"I didn't want to do it," she wailed. "I felt real bad, but Kathy was impossible today, she just wouldn't stop talking, I just had to put tape on her mouth, and I turned her chair to the back of the room."

My shock must have shown.

"Well, it was only for a few minutes," she said, "and really, she could have ripped off the tape herself. It didn't hurt, it was only Scotch tape."

My shock and disapproval still showed.

"Well, what was I to do?" she said. "Kathy wouldn't let me read during story-telling. She kept interrupting and then the others wouldn't listen. She's extremely self-centered and show-offish."

It was obvious that the teacher saw the classroom in terms of her own problems rather than in terms of a child's needs. I tried to point out the need.

"Well," I asked, "if she didn't want to hear the story, why did she have to? Couldn't you let her draw or paint or play in another corner of the room? Maybe she can't sit still."

"Well, then the others would want to do that, too," she explained.

"What's so wrong with that?" I asked. "Why must they—"

"Because it's story-telling time," she interrupted.

"And it can't ever be changed? It's immutable?" I queried.

"Of course not, but it's story-telling time—" she repeated, as if I had not heard her the first or second time.

"It's apparently your story-telling time," I argued, "but not Kathy's, and if what you are teaching is reading readiness and getting children to enjoy stories, this is one helluva way. Kathy will hate reading if she's forced to listen, and she'll hate reading if you tape her mouth because she doesn't listen."

That much she agreed with. As we talked, she laid the blame upon her supervisor, who was the head of the private school in which she worked. Mrs. Wilson believed in rigid routines. If the child didn't conform, punish that child. The child had to conform to the group at the arbitrary whim of what the teacher decided to teach. Story-telling time was inherited. The hour was set in teacher genes. Apparently, Mrs. Wilson had never heard of individual children and *their* genes.

"I have to do these things if I want to keep my job," my student wailed. "Mrs. Wilson told us to. It's how she teaches. She's very old-fashioned."

"And punitive," I answered. "All in the guise of teaching. How old is Kathy?"

"Five."

"How old are you?" I asked.

"Twenty-five."

"And you can find no other ways to teach than by taping a child's mouth?" I asked. "No matter what Mrs. Wilson says?"

She slowly began to think of several. I suggested she begin by relinquishing her grip on story-telling time. I also suggested that she might have to make the decision to talk with Mrs. Wilson, albeit her job was dependent upon Mrs. Wilson's good will, and to question some of the school's practices.

I also suggested that if she found Mrs. Wilson too restrictive, that if Mrs. Wilson insisted on story-telling hour and quiet for everyone at the same time, or Scotch taping a mouth, then it might be beholden upon her to speak to Kathy's parents.

Revolution is a very aggressive activity, and it can be more therapeutic than taping the mouths of five-year-old children.

The story did not turn out well. Mrs. Wilson was unresponsive. My student talked to Kathy's parents, who withdrew Kathy from the school. My student was fired from her job. On the other hand, perhaps it turned out very well. Kathy may have been saved, and so may that student. Maybe even Mrs. Wilson had a qualm or two after that.

Physical punishment and repression do not eliminate disobedience any more than they eliminate violence. While punishment and repression may have a temporary silencing effect, they breed depression, anger, and feelings of powerlessness and frustration; children who are continually subjected to our nominally disciplinary measures are learning to believe in violence.

Mr. Harrison, for instance, taught in a so-called rough school in Pittsburgh. Pittsburgh is the city in which the president of the Pittsburgh Teachers' Federation said, "Until somebody comes up with an alternative, we'll support it [corporal punishment]."*

Mr. Harrison felt perfectly honorable in teaching his junior high school classes that violence is acceptable.

"Keep the center of the floor clear, boys," he would say to his class. "Let them fight it out."

"What?" I cried, horrified, when he told me of his practice.

"Yes," he said, "if they're going to fight anyway, instead of them getting hurt and fighting dirty, I say all right, fight it out—here and now."

"Don't you try to discuss it first?" I asked.

"Oh sure," he said, "but if I don't think it will work, well—they don't even hurt each other, they spar around and it's all over."

"But consider what they learned," I said. "That fighting is

---

*Alan Reitman, Judith Follmann, and Edward T. Ladd, *Corporal Punishment in the Public Schools: The Use of Force in Controlling Student Behavior* (American Civil Liberties Union, March 1972), p. 3.

okay, it's condoned by the teacher, that might makes right, that the meek will not inherit the world, that issues are settled by fighting, that street values are correct, that gang wars are acceptable if the fighting is fair. You're teaching them that fighting is fine as long as it's a fair fight. Correct?''

He had never looked at it that way.

"What other way is there to look at it?" I asked.

"Before you know it, it's over," he repeated. "And they really use up energy that way."

"Well, you might as well tell them to masturbate," I suggested. "That will have the same effect."

I was being facetious, of course, but I was disturbed.

"And what about girls?" I asked. "Do you let them fight, too?"

Now it was his turn to be horrified.

"Oh no!"

"Why not?" I asked. "If what you're teaching is fine for boys, why not for girls? Some of the best fighters I know are girls."

He got my message.

"Are you saying I'm a male chauvinist pig?" He tried to laugh.

"No," I answered, "but I am saying you have a lot to question yourself about. Teaching kids that fighting is the way to resolve arguments is wrong both for boys and girls."

Teachers can condone neither the street values of crime and violence nor the values of war. We cannot teach children to believe that fighting to settle an issue settles the issue. Fighting only leads to more fighting. Violence begets violence.

"Do you believe in the principles of the United Nations?" I asked.

Of course Mr. Harrison did, but he also believed in being practical. Politics was politics and school was school.

I tried to convince him that the height of practicality was to be concerned with survival, and survival in schools and in the world ultimately depends upon rationality, not violence.

"Well," he drawled, going down hard, "it's really like a sport—"

"When boxers fight," I answered, "that may be a sport, and supposedly they're not angry or fighting over an issue. When anyone fights in anger, and in resolution of a conflict, it is war, and war is not a sport."

We cannot encourage and teach children to believe that fighting to settle an issue is acceptable, moral, rational, or justifiable. Yet, even New York City's United Federation of Teachers advocates violence. I don't think they realize it. Under the delusion that they are trying to avoid it, they have written: "With most elementary school students, teachers can *see* that an outburst is coming. And with most of them, physical restraint is the best response. If a teacher anticipates that an attack is coming, he should get as close to the child as possible; spin the youngster around; and embrace him in a bear hug that pins his arms to his body."*

Now, I am not opposed to self-protection. Teachers certainly have a right to protect themselves from attack. But, is *seeing* an outburst coming the same thing as an actual attack? Is *anticipating* an outburst reason for pinning a child's arms down to his sides? Or is a bear hug really just a hug?

Surely, teachers can be taught other ways of avoiding an assault.

Can they not prevent an assault by conciliation, by allaying of anxieties, by accepting the angers of the child and talking through those angers?

Where are the other children in all of this? Where are the child's friends, who may be very helpful in calming the child down? When children are treated fairly, when their feelings are *recognized*—not recognized as *just*, but *just recognized*—children generally do calm down, they do become reasonable. But teachers often do not give children the credit for rationality, because teachers become irrational themselves. They react to

---

*United Federation of Teachers, "Security in the Schools" (New York, N.Y., 1974), p. 4.

fear of the anticipation of violence and their fears coupled with their frustrations produce their own acts of violence.

In an effort to hold back the force of violence in teachers, the National Education Association organized a Task Force on Corporal Punishment. Their report, issued in 1972, first recommended that corporal punishment be phased out over a one-year period.

Why a one-year period? I don't know. Why not immediately? I don't know that either.

It seems that educational reformers are still enmeshed in the culture of punishment and cannot free themselves from it, even when they may appear ardently to want to.

Another recommendation in the report issued by the NEA reads: "The task force will delineate minimal conditions that must be provided *if* educators are to deal with disruptions in others ways than by inflicting physical force on children."

It is the word *if* that bothers me. Why if? Is corporal punishment still to be questioned? Why do they not say "The task force will delineate minimal conditions that must be provided *in helping* educators deal with disruptions in other ways than by inflicting physical force on children?"

In the same year as the NEA report, the American Orthopsychiatric Association and the American Civil Liberties Union cosponsored a conference to combat corporal punishment in the schools. The conference voted to urge the United States Department of Health, Education and Welfare not to allot funds to those school districts in which corporal punishment is still accepted by state law. Yet, only a few cities—notably New York, Pittsburgh, Chicago, and Baltimore—and only two states, New Jersey and Maryland, have passed laws forbidding corporal punishment. There are at present at least thirteen states that sanction the use of corporal punishment. Different conditions, however, are often set down. In Florida, for instance, a teacher may use corporal punishment after consultation with the principal. In Michigan, Hawaii, Ohio, South Dakota, Vermont, and Virginia, physical force may be used in order to maintain discipline. No permission or consultation is required. In California, Delaware, and Pennsylvania, the teachers are considered *in loco parentis*, so presumably they can hit with impunity. In Montana, corporal punishment is permitted only in the presence of another teacher and with notice to a parent—except in open defiance, when no notice is needed.

The tragedy, of course, is that so many parents are in agreement. Sometimes parents give carte blanche authority, sometimes they ask to be notified first. Either way, parents really are in the untenable position of upholding the school's right to punish their children without really listening to the child. Even if they were to listen before the punishment was meted out, they would take the risk of alienating either their own child or the teachers. If they believed in the school's version of any altercation, they would alienate the child. If they believed in the child's version and refused permission, they would alienate the school, which often makes matters worse for the child, because the parent becomes that most heinous of enemies—a "hostile parent." Parents caught in this dilemma most often agree to the punishment, not because they really do agree, but because they are afraid not to agree.

It is about time we said the eulogy for *in loco parentis*. It was a principle developed in the eighteenth century by the English jurist Sir William Blackstone, and it referred to the social custom of education prevailing in England at that time. Children of the wealthy were taught by tutors who most often lived with the family. These tutors assumed total responsibility for their charges. They were to all intents and purposes *in loco parentis*. But twentieth-century America is not eighteenth-century England, and teachers do not live with their students, standing in lieu of parents. Yet, parents today often find themselves adopting this eighteenth-century standard.

For instance, I met Mrs. Rogers in Kansas when I was speaking at an educational conference. After my presentation to the audience, during which I spoke of the rights of children to make their own decisions which is the greatest antidote to violence that I know, she came up to me visibly upset. She taught in the public school system. Her son attended a parochial school. She had received a phone call only that morning from her son's principal, Sister Veronica, asking permission for the principal to spank him. She repeated the conversation to me almost verbatim:

"Mrs. Rogers, may I have your permission to spank Jonathan?"

"Why, Sister, what has he done?"

"He's been very insolent, Mrs. Rogers, and he refuses to apologize."

"Why, what did he say?"

"I really would rather not repeat it, Mrs. Rogers. It was to one of the other teachers. He insulted her when she intervened in a fight."

"Fight? My God, Sister, what did he do?"

"He struck another boy and wouldn't apologize. Then, when the teacher insisted he do so, he used a foul word to her."

"I suppose he was angry," Mrs. Rogers said. She admitted she was looking for explanations for his behavior, not because she approved of what he had done, but because she wanted to understand what he had done.

"May we spank him?" Sister Veronica asked again. "He really cannot be permitted to be rude."

"Of course he shouldn't be rude," Mrs. Rogers agreed. "But—"

"Well, may we spank him, Mrs. Rogers?"

Mrs. Rogers was confused.

"Where is he now, Sister?"

"Waiting in the assistant principal's office."

"To be spanked? Oh my God!" Mrs. Rogers was close to tears even as she told the story. I knew she must have wept then, too.

"Shall we go ahead, then?"

Mrs. Rogers found herself catapulted into agreement.

"Yes."

The moment she had said it she was sorry.

"Well, why did you let her?" I asked.

"Because I wasn't there," she explained, "and I knew I couldn't get there today because I was scheduled for this conference. But after all, the teacher is *in loco parentis*. Oh, I don't know—" she ended. "I should have gone to his school."

I agreed with her and suggested that she could still go. She decided she would. Before she left, however, I asked her if she would have hit him if she had been there.

She said no.

I asked her if she would hit a child in similar circumstances in her own class.

She said no. Then she smiled ruefully. "But many teachers do."

We talked as I walked with her to where her car was parked.

"In other words," I said, "what your son learned, Mrs. Rogers, is that aggression is paid off by aggression. He learned the dynamics of war. Quite a lesson for a child attending a religious school."

Mrs. Rogers agreed. She realized with sudden insight that Sister Veronica had proved her authority by spanking a child, who by this time was waiting patiently in another office to be spanked. I am certain it never occurred to Sister Veronica or to Mrs. Rogers that spanking was a release for Sister Veronica's own anger. It might even have made her feel better— momentarily. The guilt would come later. How much more effective, meaningful, and moral it would have been for Sister Veronica instead to have called both boys and the teacher to her office and, over cocoa or sodas, to have discussed the reasons for the fight, the possible solutions that could have averted it, and the teacher's role in trying to stop it. Perhaps then Jonathan would have apologized to the teacher for his loss of control and for his "foul" word to her. He would have meant the apology because he would have understood the teacher's concern. It would not have been an apology grudgingly given and therefore hypocritical.

Sister Veronica should have accepted everyone's feelings of anger, the teacher's as well as the boys'. This would have been aggressive counseling. The boys could have learned that feelings of anger can be accepted in a classroom and talked about, and that in the resolution of conflicts there are alternatives to violence. The teacher would have learned that a "bad" word cannot destroy unless one lets it destroy. The teacher would have learned that it is necessary to recognize the feelings of the children rather than to respond primarily to her own.

In this kind of counseling, Sister Veronica's own need to be recognized as the person in charge could have been gratified through intellectual control; she would not have felt the need to hit.

Sister Veronica, however, merely became violent herself. Out of anger and frustration she did exactly what the boys had done; she engaged in exactly the same behavior for which she was punishing them. She hit a child.

Violence stems from impotence and frustration. Teachers use physical punishment when they feel inadequate and unable to handle a situation. Frustration mounts and violence erupts.

Mrs. Chambers, for instance, constantly prodded boys with her six-foot speared blackboard pointer. Mrs. Chambers was the forty-five-year-old gym teacher in an all-boys' junior high school.

I am trying to find reasons why Mrs. Chambers needed that spear. She used it methodically: a shove in the side to line the boys up, a whack on the backside to start a race, a bang on the head for the beginning of gymnastics, a swipe on the arm to stop talking.

Younger boys feared her. The older boys and the principal liked her. As faculty adviser to the General Organization, or G.O., as it was commonly called, she encouraged the older boys to bully the younger boys into conformity and into paying their twenty-five cents dues for the term. The principal had a well-disciplined school and a 100 percent membership in the G.O. Mrs. Chambers was proud of her G.O. It was her contribution to the forces of democracy. Other than that, she didn't believe in it.

Mrs. Chambers never used or needed the occupational trappings of a gym teacher—a whistle or a gym suit. She did, however, wear white sneakers. That's how come she could sneak from behind, front, sideways, and backwards—and *poing*! went that stick. Once she did it to a teacher, assuming that the teacher was that loathsome thing—a student. Seeing only a sweatered arm holding a swinging door and not seeing the rest of the body that belonged to that arm behind that swinging door, down went that spear.

"What are you doing, cutting classes?" she screamed at the teacher.

I looked at her, stunned. "Cutting classes?" I thought. My God, it was my arm she cut.

Mrs. Chambers recognized her mistake. She flushed and apologized curtly. I accepted her truncated apologies with magnanimity. But then, after she left, my anger took over, and after school I took my magic marker, my friend, and my revenge, and all over the main staircase we wrote, FUCK MRS. CHAMBERS. That was before I knew about constructive aggression. Now, of course, I would simply tell her how I felt about her and her methods.

Looking back at it now, I realize that Mrs. Chambers was all façade, all defense, and all fear. She ruled by that stick. The boys had a word for it. They called it her "dick." Perhaps they understood her better than I did. Perhaps she was trying to be a man herself, or perhaps she was trying to be more of a woman by castrating all the boys in that school—I don't know. All I know is that she was a bitch, that I hated her with a passion, and I made little effort to understand her until the very end of the term, the last day, in fact, when I knew I would never see her again. I was transferring to another school.

"I once wanted to paint," she admitted to me. "I used to be quite good. Pastels were my media, but—"

I never knew what the "but" was because the artist suddenly faded and she became Mrs. Chambers again. I felt sad. Somewhere within Mrs. Chambers there had been a good person. Where was that person now? Surely, not in that teacher.

Perhaps if she had been the artist she had hoped to be or had at least taught art, or perhaps if she had just searched out herself and felt good about herself, she would not have acted so violently. Her "but" was certainly a statement of frustration.

How different a person Mrs. Chambers was from Mrs. Sealy, who understood frustration and knew how to overcome it. Aggressively. Because she knew herself, she was not easily threatened. She did not need to prove her superiority in the classroom.

That first day of the term she faced her seventh-grade all-boys' class with some trepidation. She was a good teacher, she knew she was a good teacher, but the nineteenth class on the seventh-grade level in a school that groups children on achievement scores is a class to be reckoned with—for any teacher.

That class of Italian, Jewish, Polish, German, Irish, Gypsy, and Puerto Rican boys knew they were grouped for stupidity. They were a so-called adjustment class, which meant they were labeled maladjusted, and, being so labeled, they were forced to wear their armor to ward off the hurt. They were disdainful, contemptuous, and angry boys when they weren't truanting. They were, it seemed, grouped for toughness. They were individually tough, collectively tough, and massively tough.

It was a class in English. They wanted to talk sex. She let them talk sex.

"Look boys," she said quickly, the first thing that came into her head, "I have clerical work to do anyway, so I'll just give you a free period. I'll be so busy I won't have a chance to listen."

She sat and grabbed the first sheet on her desk, which happened to be the principal's useless conference notes, delivering in pompous tone the year's educational goals. She began diligently and studiedly to copy them.

There were catcalls and dirty jokes and remarks thrown her way.

"I wonder if she gets it regular—"

She wrote on silently, and occasionally muttered that if

she didn't send the report to the office, she'd be in trouble.

Boris, who seemed to her, at first confrontation, to be seven feet tall and all red knuckles, had a razor blade with him, with which he kept stripping the leather off his shoes. He sat in the seat directly in front of her and he kept his shoe with foot still in it on her desk.

"Boris, would you mind?" she asked. "I need to spread the papers on the desk—"

He removed his foot with no comment.

By the time the bell rang, the joke had worn off for the boys. Mrs. Sealy told them they'd start work the next day.

And they did.

Class 7-19 decided that Mrs. Sealy was okay. That year the Mississippi flowed into Delancey Street as those boys—tough, poor, and sophisticated in the ways of New York City's streets —dissected, fought over, amended, edited, and acted their own version of *Tom Sawyer*. It was a book they all wanted to read, perhaps because it was a current movie. And through it they learned a lot about another culture and its history.

Mrs. Sealy was not always totally in charge in terms of order in the classroom. She was, however, always in charge of her own feelings. She did not feel threatened by noise, movement, or bad language. As a result, the boys respected her authority, because she had a real sense of her own.

Teachers who feel that their role does not have to be a controlling one, teachers who learn that they can always be in control of their own feelings even if they are not in control of the feelings of others, do not feel that they have to control others. In other words, self-understanding means that one can always control one's self even if one cannot always control others. What teachers will find, and I am certain that it will come as a surprise, is that, once their own self-certainties become evident, children will respond to those certainties by becoming more receptive to learning.

A teacher who says to a child, "I can't stop you from fighting, only you can stop yourself from fighting," is giving a child an understanding of self-power and self-determination, as well as an understanding of the role of a teacher.

I listened to Charlie Gray, the assistant principal at Livingston, now retired, as she talked to Janie, a loud girl who was always ready, it seemed, to fight.

"But if she jumps me," Janie cried, "you mean to tell me to let her hit me?"

"No," Mrs. Gray answered. "If you're in a street and attacked, you have to defend yourself. That is your right, and you make the decision whether to fight or run. But if you're in school, and it's not a matter of self-defense, only a matter of pride, you can walk away and let the law work for you, the law or the teachers. You can get a teacher or a counselor to help you talk it out. You can even bring charges in court. But walking away takes guts."

Janie learned that there are alternatives to violence, and that self-power means considering those alternatives.

A teacher who says, "Let us plan what you are willing and ready to learn today," is also giving children a chance to find their own power.

In instructing children how to take the responsibility for their own decisions, teachers must be prepared to go the whole way with the decision.

"We want to play today," said a sixth-grade class. "We want to read comic books, play games, talk, do nothing."

"Why?" asked Mr. Ontero.

"We just feel like it," was the answer.

"Okay," said Mr. Ontero. "Let's plan how we'll organize our play day."

The class proceeded to organize. The children learned many things that day—not reading or mathematics, but how to plan, how to assign tasks, how to get things done.

Mr. Ontero did not feel that he was not needed. He did not feel guilty because he wasn't teaching subject matter. His inner security made the learning of that day possible for his students. He was able to give the power of decision making to his class.

Mr. Ontero's ability to give that power stemmed from his own sense of self-power. The giving of power therefore was not a threat to him.

If we were to make education what it should be, a process whereby children learn the skills of self-determination; if more decision making processes were given to children; if children were to decide what they are to learn, when they are to learn; then children would not repudiate school and their teachers as they are now doing in large measure, but would assume greater responsibility for themselves and be willing to be held accountable to their teachers for their own learning.

"I'd really rather rap today," said the ninth-grade English teacher. "It's June and it's hot, and I don't feel like work, and I know you would rather not work either, but that end-term exam is coming up soon and we need to review the grammar. What do you think?"

After discussion pro and con, the class decided to review for the test.

If their decision had been to "rap," the teacher would have agreed, because in the decision making process, decisions are not based on mere impulsive whims but on a discussion of consequences. Values are always inherent in the discussion.

When the discussion was over, and it lasted fifteen minutes, the learning that took place in exploring the question of long-term goals vs. short-term goals was as valuable as the study of grammar that followed. When the hour was over, some students discovered that the study itself was rather pleasurable because the decision to study had been theirs. However, if the teacher had commanded Study, while the students might have learned some facts, they would not also have learned that they did indeed have control over and responsibility for their educational lives.

In the same way, if teachers had greater freedom to decide what to teach, when to teach, and how to teach, and if they were permitted to fail occasionally in the process of their own learning, they would learn that this failure does not destroy them but is only a basis for exploration of how to learn to be more effective. And then they would begin to feel their potential for real power. When teachers have real power, *the power of self-understanding, the power to give power to children*, and *the power of being unafraid* when such power is given, violence in the classroom stops.

Self-determination is a process not clearly understood by teachers, because they have been deprived of it as students and are still being deprived of it as teachers. Having been made to fit the mold themselves, and still fitting the mold, they become fearful of students who refuse to be molded. They then stress not self-determination but conformity. Any child who violates the conformity process is to be feared, as violence is feared. In their efforts to suppress violence, teachers repress the children and exert their own power. They do not understand that repression does not stop violence; it causes violence. They do not understand that powerlessness is at the seat of violence and that our children are indeed powerless. If one wants to stop the violence of a powerless group, one must give them power, not take away what little they have. If we were then to give children the power of self-determination in the schools, violence in the schools would decrease.

There is no doubt that violence cannot be tolerated in our schools. Teachers, however, quite refuse to see that they are producing it.

For instance, the deprivation of food is a violent act. I have seen children come to school hungry, and because they are hungry, they become unpleasant, irritable, and sometimes aggressive or violent. The obvious solution is to give the children breakfast. Many teachers, however, react to the symptom, behavior, which is not the cause, hunger, and paradoxically punish the children with "no milk and cookies for you at recess because you don't know how to behave."

I have also seen hungry children told by teachers that they couldn't eat lunch that day because they had been too noisy in the lunchroom the previous day, and were too proud to apologize for being loud. These were children of the poor, for whom in some cases a school lunch was the only nutritious meal of the day.

A child who is drowning needs air, *not* to have his head shoved under the water so he can get used to the lack of oxygen.

A child who is hungry should not be deprived of food and told to be good. When a child is hungry, we should feed him and then help him to find his way to being good. How violent can violence be, short of death?

The prevention of violence is often no more than feeding a child, physically or emotionally. But no, teachers dwell on the unpleasant act after it happens without trying to prevent its happening again; they dwell on result, not cause, and they rationalize their right to control, quell, and punish. Thus, they repress violence and in the process manufacture it in the millions of "disobedient," "disruptive," "delinquent," and "disciplinary" cases they produce each year. They expel their own frustrations by dispensing punishment and, with the dispensing, label their victims disruptive. Both the punishing and labeling are acts of violence. In doing so they deny the child the right of self-determination and they deny that the antidote to violence is more power to the victim, not less. The antidote to violence is giving children greater rights, not less.

Children who are crying out to be heard need to be heard. The children who want to talk need to talk. Children who want to move need to move. Children need power.

Teachers are frightened of the idea. The more frightened they become, the more repressive and violent they become—and the more open about it. They advocate violence.

In a booklet entitled "Classroom Activities for Modifying Behavior," teachers are taught how to use physical punishment.

Objective: To provide effective punishment for certain misbehaviors.

Preparation: If school rules permit it, mild physical punishment can be highly effective, but it is also very risky. It should, therefore, in every instance be used with considerable judgment and discretion. I might suggest that the teacher who is perfectly sure that she has the love and respect of her students can more easily use this activity. In situations where love and respect are at a lower ebb, or where there is open antagonism between a teacher and her pupil(s), this activity could be used as a weapon against the teacher. In such a situation, any punishment involving physical contact is strongly discouraged.

Procedure: If you notice a student in the process of misbehaving, pop him on the hand, shoulder, or bottom with a yard stick. *I do not mean* taking hold of the child, positioning him, and then popping him! I mean rather utilizing the element of surprise to reach out and swat him as he is in the act of misbehaving.

It is noteworthy that punishment is discouraged when the teacher isn't loved. Then presumably the teacher may be hit in retaliation. But if the teacher is loved, the "it hurts me as much as it hurts you" philosophy prevails—a phony statement if ever I heard one.

And I have heard many.

I attended one educational conference where the main point of discussion for over two hours was how to fill out forms to make the act of teacher violence look like an accident. Little sweetheart statements like "Tell the teachers to get them where it doesn't show" were constant refrains, jokingly said, but absolutely meant. At no time was there a discussion of the immorality of teacher violence. At no time was there a discussion on how to fire such teachers. At no time was the point even made that when teaching was effective, when there were good relationships between teachers and students, beatings were unnecessary. In schools where children love the school, there is no vandalism, no marking on the wall, no stealing of equipment; in schools where children feel they belong, there is no violence.

I was at another conference where principals were told by the superintendent that when a teacher lost his temper and beat a child, it was "manly" for that teacher to apologize. It was said in admiration of his "manliness." Nothing, of course, was said about the "manliness" in the first place of a six-foot-tall burly teacher beating a seventh-grade boy half his size. I wondered at the time, rather bitterly, if a woman beat a child and then apologized, whether it would make her more "manly" or more "womanly."

How belittling for a grown person—man or woman—to have to hit a child. It speaks so for their inadequacy. Yet, I have been told by educators that children like to be beaten. It shows "we care."

I have heard this statement made seriously. Just as I have heard that it is necessary to search children daily for weapons.

"Sometimes there's no other way," a superintendent of schools of a large city once said to me. "What are we to do when kids bring weapons to school?"

I told him they wouldn't bring weapons to school if they weren't treated repressively. Repressed prisoners will erupt, as they did in the Attica massacre. Repressed students sometimes erupt outwardly, sometimes inwardly. Both are acts of violence.

My remarks produced the comment that I was "a liberal," with implications that I was also merely a sentimental woman. Did I not believe that there were disturbed children who became violent?

"Certainly," I agreed, "but disturbed people, including children, need treatment, not repression, and when they are in school settings they need treatment programs, not repressive ones. We should be past the days of beating the devil out of mentally ill people. Why are we still doing that?"

"There are times," he insisted, "when it is necessary to search children for weapons."

I disagreed, because I know that if any student really wanted to hurt another student or a teacher with a weapon, no amount of searching could prevent it. A determined student will find a way, in school or out, to use that weapon. A child who brings a weapon most often wants to be stopped from using it. He lets it be known he has that weapon. Besides, one child who may occasionally bring a weapon does not warrant the daily searching of all children.

I knew this to be the case in several schools for socially maladjusted and emotionally disturbed boys. Boys were searched daily and routinely for contraband, defined as pen knives, knives, guns, dope, candy, combs, pics, gum, money, and wristwatches.

I found the classification to defy any system of logic. It was explained to me that these were the items students fought over.

I wondered why they didn't include girls in the list. Quick—roaming girl visitor in school—seize her as contraband! Search her, even she may have a weapon. There are many superintendents, principals, supervisors, and teachers who condone searching even though it is in violation of everyone's civil rights.

"Oh that," a principal once told me. "Civil rights are all right in their place, but let's be practical. These kids are not you and me—they don't know how to use civil rights."

I thought he was stupid so I didn't bother to become angry.

"What about what searching does to the child's concept of self?" I asked. "Would you like to be searched daily at your office?"

He clearly didn't see the analogy. It was obvious he felt that no students' rights were equal to his. What he did say was, "They don't mind being searched. They know it's for their own good."

I realized then I was underestimating him. I was annoyed at

myself for not seeing below his surface. He was not stupid. He represented a large bulk of our educational hierarchy. To label such viciousness, crassness, and need for personal vindictiveness, hatred, and power as merely stupid is to minimize it. It was my own personal act of self-deception. I did not want to see the truth. These are not stupid people. The truth is, many principals feel that students going to school, like prisoners going to jail, give up their civil rights. These principals have adopted the prison codes.

"Oh," said another principal, "there's nothing formal about a search, we do an informal search."

A friend of mine, hearing him, said, "I suppose he does it with a cocktail in hand."

No, he did not. His searches were "quickies." Boys were called suddenly without warning to the gym, and were commanded to face the wall, raise hands above heads, put hands on wall. Teachers searched.

"They like it," said one principal. "It keeps them secure." It was the "we care" syndrome, stated differently. I didn't bother to answer.

"It works," said another.

I couldn't let that pass.

"So did slavery work," I rejoined, "for the slaveholders."

He flushed. I assumed he was angry. I hoped so.

"What does slavery have to do with it?" he asked.

"Everything," I answered. "Searching works for the good of the teachers, or so you think. It doesn't work for the good of the kids. Searching is immoral. Since when is expediency more important than morality?"

At this point I was close to tears because I knew that searching really couldn't work for the teachers either. It could only heighten their own process of demoralization. How could teachers respect themselves? How could students learn under such indignities?

We teach, it seems, for self-deformation as well as for deformation of our students. We cripple ourselves as we cripple them. Then, when the children react violently to our programing of them, we ask in seeming surprise, ''But what else can we do?''

The question points the way to prison.

6

The Prison Syndrome

Fearing the children and decrying their violence, we commit the most violent act of all. We send the children we have failed to prison. Sometimes we assembly-line them through a court process, sometimes we do not. We punish with and without legal sanction while we completely blind ourselves to our own aggression, violence, and immorality.

Teachers can very often handle most successfully the children whom educators like to call special, the children who are hard-of-hearing or crippled or blind or intellectually retarded. As a matter of fact, our best classes and our best teachers throughout the country are often in these special classes for physically disabled children. These children have an overt disability that we can recognize, see, and treat, and we have real and true compassion for them. With these special children, teachers are often involved in self-exploration. They know why they are there, what their special penchant is, and why (often because a friend or member of the family is so impaired).

But the children without an obvious disability, the twenty to thirty million abrasive and obtrusive children in our schools who are the "holdovers"— the nonpromoted, the poor learners, the disruptive, delinquent, truant, and difficult children, whom teachers call underprivileged or culturally deprived or disadvantaged or emotionally disturbed or socially maladjusted—these are the "discipline" cases—the children we cannot beat down, the children we therefore hate and want to punish.

148

Let me make a distinction. Certainly there are children who are mentally ill or suffering from emotional disturbances. They are not troubled or abusive simply because they are the products of an inadequate school system. They are disturbed because of deep-rooted personality disorders, which poor school experiences can, of course, exacerbate. They are of special concern and should be given special therapeutic programs. These children are not necessarily unmanageable even though they might be seriously emotionally ill. Some emotionally ill children are quite manageable, passive, and conforming. In fact, their passivity might well be the core of their illness. On the other hand, many so-called unmanageable children are not ill at all, although some may be. Unmanageability is not synonymous with being disturbed.

The fact is that millions of children are troubled, not mentally ill. They are suffering because of the ineffectiveness of their schools, the obdurateness and intransigencies of their teachers, and the unfairness of their own lives. Their open troublesomeness is their major source of strength and health. Refusing to give in to tyranny, refusing to be victimized, standing up for one's rights is, after all, very Pioneer American. Why do we fear them so?

Can't we use their strengths of defiance and aggression? Can't we build upon their ability to fight back against a society that has failed them? Can't we take their potential for aggression and teach them how to use it constructively?

We do not even try. We put them away. In prisons. Moreover, we don't even put them in prisons in their own cities or even in their own states; we send them instead far from home, where their own parents cannot afford to visit, because we must not forget that these are children of the poor. Thus, we provide not only geographical banishment but emotional banishment as well, and we kill any hope we may have for the rehabilitation of a child within the child's own family. Under these conditions, the professionals who do care, and there are many, often become defeated and give up trying. So do the children, who, at the age of seven, eight or nine, often suffer the pain of seeing themselves as human failures.

For how can treatment or therapy be effective, if indeed it is even provided, when it is provided for the child alone but not for the family? Yet, we all know that the problems obviously cannot rest with the child alone but must be related in part to the inadequacies of the family. Shouldn't the parents be involved in any treatment that is provided to the child, so that whatever problems the family and the child may experience together can be resolved together? How can such resolutions take place, however, when children from Illinois are sent to Texas, and children from Massachusetts are sent to Maine, New York, or Pennsylvania, and children from Alaska are sent to Colorado? By this lend-leasing of children, many states avoid their responsibilities to provide appropriate treatment, because it is cheaper to export children than to treat them.

George Bernard Shaw once said, "It is not our disorder but our order that is horrible." He was so right. We are not incidental in our abuses of our children. We provide a definite system of abuse. That system is prison. But because we all know that prisons are not for children, we delude ourselves and call them training schools, juvenile schools, youth houses, youth centers. Call them what we will, they are miniature prisons operating under the name of school. In the different states the teachers are responsible to different agencies and different authorities, to the county, the city, or the state; to the Department of Correction, Department of Social Service, Department of Mental Hygiene, or Department of Education.

One-third of the children in such institutions are imprisoned because they have been labeled "bad," "difficult," "incorrigible," "disturbed," "maladjusted." They have been fresh to their teachers and slow to learn, and they look for their significance outside of school and in the streets. They can sometimes manage to feel big and sometimes even tangentially happy. They stay out late at night and they run away from home in their search. They seem to offend everyone—the school, social agencies, the community, and even their own parents, who are desperate with concern or who have simply given up.

The second third of the children in our miniature prisons are our "neglected" and "dependent" children, our children, the agencies say, who are "in need of supervision." We strip them of their civil rights and put them into prison. Yet, they have committed no crime. Their "crime" has been to be born into families that are inadequate, overburdened, troubled, and poor. Their "crime" has been to be insolent and rude to their teachers or to ignore their teachers by not attending school at all.

The last third of the children in our miniature prisons are children who have been judged "delinquent" after a court hearing. Delinquency is a legal term. It means that if an adult committed the same act of which the child is accused, it would constitute a crime. Children are adjudged "delinquent" and sent to prison if they truant from school. Yet, no adult is sent to jail for not going to work. Neither are teachers sent to prison when they are absent from school without reason, when they commit offenses against children. We don't even fire them. Organized labor comes to their defense.

Who defends the children? *Not* our governments. Are we so different, therefore, from the totalitarian countries that banish their political dissidents? Are not our children our dissidents? Do we not institutionalize our dissidents, the children, for daring to cry out against the injustices of their lives?

Rich children don't get sent to our prison-schools. Rich parents can afford private boarding schools for "special" children, private treatment, and private hospitalization. Poor parents turn to the schools, to the social agencies, and to the courts for help.

Our "delinquent" children are not psychologically different from the children we call "dependent" or "in need of supervision," or the children we call "incorrigible." Labels vary, and often are dependent upon sheer chance and who is doing the labeling. The children are the same. A truant is a truant, yet one child may be labeled "delinquent," another may be labeled "in need of supervision.'' There is very little difference between a delinquent child, a neglected child, or one in need of supervision. One may need a home. Another needs treatment. All need help. All need education. We give them prison and call it school. It is an affront to our civilization.

In one such prison-school in Nebraska, the children are given a welcome manual to read. Perhaps it is just as well that most of them can't read. It states:

> There were some problems and things did not seem just right with your family. You were sent here to find out what went wrong and what can be done to make things better. . . . The decision as to where you will go will be up to the county court that cared enough about you to send you here to find out how your life could be made better.

The children were obviously expected to be grateful—grateful to the court for uprooting them from their parents, often against the wishes of both the child and the parents—grateful to the institution for the public condemnation of their parents.

It was a great welcome!

I visited Betty in a counterpart prison-school in New York, where she was similarly welcomed. She was very lucky indeed to have the ''county court that cared enough'' about her to send her to a place where her ''life could be made better.''

The school was two hundred miles away from home in a quiet, uninhabited countryside. No one could visit her who didn't have a car. This meant her family and friends. At any rate, that particular institution was situated where it was, not out of concern for the students who would eventually go there, but because the area was economically impoverished. The people in that area needed jobs—building the place, running it. The politicians needed votes.

So, ''the prison'' was built there.

Betty didn't get a chance to see much of the lush countryside because the building was surrounded by high walls and barbed wire, and no prisoner ever was permitted out. When Betty did get out into the air, which was rare, it was into the inner courtyard. The flower-grown fields could not be seen.

It really didn't matter. Most of the time Betty was in isolation for the infraction of one rule or another. Isolation meant a mattress on a floor in a prison cell. There was a tiny peephole for a window, through which Betty could not see, because it was too high and there was no chair on which to stand. The door leading into the cell also had a peephole. This, also, was too high, and she could not look out.

Betty had been in that isolation room for four days when I chanced upon her. Because Betty had been one of the girls who had gone to Livingston, I was permitted to speak with her.

She had been a boisterous student in school, annoying girls with her banter and her laughing threats to beat them up. She never really meant it. Most of the time, however, she had been a truant; that is, she didn't come to school when she ran away from home.

Betty was different now, apathetic and depressed. I preferred the old fighting spirit. At least she was alive then.

When I asked what had happened during the summer that landed her in the prison-school, she told me her mother had taken her to court for running away.

"Why are you in isolation?" I asked. "What did you do?"

Betty told me that her "cottage parent" had put her in isolation for cursing.

Cottage parent is another euphemism, of which institutions are so fond. Cottage parents are really attendants or aides who supervise the girls in their sleeping quarters, the dormitories or cottages. Cottage parents aren't parents at all. They do their "parenting" in eight-hour shifts. Betty's "parent" had grown up in the country. She had little knowledge or understanding of an inner-city child such as Betty; actually, she had had as much preparation for her job as I have had to be an astronaut.

"Why did you curse?" I asked Betty.

It seemed Betty had wanted to set her hair on Sunday morning before she went to chapel, and the cottage parent had refused.

"Why, Betty?" I asked.

"Because there wasn't enough time," she said. "I got through scrubbing the floor too late."

"Why were you scrubbing the floor on Sunday?" I asked.

"I had an argument with another girl. It was punishment."

"Did you hit the other girl?"

"No—but you don't understand, Dr. Rothman. I lose my temper a lot and then they make me wash the floor. They give me this little piece of floor and make me wash it with a toothbrush."

"Toothbrush?" I was furious.

I believed Betty. I had met her cottage parent.

When I confronted the superintendent of this institution with Betty's story, and asked for her to be permitted to return to her cottage, he explained why he couldn't.

"She went into a rage, she was so upset, we had to put her in isolation to calm her down. She would have hurt herself."

"She's calm now," I told him.

He thought a moment and called on the intercom—whom, I don't know.

"Sorry," he finally explained. "The cottage parent would be upset if I took her out. She has to maintain her authority you know—"

The cottage parent would be upset? I couldn't believe it. He was more concerned for an adult working there than for a child imprisoned there.

I told him the toothbrush story, which I hadn't mentioned before.

He adamantly refused to believe it. He also refused to check with other girls.

"Are you going to believe the story of a girl who is so disturbed she's probably psychotic?" he asked.

"If, by your admission, she is psychotic, is this how you treat psychotic people?" I answered angrily.

He told me to mind my own business, and in the end I served

no purpose. Betty remained in isolation, even though it was four days after the fact, and she was no longer cursing.

I went back to see Betty in her cell. I peeped through the hole and banged at the small pane. She looked up and saw me. She waved back and smiled. I fought back the tears. She was in bedroom slippers and pajamas. No clothes permitted! No dignity allowed.

The nurse was standing next to me—she saw nothing but her duty.

"You see," she stated piously, "she has to learn to show respect to staff."

"Some staff members aren't worthy of respect," I answered.

"We're not cruel," I was smugly and stonily told.

I didn't know what else to call it.

Betty was not mentally or emotionally disturbed. She was unhappy. She didn't have a supportive home and she didn't like school. She kept running away from both. The school system and her home had failed her as much as she had failed in coping with both. Yet, for our failures and her truancy she was punished and sent to a prison-school.

Betty is not unique. There are thousands of Bettys who go through our juvenile justice system and training schools and eventually find their way to adult prisons. Over 70 percent of adult prisoners have been the children in our training schools. It is a cringing thought when we remember that over two-thirds of that 70 percent were children whose "crime" was that of inadequate parenting and a tremendous need for help. Like Betty.

The most terrible part of this prison syndrome is that the professionals—the social workers, the teachers, the probation officers, the psychiatrists, and the clergy—really know that in the name of treatment we are committing atrocities. I can think only of Hitler's Germany as an analogy. In Betty's case, for instance, the isolation cell was part of the hospital wing of the school. A doctor was on call, a nurse on duty. They accepted without question what was.

In Betty's case, there were two clergymen of different faiths who conducted Sunday services. They, too, accepted without question what was.

There was also a staff of social workers and a psychologist. They did not question either.

And a principal, a secretary, and sixteen licensed and qualified teachers. Not one of them questioned.

The training school was the best of all possible worlds. The question was—for whom? Obviously, for the people who worked there!

I talked with the young reading teacher, who had just earned his master's degree. He was proud of his degree and smug about his accomplishments.

One girl was in the classroom, her head on the desk. She was dozing. The teacher was sitting at his desk, reading the newspaper.

"I gave her the period off," he explained jovially. For one reason or another, the other girls in his class weren't there, one was seeing the doctor, one went to court, and so on.

"As I couldn't have a lesson, I told her to take it easy. She's happy."

It apparently never occurred to that teacher, that master's degree graduate, that he had the girl all to himself and therefore had a wonderful chance to get to know her, to relate, to talk, to be friends—even perhaps to teach reading.

The principal was no better. "We have forty-minute periods. Students travel from subject to subject. We have the departmental system. Our big problem is money. We need more equipment."

For what, I wondered. I had seen ten typewriters in the classroom; two were in use. I had seen a beauty shop fully and adequately equipped—it was closed. I had seen two dressmaking rooms, both with high-powered sewing machines. Both teachers were in conference.

I tried to be gentle, nonthreatening, offhand, and flexible.

"Do you have an experimental program?" I asked. "This

school seems just like their old schools. The ones in which the kids failed in the first place."

"But of course," he explained condescendingly, "they have to go back to what they came from. If we had a different program here we'd only confuse them."

"I wonder," I said, "why we feed children when they're hungry? After all, they have to get used to being hungry again."

But he didn't know what I was talking about.

I tried talking about life at the school in general, and about isolation procedures in particular, about cruelty, about the responsibilities of the staff—any staff—who work there.

Is the sole function of teachers to perpetuate the system?

Are they to hide and ask no questions?

Have they no morality—or conscience?

Do they not see?

"Oh," said one of the teachers, "I've been here seven years—and I never go to the cottages where they live. My job is teaching mathematics."

"Aren't you ever curious?" I pressed.

"Well, I'm so busy teaching mathematics, you see."

She showed me her grade book. There was a list of names, and next to each name a series of red marks.

"What happens," I asked suddenly, "when you have trouble with someone in class, when a girl gets angry or upset, or curses, or something?"

"Oh, I send for the principal and he sends for an attendant, and the child gets sent back to her cottage for a few days."

"To wash a floor with a toothbrush?" I asked sharply.

She stared at me vacantly.

"But when they come back in a few days," she continued brightly, "they're really so much better behaved."

I left, totally disheartened. Where was the beginning of change? It seemed so hopeless, and yet there had to be a beginning.

I went to another prison-school equally beautiful from the outside, equally corrupt from the inside. This one did not even

have teachers. Many prison-schools don't. For instance, New
York State imprisons children because of truancy. Thus, the
state sends them to a "school" in order to go to school. Only
when they get to the "school," there is often no school. The
state, like the children, violates the compulsory education act.
Not only do they not provide a school, they go one better. They
put the children out to work. Some children work for fifty cents
a day, some for five cents an hour, some for no cents a day.
They work in institutional laundries, kitchens, and yards, cleaning and caring for patients who, by the way, deserve better care;
they work in farms and forests, cleaning and caring for land;
and they work for small local businesses. The state calls it
volunteering. I call it slavery. What do our children learn about
the work ethic? That prostitution pays better. That stealing is
more lucrative. That welfare is easier. That gambling is more
fun.

It is clear that we are teaching children one thing: only fools
work.

"It's good for kids to give service," I've heard it said. "They
have to learn to give—not to receive."

When I tried to make sense out of this madness—only it is
more than madness; madness can be moral, and hypocrisy can't
be—I was told that the "children simply were not motivated to
attend school or to learn, so why provide a school?"

So—I ask—what are they doing there in the first place? Why
are they sent?

Rosa was scheduled for one such prison-school that didn't
have a school when I met her for the first time in the family
court. She was about to go before the judge to be sent to the New
York State training school because of truancy. Her lawyer,
appointed earlier by the court, had taken one look at Rosa, at her
school record, and had sent for me. He knew something was
wrong in the state of educationhood, but he didn't know what.
He also knew that I was opposed to sending children to correctional institutions for the crime of fearing schools. All the
truants I have ever met have been afraid of school in one way or

another and have tried very hard to hide that fear, from others as well as from themselves. The arrogance and braggadocio of many truants is most often a reaction against admitting into awareness the truth of fear.

Rosa was three months away from her sixteenth birthday. At age sixteen, of course, her obligation to observe the compulsory education law would have ended. Sixteen is the age of legal departure from school in most states. Yet, at the age of fifteen years and nine months, she was in danger of being "sent upstate."

Rosa was sweet and apathetic that day in court. She answered in monosyllables. She seemed not to absorb the distinct possibility that a strange man talking unknown words could alter her life and send her far away from home to live in a miniature prison. When I asked her why she hadn't gone to school, she told me simply that she didn't like school. I knew, of course, that not liking school meant she was failing in school and that she was afraid to face her failures. When I asked her to read a simple sign in the room, Rosa couldn't do it. She was a nonreader. Her shame was apparent.

Rosa did not do what other girls might conceivably have done under similar circumstances: promise to attend school in the future if the judge would let her go home. She simply said no—she wouldn't. There was no deceit in Rosa. She was completely honest. It was an honesty to be respected. I spoke with the grandmother, who seemed to be Rosa only doubly grown. When I asked her why she hadn't made her granddaughter go to school, she said that the girl didn't like school.

Rosa's school records, copies of which her lawyer had obtained, were astoundingly bare. As far as the school authorities were concerned, she was a tabula rasa—they knew nothing about her. There were no grades in reading or mathematics, no reference to family contacts, no referrals to parent-teacher conferences, no requests for clinical help. Not a teacher, social worker, paraprofessional, or principal had ever tried to find out why Rosa had not attended school.

Yet, for the ten years that Rosa was supposed to have attended, she had actually been in school less than one year's worth. One year of schooling, scattered erratically by days over a period of years—the neglect by the school authorities was incredible. Now, three months before her sixteenth birthday, the girl was being noticed for the first time.

Rosa did not go to a training school because I asked the judge to permit me to work with her and to permit her to attend Livingston while she continued to live at home. Permission was granted and Rosa attended school at Livingston. The damage of neglect, however, had already been done and Rosa dropped out of school at seventeen. In that year she learned to read a little and to smile a little, but she was still withdrawn, depressed, afraid, and still a psychological truant. Attending Livingston had made no real dent in her life except, of course, that it had kept her out of a correctional facility, where she did not belong.

Other Rosas, however, are still being sent up. And other Bettys.

What part do the schools play in this process of migration from school to training school to prison? How much responsibility must the schools assume?

A great deal.

We exile our failures.

We proclaim our innocence.

We silence our consciences.

We tolerate evil, we excuse it, and then we encourage it.

7

To Be Loved, Young, and Immortal

The need for power is not the only substrata motivation for teaching. Other needs are equally dominant, equally repressed, and equally struggling to find expression in the classroom. They are the needs for love, youth, and immortality.

The need for love is a basic human need. It is a need that centers on the search for immortality. Through love, we procreate. Through our children, we seek immortality. Our children bear our image and our name. They also bear within them the memory of our lives. We are kept alive after death by those who have loved us and who remember us.

Work, like love, is also a bridge to immortality. It is an extension of ourselves as much as our children are an extension of ourselves. It is our imprint on this world, our way of saying, "See, I was here and this is what I have left behind."

One's investment in immortality, therefore, is through love and work. After their death, teachers leave behind them the memory of themselves in their students and the significance of their work.

When work is meaningless, the self often becomes meaningless and immortality becomes threatened. Can one feel important selling artificial fingernails? Is this the work that leads to immortality?

The search for significance in work is therefore the search for self-meaning and immortality. We are what we do. We leave behind what we have done.

The work of education is a work to which society attaches great importance, because the children in our schools are important. We convince ourselves that it is our children who are the future leaders of our country, if not the world, and that the education of our country rests largely on us. It makes the future ours; it makes immortality seem almost possible.

In search of immortality teachers seek the physical presence of youth, because they are also seeking eternal youth. Surrounded by youthful bodies and youthful zest, they feel that the aging process is distant. It almost becomes possible to believe that one will never get old and therefore that one will never die.

In their need to be young, teachers often adopt the dress and speech of their students. They often succeed, however, only in looking inappropriate and sounding ridiculous. Often, too, and far worse, they adopt the values of their students even when those values are not basically their own. It is their way of trying to be young by buying youth from their students. They feel they have to sell out in order to be accepted.

"Poor kids," a teacher once boasted to me, priding himself on his rapport with his students, "when they buy pot they get cheated, they're only kids and the pushers cheat them, but when I buy it for them I get my money's worth and at least it's good grass."

I don't know which shocked me more—the fact that he told me he was buying drugs for his students or the fact that he *was* buying drugs for his students. He didn't appear concerned about either, perhaps because he did not consider marijuana harmful and perhaps because we were at a party.

"But it's illegal," I said. "Even if you don't think it should be, it is. Aren't you afraid of getting caught?"

"Well, I don't do it that often, and of course they don't smoke it in school. Actually, I don't think it's any worse than taking a martini," he said, pointing to the drink in his hand, "but they're great kids, they're in my special science program, and they're damned talented, I can trust them. They remind me of the way I used to be.''

I knew he taught at a high school for supposedly intellectually gifted students. I had the feeling that he was a marvelous teacher in the classroom. It was what he did outside the classroom that bothered me. He must have sensed my discomfort.

''Look,'' he went on, ''I don't want you to get the idea I approve of drugs, I don't, not at all, but marijuana is not a hard drug and I know these kids and they're interested in science, really interested. We spend a lot of research time together, they're doing independent research. Besides, I know how it is to be young and to get a kick out of something illegal, like stealing cookies.'' He smiled ruefully. ''Wouldn't it be ironic if someday they legalize marijuana and we'll all find that half the kids wouldn't bother to smoke at all?''

He might be right, of course, but I wondered if he wasn't getting his own kicks out of doing something illegal, if this wasn't his way of being accepted by his students, his way of being young, of psychologically seducing his students to accept him, of reliving his own youth.

Many teachers pursue the condition of youth with a frenzy and dedication that is continually being fed by the modern madness of our culture—the worship of the state of being young. This form of worship should not be confused with the worship of those who are young. There is a vast difference between the two. Many teachers yearning for the state of youth are often envious of those who are young. Envying them, teachers hate them, even as they strive to be like them.

''Cut off your hair,'' they decree.

It might as well be ''Cut off your head.''

These are the teachers who play all the power games because they have not accepted their own authority and thus their own true adulthood. Outwardly they bear the appearance of a distant psychological and chronological past. Inwardly, they live out their own repressed fantasies through their students.

I have seen teachers enjoy the aggression of the "bad" child when that child uses a profanity that the teacher would like to use but doesn't dare.

I have seen teachers become titillated by the sexual experiences they elicit from their students under the guise of counseling.

Teachers like these always remind me of the times when I was twelve and hid *Bad Girl*, a notorious novel of the time, under my pillow for my mother not to see. These teachers, it seems to me, are still in that period of adolescence.

Teachers who accept adulthood as a period of growth and power, as a period of full control over one's own life, will not need to remain in adolescence. They will not need to imitate youth as many do in dress and speech. Nor will they need to be envious of youth and, in reaction to their envy, to be critical of youth and to punish youth.

If they were to live with the power that the full authority of adulthood can give them, their own styles of living would not seem, in comparison to youth, to be so depressed, unglamorous and prosaic. They would not then need to live imitatively or vicariously.

There can be no doubt, of course, that with each succeeding generation, young people have greater freedom than they have ever had. Their freedoms place greater responsibilities upon them. Should they use drugs? Should they live with a lover without marriage? Should they work, finish school, or just roam the country as thousands of young people seem to do?

These are truly awesome and terrible choices, but teachers don't seem to see the awesomeness, the terrible consequences of choices, or the heartrending contemplations that must enter into such decisions. They see only the ever-unending, beckoning choices and the freedom to make the choice. It is a freedom they have never had, simply because teachers go farther back in time; and even a five- or ten-year difference between high school student and teacher makes for a difference of cultural time and style. Teachers have always been at any time in history more repressed than their students. Easily angered by the freedom of their students, angered by their own needs to live vicariously through their students, the pseudo-livers—the teachers—resent, envy, and hate their students.

Jennifer Christian, for instance, was twenty-nine years old. She taught English in a high school in Philadelphia. I had never seen her teach, but somehow I assumed she had to be a good teacher, perhaps because her mother, Lenon, was a very good friend of mine, and a superb teacher, or perhaps because I had known Jennifer since the time I burped her when she was three weeks old.

Jennifer was more than irritated one weekend when I met her at her mother's house. She had just been told that Latin was no longer required for English majors in the college she had attended.

"They're constantly lowering standards," she complained.

"Hold on," said Lenon, "why are you so mad? What standard does the memorization of Latin uphold anyway?"

"Oh, Mother," Jennifer cried, "don't start with me." She turned to me for support. "Here we go again. Mother is going to tell me I'm too establishment and rigid and all that and I resist change."

"I am not." Her mother laughed. "I'm going to tell you that you're just plain jealous because you had to struggle for four years through Latin, which you hated, and now the kids don't have to."

"Well, it's certainly easier now to get a degree than it was for me," Jennifer complained, "and that's not so long ago either."

Lenon and I both knew how she felt. We knew it from our own pain.

I remember the times Lenon and I had discussed our own learning process. We had met at graduate school and were taking courses together in methods of teaching retarded children. We had learned more from each other outside our class than we had from our instructor inside the class. We talked about the children in our classrooms, but we also talked about ourselves. I remember the day vividly when Lenon had cried almost in anguish, "My God, I feel old, those damn kids make me feel old. I feel like I'm on the finishing line, and they're just starting."

Lenon was twenty-three at the time. I was twenty-four.

Now, here was Jennifer at twenty-nine, going through the same process. Nothing much seemed to have changed in teacher-training classes since the time we went to college. Jennifer's college training both in undergraduate and graduate schools had not prepared her to face her own feelings any more than my college training had prepared me for mine, or Lenon's for hers.

Lenon and I both knew what was really troubling Jennifer. She was jealous of her students. They had so much more flexibility and ease of movement than she had ever had. She felt keenly the difference between her generation and that of her students.

Her awareness of time and cultural differences was a reminder of what she herself had missed. It was also a reminder that her time could not be relived. Her students were reminders of her own aging process, harbingers of her own death.

Understandably, therefore, the fear of aging and the fear of death keep teachers searching for youth, immortality, and love. They want to be loved as once they were loved in childhood. They long for its return.

Lucy George was such a teacher. I met her during a course I was giving in human relations. Any course entitled "Human Relations" has always been a catchall course as far as I'm concerned. The students came not knowing if they wanted to study psychology, social work, anthropology, sociology, or education. They wanted everything, but they wanted it without a label, which is all right with me. We have too much fragmentation in our society anyway. In class, therefore, we mostly discussed ourselves, our perceptions, our values, how we related to others, and how society impinged upon us.

Lucy was grasping for knowledge and for insight. We spent

many hours talking privately during that year, and from those hours and group discussions in class, I got to know her very well.

She had graduated from college magna cum laude only two years earlier with a major in history, but she had taken the necessary courses in education to qualify for teaching.

She loved history, but she knew she did not want to teach it, although she wasn't certain why. She said she would have loved to have found a job as a historian, but she had no idea where such a job existed or whether it existed at all. She decided, therefore, to become an elementary school teacher, and upon graduation she immediately enrolled in a master's degree program in elementary education. She had enjoyed student teaching and expected to enjoy teaching. It did not happen that way.

She began to teach the same year I met her and she was suffering. Somehow, all her formal preparation had not helped her in the classroom.

She was teaching in one of the most difficult schools in New York City, at the close of a very bitter teachers' strike. The community, mostly Puerto Rican and black, was angered by most of the teachers who had gone out on strike. As most of the teachers were white, all the teachers were seen as social enemies, whether they had been out on strike or not. Lucy was one who had not gone on strike. Nevertheless, she was regarded as an enemy by most of the parents and the majority of the teachers who had gone on strike. Teacher dissension was high. There was a great rift between those who had struck and those who had not.

None of these factors bothered Lucy. She had accepted the job knowing full well that a strike was brewing. She had taught during the strike because she felt committed to do so. Those were not her problem days. It was during the aftermath, when the school was supposedly settling down to normalcy, that Lucy found her greatest difficulties. During the strike she had been occupied with her particular struggle to keep teaching. Now that she was teaching without a political struggle, her internal ones were beginning. She could settle upon a political and social viewpoint. She could not find an emotional one.

"But I really am trying," she complained, "and it isn't that the children aren't learning—they are. I'm following the curriculum and all of that, and my principal seems pleased with what I'm doing, except how would he know really, he's running all around that building like a madman. My class is the best in the grade, thank God—but some of those kids are nuts."

"But," she continued, "I don't know—" her voice dropped to an intense whisper, "it isn't just the school, my kids are nice—I feel so—" she paused, sought the word, found it, and both her voice and face showed the shock at her own self-discovery—"vulnerable. I feel vulnerable." She found it hard to explain what she meant. Later she said, "Teaching hurts."

We explored her feelings and that particular statement for many hours, at different times. It became almost a password between us.

"How was today, Lucy?"

She would smile ruefully. "Still hurting, but unbandaged." She had a genuine sense of humor, which meant she could laugh at herself, even sometimes in the midst of some of her most acute depressions. It helped.

"One girl asked me if I ever made it with a man," she once said. "She was being nasty, not a kid in my class. She must have been about fifteen. I'm not even sure she goes to the school, sometimes people come and go, hang out in the halls, you never know who they are. She came in, I asked her to leave, she wouldn't. I told her I'd send for the principal, but still she wouldn't go, she didn't seem scared, but maybe she was, I don't know. Anyway, just before she left, she asked it loud and clear to shock my class, I guess."

"What did she say?" I asked.

"Just that. She stood in front of the room, almost straddling, if that's the word, feet firmly planted wide apart on the ground, and said, "I wonder if you can make it with a man?""

"What did you do?"

"I was in shock," Lucy said. "I wanted to get her out of my room. I said the first thing that came to my mind.

"What was that?" I asked.

"I said, 'What man would want someone who never got out of the sixth grade?' I guess it was right," Lucy continued, "because she just laughed and left."

I felt Lucy had handled a difficult situation well. Her humor had saved her, although the girl probably would have left anyway. Nevertheless, in discussing and exploring Lucy's flip answer, we discovered that it was a key to her problem.

Lucy, indeed, did feel like a sixth-grader. She had never left the classroom. As an adult, she sought the kinship of children as her peers. She still felt vulnerable.

"Every time I go into a teachers' meeting," she confided to me once, "I say to myself, 'What am I doing in this room full of grownups?' "

Lucy was the youngest of five children, the only girl. She was the baby of the house. Her mother and father both coddled her. Lucy never was given household chores, not even to clear the table after supper, because as her father said, "Poor child, she studies so hard."

Her parents' name for her when they talked about her, either in her presence or without, was "the child."

Lucy's parents were proud of her excellent grades throughout school. They were also proud of her manners, her sweetness, her willingness to do what she was told. Lucy didn't ever seem to have periods of anger. She was always good, and her goodness netted her the reward of love. She knew her parents and her brothers loved her. She never wanted to hurt them or even leave home. Even when she was awarded a scholarship at a prestigious college, she refused it, because it meant leaving home. Lucy chose a city university instead.

Lucy did not know how deep her resentment went against her parents for viewing her as a baby. She did not know how deep her resentments against herself went for her willingness to remain a baby and stay in the role in which they put her. In a classroom with sixth-graders before her, she began to find out suddenly that she was an adult. She was in charge. The children expected her to give orders, to tell them what to do. She expected herself to give orders, to tell them what to do because that's how she viewed teaching. She couldn't do it. She could make teaching plans the night before, but when it came to following those plans, she found her heart pounding, her palms sweating, her knees trembling. She got through the day some-how, but she would go home exhausted, fall into a deep sleep, and be awakened by her mother, urging her to eat.

"If it weren't for my mother, I'd forget to eat," she once said.

"That's too bad," I answered, "because how long do you want to stay a baby?"

She didn't hear me. She went on to explain that the rest of the evening would be spent worrying about the next day's teaching.

Did Juan really belong in the slowest group in arithmetic?

What could she do with Judy in reading?

What if Susie kept on talking all through spelling?

"Miss George, how old are you?" Susie asked unexpectedly one day. Before Lucy could answer with some inane remark that ladies don't tell their age, the child answered herself.

"I bet you're at least thirty."

This one remark put Lucy at her lowest ebb. Tears came to her eyes and she could not explain why. She knew children were abysmal age tellers, and she knew she didn't look thirty; in fact, she looked much younger than the twenty-four she was, but Susie's words struck hard.

"I don't feel grown," she said. By this time, Susie wasn't even listening, but Lucy heard herself and knew why she answered. She continued to weep silently.

How old did Lucy feel? She didn't know. Suddenly, she seemed to know that she wasn't a child. The problem was, she felt like a child. Even worse, she wanted to continue to be a child. This recognition upset her more. What was wrong with her that she couldn't accept her own adulthood, which later she came to realize was acceptance of her own womanhood and her own sexuality? Yes, she occasionally dated, but men were not serious considerations for her. She had never loved a man, never had a serious friendship with a man. They were very peripheral to her life. Sometimes there were dates arranged by friends. Mostly, they were casual, and unmeaningful. Lucy wanted love and romance. Yet, she was fearful. Her need to remain a child was certainly related to her fears of growing up and being a sexual woman. Somehow, Lucy always rationalized there would be time. She was not ready.

She looked up at one point when she was discussing this and said, "You know, there's an old Hebrew song that I learned in Hebrew school. The Jews used to sing it when they declared the need for a Jewish state. 'If not now—when?' It's a good question. When is when?"

Lucy began to search for the when of her adulthood. She began to realize that she resented her parents for keeping her a child. This partial realization, however, brought guilt. She began to hate herself. Self-hatred and hatred of her parents were not easily admissible. It was much easier to find a substitute target to hate. She did. The children. She began to look for their imperfections. She found them. The children lied, were fresh, were rude, were impatient, were "impossible." And, as she saw them and treated them, so they became.

"I told you once how to do that example, Anton, I won't tell you again. Listen next time."

"You can't go to gym today, Murray, you ran around the room too much."

Only later did she realize that Murray needed that gym period, and needing it is what probably made him run around the room in the first place.

Lucy was covertly angry most of the time. She was angry at herself, and in her search to prove that she could be an adult, she overreacted to the normal behavior of children. She responded to their normalcy by administering punishment.

Her own sudden strictness, however, which she saw as adulthood and her punitive behavior did not ease her pain. In fact it exacerbated it. Her guilt and anxiety increased. The children felt the burden of her tensions. The classroom was an angry place. Out of retaliation, the children fought back. They were rude to her and they fought with each other. The classroom became the setting for Lucy George's internal questions, anguishes, and conflicts, and the students in covert battle became the unsuccessful antagonists.

Only when Lucy began to understand her own mechanisms was she able to realize how she was using the children. She realized that her desire to remain a child was conflicting with the reality of her adulthood. She also realized that it was her need to remain a child that made her choose teaching as a career. Why not pursue her interest in history and try to find an occupation that would bring her into contact with more adults? Why remain with ten-year-olds? Lucy had found her answer—to be a child, be loved as a child, and remain forever young.

When the children could not accept her as a child—as indeed she was not—when the reality of the classroom faced her with the knowledge that she was no longer a child, her anxiety became overwhelming. In response she tried to prove her adulthood in the most damaging way possible. She became a disciplinarian. She punished children. She told herself it was for their own good. The damage, however, was both to herself and the children, because she did not like herself for what she was doing.

Her outer need, she told herself, was to teach, to help, to guide. It was in keeping with her concept of being a "good person." Her inner need was more human. She did not want to grow up, but could not admit this to herself. When she finally did, she was able to find ways in which to grow up. She was able to admit her resentment against her parents and she was able to accept the reality of her feelings without guilt. She began to put herself in positions of making her own decisions. For instance, she didn't go home and sleep every afternoon, later to be awakened and coddled by her mother. She didn't need to be reminded to eat, to be urged to eat. When she didn't put herself into the position of acting like a child, her mother didn't treat her like a child. Lucy began to discover the pleasures of self-decisions and to realize that as she made decisions about herself, other people reacted to her as an adult.

"The fault, dear Brutus, is not in our stars, but in ourselves, that we are underlings," she quoted to me once. "*Julius Caesar*. See, being a history major pays off."

She began to see more people socially. Her feeling about herself translated itself into the classroom. Because she felt better about herself, she didn't have to prove her authority to the children. The classroom became more casual; children responded to suggestion far better than they had to coercion. The classroom became a healthier place for both teacher and children, and they began to learn and make decisions for themselves.

I was certain Lucy would continue teaching. I was very surprised, therefore, when Lucy called me the following September at the beginning of the school year to tell me she had left teaching. She had found a job as research assistant in a museum. Her salary was lower but Lucy sounded very happy.

I felt strangely defeated. I also felt unhappy that I felt defeated. Why should I take Lucy's decision to leave teaching so personally? Then I knew. I had failed to make Lucy in my own image. My stab at omniscience and immortality had been thrust aside.

I had hoped that Lucy would find the satisfaction I had found in teaching, the awareness of one's own sense of authority, the enjoyment of being with children, the fun of exploring new knowledge with children, and the excitement of teaching children how to make their own decisions. Wanting to stay with children, liking children, identifying with children, are healthy reasons for teaching. They become wrong reasons when the classroom becomes a barricade against one's own true and adult authority.

Yet, being the child one was is tremendously important. A

teacher must never forget what it is to be a powerless child—a teacher must never forget the need to play, to enjoy, to have fun, because through play one finds one's own values. The good teacher in part must always be a child somewhere deep inside.

A power-driven teacher, however, wants to forget childhood, wants to be eternally serious, and to suppress the needs of childhood. The result is a damnation of children.

Lucy, who struggled with the meaning of her own childhood, found her own adult authority when she realized that she had come to teaching out of the wrong motivations. She then realized that she indeed did not want to teach.

The last time I heard from her she had been given a promotion in the museum and had matriculated in a doctorate program in history. She sounded ecstatic. Her decision to leave teaching obviously had been right for her. She no longer needed to use the children as a refuge against growing up.

Lucy sought love by remaining with children in a child's setting. She at no time, however, acted like a child. It was her struggle to act like an adult while wishing to remain a child that caused her so much pain.

Other teachers, however, with the same needs as Lucy's, do not make the same fight. Out of a need to be loved, they assume the values of the children and completely give up their own. For fear of being rejected, they never say no to a child. They purchase love with gifts, good grades not necessarily earned, trips to movies, and a complete laissez-faire attitude in the classroom.

Mrs. Diamond, a teacher I met at a conference, told me that she did not believe in saying no to children. She was rather proud of it. She equated it with loving them. What she really wanted, however, was for them to love her.

It is curious that while teachers are unable to admit to their need to be loved by the children, they can admit to their need to love children. After all, giving love is the idealized image they have of themselves. Taking love does not fit into their glamorized self-portrait.

The irony is that, needing love, teachers often cannot give it. They can take it, absorb themselves in it, nourish themselves by it, and deny that they are the takers.

Mrs. Diamond invited me to visit her class in Brooklyn after I told her I was writing a book on teachers. I am certain she considered herself a good and loving one.

When I did visit, I could see her philosophy in action. Children pushed, walloped, played, read, climbed, dallied, threw, painted, and ran at will in and out of her room. At one point, when Mrs. Diamond mildly asked a boy not to throw chalk, he cursed at her. Another child, a girl, became very angry.

"Don't you yell at teacher," she cried, "when she spends so much money on you."

"Fuck you," the boy answered.

Mrs. Diamond appeared not to notice.

I was sorry for the children. It didn't help that little girl to feel her teacher was inadequate and helpless. What can a child learn from a teacher? A teacher is supposed to teach an approach to life. What kind of approach is helplessness? And it didn't help the other child to look with derision upon his teacher.

In talking with Mrs. Diamond later, I began to understand that setting limits for children, and guiding them into setting limits for themselves, was too threatening to her. She was afraid they wouldn't like her. She could not tolerate being disliked.

Her need to be loved was as much a controlling mechanism as overt aggression. Only it was more subtle. The loved child controls parents by the very nature of dependency. Children cry, parents hold. Children are hungry, parents feed. Children are sick, parents stay home.

Mrs. Diamond's dependency was also a controlling mechanism. "I'm weak," her behavior said, "so love me. I'm vulnerable, so love me. I'm overwhelmed, so love me."

It was ironic that her need to be loved produced the opposite of what she wanted. Children did not love her. Either they felt sorry for her or they had contempt for her. No children learned from her. She hid the truth of their feelings from herself.

Mrs. Diamond was a woman in her mid-thirties. She was of Puerto Rican descent. She had been teaching for seven years and had married a man of German-Irish ancestry soon after she started working.

She was brought to the mainland when she was four. Her childhood was rather uneventful, except for yearly summer trips to Puerto Rico. Her parents did not approve of the streets of New York for her during the summer. They worked and could not supervise her. Her brothers were much older than she, and they were permitted to stay home during the summer.

"My parents always trusted them," she said, "but not me. I had to go back to P. R."

"Was it a matter of not trusting you?" I asked.

"Not really," she conceded, "just that old Puerto Rican machismo thing. Boys can take care of themselves—like hell they can—but girls need to be protected, nonsense like that. You know, my brothers were never expected to do a lick of housework, not one single thing. I had to help in the house, do the dishes, wash the floors, help with the washing. Right from school, I had to go home and help my mother. If I was an hour late, no, a half hour, 'Where were you Rosie?' Even during college they were very strict. My God, there were times—" She stopped suddenly. The tiny anger that I thought was emerging was suddenly aborted.

"Times, what?"

"Well, what's the use talking of it now?" she laughed. "It all worked out. I owe my parents a lot! They put me through college. That was not easy."

"I'm certain it wasn't," I agreed, "but they made so many demands on you. Weren't you ever angry?"

"Me?" She seemed astonished at my question.

"No, that's the way it is with a lot of people from Puerto Rico."

''Not even at the unfairness?'' I asked, ''between you and the way your brothers were treated?''

''No.'' Again she laughed. ''They're not so bad. You should hear my husband on the subject of women's rights—he's worse than my brothers and parents, and he's not even a Puerto Rican. He doesn't really want me to teach. Of course he likes the money. We're saving for a house, but he wants me to quit soon, and I will, I suppose.''

''Do you want to?''

''Well, I'd like to have a family—''

''That doesn't mean you have to stop teaching, does it?'' I asked.

''Well, I could take a leave, I suppose—but once I have a family, he'll want me at home. He thinks mothers should be at home—''

''Fine for him,'' I said. ''But what do you want?''

From what she had told me about her husband, I didn't like him very much. I suppose my feelings came through.

''I really don't know,'' she admitted.

I felt myself getting impatient with her. I also felt myself trying very hard not to let it show. But I was annoyed. My God, hadn't she ever heard about Women's Liberation?''

''Well, do you believe that women have to stay at home?'' I asked.

''Well, I suppose so,'' she said.

''Do you really think that?'' I asked, ''or is it what your husband thinks?''

''Oh, he thinks it all right,'' she promptly agreed.

''And you?''

''Well—I suppose so,'' she said again.

''Do you always agree with him?'' I asked.

''Well, generally,'' she said.

''Why?'' I asked.

She seemed startled and didn't answer for a moment.

''Well, is that wrong?'' she finally asked.

Suddenly I felt very sorry for her.

"Don't you ever get angry?" I asked.

She seemed genuinely surprised.

"What's the use of anger?"

For the first time I saw how really defeated she was. Her acceptance of what she believed to be her culture and her role in that culture made her see passivity as the only way for a woman to behave. Passivity was a guarantee of love. Her classroom performance was but a mirror image of her earlier life and her marriage. She bought the assurance of the love of her parents by passive acceptance of their demands. Her husband's love was guaranteed by her always agreeing with him and never speaking up for herself. She saw herself as a person who lives at the expense of her own desires. Her purpose in life was to gratify the needs of others. She saw no future in a woman's own life. As a result, she negated her own individuality.

In the classroom, she hoped to buy the children's love with gifts and letting them do whatever they wanted. She used love as a barter of exchange. She gave total agreement in exchange for love. The problem was, passive agreement to everything did not give her the love she sought. Instead, her attempted purchase brought resentment from her students, and she responded by adopting a martyr's role. Martyrdom served two purposes—first, to punish herself for being unworthy as a person, and unworthy she must be or why else was she not loved; and second, to fantasize her own heroism. Through fantasy she sought an ego. Obviously, however, her mechanisms for obtaining love were not working for her. She was a deeply unhappy person who hid her unhappiness even from herself. The result was a bland, ineffective, unfeeling, totally dependent person.

Mrs. Diamond tried to receive love through dependency. There are teachers, however, who use dependency differently. They are not dependent upon the children. They reverse the process. They make the children dependent upon them, because dependency makes them feel loved. It also makes the children afraid to succeed. Success might give them independence, but it also might deprive them of love—the teacher's. It is a risk many children are afraid to take. One must ask, why should they have to?

"Sweetheart," I once heard a first-grade teacher say to a child, "it's too hard for you to color that picture. Wait until I can show you how to stay in the lines."

The child waited. When the picture was colored, it was as much the teacher's as the child's.

"See, what did I tell you?" the teacher repeated. "It would have been too hard for you to do alone. Aren't you glad you waited?"

The child said yes.

She kissed him for saying the right thing. She felt needed. But what *if* that drawing had been hard? Couldn't she have let the child try it? And what if some of the lines were smudged? How could a drawing be wrong, anyway?

This phenomenon is not unique to teachers. Psychotherapists treating disturbed children often see it in family relations. As the children become better in treatment, begin to change, become healthier, the parents of the children often become resistant to the treatment. They do not really want their children to be independent of them. Such parents and teachers need to be needed. They keep the children feeling inadequate and dependent.

Children who are poor learners are certainly more dependent on their teachers than are bright children. In order to keep them dependent, it behooves the teachers to reward their nonachievement. The rewards are in the form of attention, approval, and affection. Thus, through failure, the children seek the reward of the teacher's approval or love. The most crippling aspect of this process is that children who want a teacher's approval, attention, or love often have to give up their own self-esteem, their own independence, their own successes, in order to receive it.

All beings, of course, need love. The need for love should always be gratified. Needs for love should be met by the significant people in everyone's life—parents, relatives, friends, teachers, lovers. Teachers in classrooms are gratified when children love them. It is truly a beautiful relationship when teachers and children give love in mutual satisfaction of each other.

It is when the satisfaction is not mutual, when it becomes unequal, when the teachers need more love than they can give, when the children are used as substitute lovers for the lovers the teachers do not have outside the classroom, that the need for love damages students.

Teachers must learn that in order to receive love they must be able to give it. Moreover, it must be freely given—without strings attached to it. "I'll love you if you fail" or "I'll love you if you're quiet" or "I'll love you if you memorize the three-times table" is not love. It is control and a demonstration of power.

Some teachers exert such control, not by demanding love, but by offering gratitude. Gratitude is not love. Gratitude can be a part of love when neither gratitude nor love is demanded by one person of another. When gratitude is subtly demanded or expected, it is rarely given. When it is given in words because it is demanded or expected, it is rarely meant. The demand of gratitude, spoken or unspoken, demanded or subtly elicited, provokes hostility. No one wants to be mandated into gratitude.

Demanding gratitude is a hostile act in itself. Teachers who demand gratitude require tit for tat. They will not give unless they can receive. They do not realize that they are cheating themselves, that the act of giving can be recompense enough. The act of giving is love. Expecting gratitude is not.

Mr. Horman was a teacher with whom I once worked. I knew that he was deeply committed to the welfare of his class. He knew about each child in his room. His teaching was not confined to the classroom alone. There were Saturday trips, evening theater parties. Mr. Horman often stood the total expense. The problem was, Mr. Horman needed gratitude.

"Look what I did for Joseph," he once complained to me. "I

really put out for that child. I really did. He had no clothes, so I bought him new ones. I really bought new ones; he has had hand-me-downs all his life. I wanted him to feel good about himself. I thought he would be grateful—I really did. So what does he do? He steals from me—from *me*. Wouldn't you think he'd have some feeling for me?''

The answer was yes. Joseph had a lot of feeling for Mr. Horman. He resented him.

Joseph and Mr. Horman were not on equal terms because Mr. Horman let himself be known as the giver and Joseph as the taker. Joseph did like Mr. Horman but the resentment was there nonetheless. Joseph's father did not seem to care for him. Mr. Horman did. Joseph hated his father and hated Mr. Horman for not being his father. Joseph had many feelings about Mr. Horman. They were love and hate combined, and even gratitude.

Joseph became a thief out of many mixed emotions; one was resentment. He stole from Mr. Horman in order to prove to himself he was not grateful. Perhaps Joseph would have stolen anyway, out of frustration for not having a loving father or even out of envy. Mr. Horman, however, made it easier for him to steal. He provided the stimulus by his subtle communication.

"Joe," I once heard him say, "did you ever finish that book I bought you?"

"Yeah," Joe answered.

"Did you like it?"

"It was okay."

"That's all?"

"Yeah, it was okay—"

"Oh—I thought you'd like it a lot. I went to a lot of trouble to get it."

Joe didn't answer.

Genuine love does not demand gratitude. A genuine exchange of equal and open love between teachers and students is beautiful.

Unfortunately, teachers often misinterpret their own roles.

They try to model themselves after the role of analytical therapist, who is a receiver of feelings, not a giver, a receiver of love,
not a giver of love. Their motto appears to be "Accept all
feelings, don't give feelings back, don't exchange feelings."
The exchange of emotions is interpreted as not only embarrassing but wrong.

The modus operandi of the therapist is to remain uninvolved
emotionally but to elicit and to get intensity of feelings from
patients. Thus, the patient lives closely to the therapist, but the
therapist does not necessarily live closely to the patient.
Teachers who accept this role model are willing to receive love
but often are not willing to exchange love. How they cheat
themselves! What a burden for a teacher who truly loves the
children and who fights inwardly not to love them back.

Anita Jessica was someone who fought such a battle. Luck-
ily, she lost.

I knew her well. Her classroom was an active place of
learning. Children were happy. So was she. She was married to
a lawyer. Her marriage seemed a gratifying one. Her two
children attended the school in which she taught. She was active
in the parent-teacher association and was respected by both
parents and teachers. In times of mild conflict between the
groups, she served as a good conciliator.

Anita denied herself the great pleasure of letting the children
kiss her or bring her small gifts, because she felt that she could
not accept a gift without returning a gift. She was wrong. She
could have accepted a gift that was given in love. She also could
have permitted herself the luxury of giving a gift to a child out of
love. It need not have been out of reciprocation but simply out
of her need to give.

Anita, however, tried very hard to convince herself that it
was wrong for teachers to accept overt offerings, because then it
meant they had to return them. Somehow, it spoiled her concept
of the therapeutic role.

Then, one Monday morning, seven-year-old Jerry brought
her a yellow tulip, with a note painstakingly printed. It must

have taken hours for that little boy to write each letter so straight.

> Dear Miss Jessica
> I love you. Please keep my flower forever.
>> Love,
>> Jerry

Anita knew then that she had been cheating herself. There was nothing wrong and everything right with accepting love freely given. She realized that her pride in not accepting affection and the tokens of love acted as a barrier to her full unfolding as a human being. Reading his note again, she permitted herself to be what she really wanted to be—a truly loving person, one who could both give and receive. She wrote Jerry back a note, almost as painstakingly written as his.

> Dear Jerry,
> I love you too. I shall never forget you.
>> Love,
>> Your teacher, Mrs. Jessica

To receive love genuinely, to receive love with love and to return love with love, can be the joy of teaching. Too often, however, teachers are only the receivers, and the love they return is mere form.

I know of one private school for severely disturbed children in New York City, for instance, in which it was the responsibility of the teachers to kiss and to be kissed by every student every day when they met. The practice was based on the theory that children, and disturbed children particularly, need human contact. I agree. They do. So do teachers. But any love that is based on the standardization of kissing is not genuine love.

How sad that this kind of greeting is perceived as a responsibility rather than as an expression of love and therefore of joy. If teachers were truly to love their students, they would not be *required* to kiss them. Love would be willingly and spontaneously demonstrated instead of a kiss perfunctorily bestowed.

A kiss at the end of a movie, after all, does not necessarily make for a true happy ending. Teachers who lend themselves to the pretense of love may only be living a one-sided fairy tale in which they live happily ever after at the expense of the children.

8

The Romantics

Teachers are notoriously romantic. It is their romanticism rather than their economic class that prevents them from understanding the realities with which their students live. Yet, the militant leaders of the poor as well as the intellectual elitists of the colleges and universities place the blame for the failure of our schools on the statistical fact that the majority of the teachers in our nation's classrooms are predominantly white and come predominantly from the middle class. They claim that being middle class denies accessibility to understanding poverty or prejudice, and that therefore middle-class teachers do not and cannot accept and teach the children of the poor, the children of the ghetto.

In the same manner that the word *ghetto* stems from the Hebrew word meaning divorce, or separation, they believe that middle-class teachers are so separated and divorced from the children they teach that they cannot understand and empathize with the realities of poverty and prejudice. Following this reasoning, logic would require that one cannot understand the horror of cancer unless one is afflicted with it.

I cannot take that stance. I cannot agree that only the victimized poor and the minority poor should be the teachers of the victimized poor and the minority poor any more than I would argue for middle-class children to be taught only by middle-class teachers. On the contrary, the need for middle-class children to be exposed to minority-group teachers is, in my opinion, far greater than the need for minority-group children to be taught by teachers of their own group. If white children are to unlearn prejudices, the place is in a classroom with teachers racially unlike them.

It is not economic class that separates teachers from their students. It is a psychological mechanism that is rooted in the firm belief in the inevitability of the happy ending. It is known as romanticism. Toward this end, teachers negate the real if the real is unhappy, in favor of the fantasy, which is always happy.

This does not mean that teachers negate only the ugliness of the outer realities, such as poverty, disease, and injustice. That they do. They also negate, however, the intensity of basic emotions, such as hate, anger, and even love.

Romanticism, therefore, is the mechanism by which teachers substitute shallow values and hollow feelings for real feelings, and deny the imperfections of our outer society. In much the same way, they deny what they consider to be their inner imperfections. In other words, they try to live a fairy tale.

Romanticism dictates that all emotions must end in happiness although they may start with sadness, and that all obstacles must be overcome. Romanticism dictates success for everyone, with the teacher bearing the banner of success for every child. Romanticism dictates a version of life in which the teacher is the transmitter of culture and success, and success is achieved by education and hard work. The teacher as the catalyst of success is therefore also the hero.

The American style of life, following the American myth of life from pioneer to tycoon, from killing Indians to settling large cities, from killing the bad people and saving the good, sets the romantic mold. Teachers believe the myth, and they therefore teach it. Thus, they are as damaging to middle-class children as they are to children of the poor and of the rich, because they teach a lie.

Work and education do not always lead to economic glory. Hatred does not always turn to love. Prejudice is not always overcome. The good guys do not always win. There are unhappy endings.

Yet, negating unpleasant realities, including the fact that emotions can be intense and that love can be a burden, teachers seem to say to their students, "You too, native American white child, you too, child of the native poor, child of the black man, Mexican, Puerto Rican, Indian or immigrant poor, you too can become President of the United States, or wealthy, or famous."

Can teachers possibly believe the lie they teach? Can there be no moments of sudden and sharp doubt, moments of intrusive reality, moments of guilt associated with teaching the lie?

There must be. There are. But teachers have so long been brought up with the romantic myth themselves that they choose to believe in it, or they pretend to believe in it, or they delude themselves into believing it. It is hard to resist the idea of heaven.

Success through work and education is the hallmark of romanticism. In the pursuit of success, fraud, poverty, disen-franchisement, brutality, racism, and injustice become almost desired evils, if not virtues. If these conditions did not exist, how could they be overcome, and if they were not overcome, how could we prove our mettle, how could we reach the happy ending?

"Hey, Teach," I was once told by Tony, who was a lot wiser in his sixteen years of living than I was in my twenty-six, "Howard Hughes never hadda overcome nothin'. He was born rich."

Over twenty years later, Lavinia, a girl sophisticated in the ways of New York streets, had the same point of view.

"Marilyn Monroe didn't need an education," she told me, "she never got outa school, and she got diamonds to show for it."

In between Tony and Lavinia—there was Martin.

I met him when he was fourteen and a psychiatric patient at Bellevue Hospital. I was his teacher. He had been at Bellevue three weeks. It was my first.

I could see nothing wrong with Martin. He was sweet, lovable, charming, courteous, affable, and bright. I therefore decided he had no problems.

I was certain that Martin did not belong at Bellevue, that either his doctors had railroaded him in, or that his mother had simply dumped him out. Martin agreed with both my diagnoses. I decided that as nothing was wrong with Martin, what he needed was an education. I also decided that the education he needed was a knowledge of New York City. Accordingly, I made known my decision on the movable blackboard in my classroom, which also served as a waiting room for court hearings on those two days a week when a judge came to Bellevue.

I wrote on that blackboard: "The aim of this lesson is to study about New York City." I don't know why I did that, because surely the judge didn't care what the aim of my lesson was; and, as there were no other students in my class besides Martin, I could simply have told him.

Anyway, Martin accepted my largesse and my lesson plan. I told him we would make a map of New York City on papier-mâché, which we would model after subway maps. It was important, I told him, to know the subway system. He agreed. We went around to all the rooms on the seventh floor, collecting old newspapers to soak in paste, but there are five boroughs to New York City, and there weren't enough newspapers. I decided to take Martin to the fifth floor and round up old papers from the ward. This was not as easy as it sounds.

The elevator bells at Bellevue had a will of their own. While I am not a believer in animism, I was fully convinced and I still am that the bells that signaled those elevators were definitely stubborn. When I pressed UP, they invariably voted to go down and vice versa. Only when someone as angry at them as I outfoxed them by hanging a sign on each floor that read RING UP FOR DOWN did the bells permit those elevators to go in the correct direction. Victory, however, was short-lived, because—I swear it—no one quite believes me, but I will attest to it even now that those bells learned to read. We were right back where we started from—on the wrong floor.

At any rate, that's why I decided to walk. I took Martin into my confidence about those elevators, but he thought I was crazy—which only convinced him, of course, that he did not belong there.

I don't know about today, but in 1949, the doors leading to the stairway were always locked from both sides. It was possible to go from the basement to the eighth floor, which was the top, without getting out at any landing if one didn't have a key.

I entered on the seventh floor, gave my key to Martin to hold, and I started blithely down to the fifth floor. He was behind me.

Suddenly I felt Martin on my back trying to grasp at me, kissing me on the back of my neck.

I was stunned.

"Martin," I said firmly, "you know I will have to put this on your record card."

He immediately jumped off me. I walked ahead. He followed. We got off at the fifth floor, and we proceeded to make our papier-mâché map of the subway system of New York City. We never said a word about it. I never told his doctors. Much later, long after Martin went off to a treatment center, I looked at his psychiatric record. Martin had been in Bellevue for attempted rape of older women on subways.

Funny? I thought so then. Now I don't. I was indulging in my own sense of fancy. I had not helped Martin. I had hurt him. The romanticization that nothing was wrong with Martin because I chose to see nothing wrong was a denial of his illness. Martin did not need me to stimulate his behavior or his imagination.

Many years later Martin visited me. He was going to college and he appeared well. I believed he was well—or was that my romanticism again? I don't know, because I haven't heard from him in over twenty-five years.

A teacher's reality is not necessarily the child's reality, and the child need not be a patient in a mental hospital. That child can be white, black, Indian, Puerto Rican, Mexican, or Chinese; poor, middle class, or rich. That child can be attending the public schools in any city or town in this country.

The teacher's reality may be economically different. It is not the difference of economic class, however, that is the barrier. There are many middle-class teachers who can and do understand the lives of poverty that their children live. They can be good teachers if they expose themselves to the psychological realities of their students. No, poverty and race are not the prime dividers. Romanticism is. It promotes emotional distance. Teachers who believe in romanticism will never believe that children hate their mothers, that children can murder, that parents can abuse their children, that they themselves can hate their students. They cannot believe in a "bad" feeling, except as those "bad" feelings are overcome and converted into good. After years of living the lie of being good little boys and girls themselves, who never expressed anger or hate or aggression because these are not acceptable emotions, they convert their own denials into romantic distortions of life.

I met Jonathan Evans at a teachers' meeting. He taught in a suburban high school and was quite pleased with his school and his students. He told me how shocked he had been when he had learned that a fifteen-year-old student of his, an honor student, in fact, had attempted suicide. He refused to believe it.

"Why?" I asked.

"Because he comes from such a good family," Jonathan explained, "there are no problems in that home, I'm sure of it, or if there are, well of course there are some," he amended, "what family doesn't have some, but suicide?—"

"Why not?" I asked.

"Oh, I'm certain he didn't mean to kill himself," Mr. Evans repeated. "Maybe he just wanted attention or something like that—"

How often I had heard that naive statement—as if the need for attention, and seeking it in such a drastic way, is not as serious as a real suicide attempt.

Again—romantic distortions—because suicide is an ugly thought.

But Mr. Evans saw only the student's private house, two parents at home, economic security, and ergo mental health and a happy ending; his student could not have meant to kill himself.

Yet, what was that student's emotional reality that prompted him to slash his wrists? Whether he meant to kill himself or not was really irrelevant. He did slash his wrists. Why was Mr. Evans not believing and not accepting the boy's anguish?

Romanticism demands that teachers believe only in surface people and surface emotions. They do not see that the surface child is not the real child any more than the surface teacher is not the real teacher. It takes a great deal of digging to find both the child and the teacher.

Children, like teachers, have layers and layers of defense. Teachers, however, believe in only one. Scratch surface and find innocence. Scratch innocence and find motivation to learn. Every child has an interest. Just find that interest, build your lesson plan about that interest, and the child will learn.

Children, however, are far more layered than that, and they are resistant to the gentle tapping of teachers. The process of growing up is not easy. Children suffer chiefly because the emotions they are experiencing are looked upon with disfavor by their parents and teachers. Yet, they themselves are aware of the truth of their emotions. They suffer because the truth is stamped a lie by those who should know—their teachers.

Feeling misunderstood by their teachers and guilty because of their emotions, they are resistant to what teachers have to tell them. Their motivations to learn, therefore, do not lie just below the surface. One has to dig deep to find them. One has to dig deep to find the child.

Teachers who look for surface children gear their thinking for surface values and they teach without depth.

I remember kindergarten. I remember standing on a long line

before Miss Leslie's desk to buy chocolate-covered graham crackers, two for a penny. Usually I gave my penny to my friend Lilly to stand in line because she knew what to say. I didn't. This time Lilly refused. I stood on that long line. I had never talked to the teacher alone before.

When I got to Miss Leslie's desk I put out my hand with the two pennies in it.

"Well?" she said.

I hung my head.

"Two," I whispered.

"Is that the way you ask?" she said coldly.

I tried again.

"Two."

"Well," she said again, "I see you have to learn your manners."

I stood frozen.

"Stand aside," she ordered, "and listen how someone else asks for it properly."

I moved aside while the child behind me made her request.

Miss Leslie turned to me and smiled. "Now do you know how to be polite?"

I shook my head yes.

"Say it then—"

My voice cracked. "Could I please have two cookies?"

"Well, what kind?" She became impatient with me.

"Chocolate-covered graham crackers," I could barely speak.

She gave them to me and I turned away. I could not eat them.

I am certain that Miss Leslie thought she was teaching me manners. But where were hers? Did she not know that politeness is a surface mechanism? When it is genuine, it springs out of concern for other people's feelings. Where were her feelings for me?

All she saw was a fresh little girl—or a stupid one. All she saw was the surface child. She didn't see me—the core of me. I was afraid.

That moment is still with me and I strive to keep it alive. It would be more comfortable to forget it, but I feel strongly that teachers must consciously train themselves to remember their own hurts—because only in remembering can they alleviate the hurts of others.

Surface teaching, however, does not call for memory. It calls only for surface dedication and surface intellectualization.

Teachers know, for instance, that the functions of the human mind are common to the whole of humanity. Yet, when they deliberately misunderstand the complexities of children, they negate those complexities, believing in the primitive human mind. The child is simple, they say, and they fail to understand that it is their own denial systems, their own romanticism, that make the child seem simple or primitive or innocent.

Teachers unfortunately refuse to believe in the depths of which children are capable. They do not see the inner children who try valiantly to hold on to their own integrity but who very often can't because of the torrents of brainwashing to which they are continually subjected. Children are urged, coerced, and made to conform to the teacher's version of what is their innocence.

I learned this when I was about twelve, although of course I could not conceptualize it until long after I had hurt my share of children.

One of my first encounters with a school librarian was asking her for the book *Joseph in Egypt*. I had never heard of Thomas Mann, but I had seen the book prominently displayed in a book store. I wanted to read it because I was going to Hebrew school and had just finished reading the biblical story of Joseph in the original Hebrew.

I did not tell that to the librarian. Consequently, she looked at me in disbelief.

"Oh, you don't want to read that," she told me. "That's way too hard for you."

She then suggested I read something else and handed me a copy of *The Bobsey Twins*.

Of course I could have read *Joseph in Egypt*, because I was a very good reader. I may not have liked it, but why not let me try? Why anchor me to the children's book section?

The romanticism of teachers is constantly to be fought, because living the fairy tale is damaging.

We are not all Doris Days. We do not all live in suburbia. We do not all sleep with pillows on our bed, and we do not all love our mothers.

I too would like to be a romantic, especially as I am a teacher and talk of maintaining the dignity of the teacher, keeping the authority of the position, and the right to privilege. It is an easy way for a teacher to live. So sometimes I slip into the fairy tale.

Very recently I remember talking to some girls at Livingston about the American War of Independence.

"That ain't my war, honey," Evelyn shouted.

I was peremptory. "Don't be silly," I said, "it was every-body's war. The trouble is, you don't know anything about history."

"Not mine," she repeated, snapping her fingers at me. "The Constitution wasn't written for the black man. It says all men are created equal, but it don't say no black man was created equal to no white man, do it? Why, when that thing was written, black people were in slavery. How does that Constitution talk to me—tell me that? When it was written, we was written out and we're still out. What you telling me?"

Evelyn was right. What was I telling her? Her history was different from mine, yet I was teaching as if mine were the only history.

Over and over again I become acutely aware of the disparity between reality and romanticism. It is a lesson I must constantly bear in mind. One summer I visited a small town in New Mexico with a large Indian population. I met a teacher and spent a lot of time talking to her.

"Oh," she said to me, "there is absolutely no tension in this town. Everyone gets along just fine."

I mentioned the obvious disparity between some of the homes

I had seen, in which the white landowners and shopkeepers lived, and the hovels, in which the Indians lived.

"Well, that's their culture, you know. Now, if only they would get out and make those beautiful rugs and Indian jewelry, they could put every store owner out of business."

I somehow doubted that.

"But they're so lazy, they prefer to get food stamps or welfare."

"What industry is there around here?" I asked. "What jobs are available? What jobs could they get?"

"Well, that is a problem," she explained, and she emphasized the word *is*. "This is a very great poverty area. There aren't many jobs. This is mostly a tourist town, skiing in the winter and we're also an art colony, not much agriculture, and of course the Indians have been living here for hundreds of years, but as I say, if they wanted to work they could."

"At what?"

"Well, as I said," she drawled, "they could make those rugs, and their jewelry is fabulous."

"I can't believe there aren't tensions," I insisted. I pointed out that only a few months earlier there had been an Indian resistance movement in Wounded Knee in which several people were killed. "The pueblos may be a cultural style of living, but you can't convince me that Indians or anyone else for that matter enjoy poverty. Indians may want to live in pueblos, but why isn't there electricity or running water in those pueblos? You can't tell me they don't want to live under sanitary conditions."

"Well, I guess they just don't mind," she said.

Whose reality?

She was white. The children she taught were Indian. She lived in a wooden frame house and went to Europe once every three years. The children she taught lived in adobe huts and often did not have enough to eat.

Yet I am certain she could have overcome her middle-class mentality if she had but tried. I wondered if she would ever be able to overcome her need for a romantic vision of life.

Teachers, it seems, produce their own blind spots. Blinking and shutting out their own intense feelings from themselves and hoping that their own wishful thinking processes will replace their lack of vision, they introduce their romantic distortions as if these distortions were the psychological and social realities of their students.

I was going over some record cards of a girl who had just been referred to Livingston because she had been an assaulter. In her guidance record I read the following account:

"Student requested a change of program indicating she wanted to drop Spanish because a Spanish man killed her father."

"I interviewed the student regarding this change. She agreed that it was not a valid reason for dropping a subject. I used this as a classic example of the irrationality of bias, whereas an entire culture is held responsible for an individual's act."

I continued to read the record. Apparently, the girl supposedly agreed. She went out, however, and assaulted a child.

I have no doubt that the counselor was pleased with his preaching, which he called counseling. I also have no doubt that he took no responsibility for the child's assault. Could he help it, he must have told himself, if the student was really a violent child? Yet, he had committed a more violent act than she. He had preached a frozen intellectual morality that had no relationship to the reality of her feelings. He had in fact denied her feelings, as if her problem were only one of prejudice. Did not that guidance counselor understand what murder meant? What hatred meant? Could he not have let her talk of her mourning for her father, her feelings of anger and loss?

He did not hear her emotions because it was easier for him to intellectualize rather than to accept them.

"Uh huh," he must have thought, if I judge his report correctly, "now I can teach a lesson on the meaning of prejudice." Problem: Prejudice. Aim of lesson: Eradication of Prejudice. Method: Teacher.

All surface mechanisms.

What that child needed was not a diatribe on prejudice. She needed to sort through her feelings. Did her refusal to learn Spanish really mean that she was prejudiced? Perhaps it was just a constant reminder that her father had been murdered. And what if the murder of her father did result in prejudice? Was this the time to discuss it? That child was a mass of undifferentiated feeling—love, hate, anger, loss, frustration. When her counselor denied the reality of her feelings and substituted a surface morality, she struck out in anger at him and hurt another child.

The irony is that teachers are adept at teaching the dynamics of prejudice when the prejudice is on the part of their students. Yet, they romanticize their own.

The rationalization of prejudice finds its greatest outlet where black children are concerned.

Teachers who live in the romantic tradition absolutely refuse to see that the fatherless black family is the production of white history. Slaves were urged to reproduce. It was profitable for the slave owner. When families were separated and sold separately, it was also profitable for the slave owner.

Now that slavery is no longer profitable, we expect patterns that we have foisted upon the black people to disappear. Patterns are now a hindrance. They are no longer profitable. They embarrass us. We demand change. But history dies hard.

Now that our society no longer finds slavery economically, socially, or culturally profitable, we want these patterns to disappear as if they never existed. Moreover, we resent reminders that it cannot disappear. Therefore, we negate our responsibilities by negating our history.

The following letter, for instance, was written to a newspaper by a white teacher:

"It is demeaning and condescending to all black people to be told that there is such a thing as 'black culture'—culture is democratic and should not be given ethnic limitations."

Now, there is a blind spot indeed. Can teachers really believe that there is only one culture—and that it is only a democratic one?

Black children in a classroom in which a teacher negates their past existence are bound to suffer. Their resentment against the teacher would either be expressed in direct rebellion, if they were able to do so, or in suppression of their own hostility. In the latter case, suppression would be self-defeating. They would become what she knew they were in the first place, nonverbal, silently hostile, and unmotivated to learn.

Children do not achieve when they suppress hostility. Black children are no different. They cannot achieve when in the process of suppressing their hostility they also suppress their spontaneity and creativity. Black children cannot learn when in the process of accepting their teachers' values of their own unacceptability they themselves begin to see themselves as unacceptable. Self-hatred cannot be the foundation of learning.

Whether we like it or not, the patterns of slavery do remain, patterns of apathy, ignorance, frustration, and violence. These are negative patterns. Many positive patterns, however, also remain. Unfortunately, teachers often do not see these patterns, the patterns of larger familial love, when the immediate family is decimated; patterns of music, poetry, and the greatest pattern of all—sheer survival.

There are many routes to survival. Work may not be one. Nor education. Many students, for instance, have parents who will support them. This is particularly true of rich and middle-class students. Or they can run away from home and fend for themselves. Over one million children from middle-class families take this route. They have learned that they can survive without work. The children of the poor know this already.

Work is not the sine qua non of existence. Yet, we teach in the romantic tradition as if it were. To the worker go the spoils.

Work should be a part of education; it should be a meaningful part. Children should learn that through work we can find great personal satisfactions even if we cannot find immortality. Work for which children earn money should be a part of every school.

As they now exist, however, work programs in schools are, more often than not, a sham.

Work programs are created most often during June in order to keep students quiet during July and August. The money generally comes from the federal government. What a waste—because the money could be spent more profitably. Students could be assigned to real jobs. Instead, they are assigned to makeshift jobs, meaningless jobs. Often, the only skill required of a student is to appear once a week and sign for a paycheck. Students soon learn that bribery is very acceptable. Corruption is enticing.

During the school year the jobs that are created are often equally meaningless. Students work either in their schools or they are assigned to cooperating agencies, including private industry. Most often, the employees in industry do not wish to make way for students, nor should they be expected to. They fear the loss of their own positions. In schools or agencies, often there is little for students to do. Three students may be assigned to one job site in which there is not enough work for even one student. As a result, those in job programs, either in schools or outside schools, quickly learn that jobs are meaningless at best, or boring at worst. Students soon clamor that there must be more to life than the prospect of looking forward to twenty-five years of boredom.

The children in our public schools see many of the work programs for what they are, unreal and simulated. There is no investment in the job. Students want not only money, they want importance. To be kept busy at an unimportant, unnecessary makeshift job is to be unimportant and unnecessary oneself. The value of work is that the worker develops a sense of achievement and pride in the work accomplished. Whether one builds a ship or types a letter correctly, the worker, seeing the importance of the work, feels important.

There can be no self-importance attached to a job that does not need to be done.

Is it any wonder then that the children turn to the streets and learn to develop the survival skills that are necessary there but that threaten teachers so?

Teachers steeped in the romantic notions of education know little of survival except the survival of American pioneers conquering Indians and the wilderness. They can understand that a man shot buffalo to feed his family—but they cannot understand a child carrying a knife in a ghetto street or a child using drugs in suburbia. Yet both are methods of survival. We may not approve of them, and they may not work even for the children who are using them, but the children are trying to survive in what to them is an otherwise intolerable world.

"You're full of shit—" Debbie, a thirteen-year-old, screamed at me. "You're more than bull, you're buffalo—"

Anger, obscenity, knives, were her forms of survival.

"Look," said sophisticated seventeen-year-old Susan, who lived in one of the best areas of New York City, "in this city a girl has to protect herself with a knife or a birth control pill. I prefer a birth control pill."

She was also surviving.

Both Debbie and Susan, worlds apart, were trying in their own ways to survive in a world they were struggling to understand, and a world in which, unfortunately, most teachers do not understand them.

Children develop survival skills and teachers label them deviant or disturbed or neurotic or even spoiled brats. Children fight and teachers label them aggressive. They may be merely transferring the right to walk down the violent street on which they live to the right to sit in a seat of their choice in a classroom. Children curse and teachers call them aggressive. They may merely be transferring the communication of the streets into the life of the classroom. Children carry weapons and teachers call them antisocial. They may merely be carrying into the classroom their world and the need to fight in order to survive.

Would these same teachers call disturbed or antisocial an Arab child who walked in the streets of Israel with a weapon? Or a Catholic child walking in the streets of Protestant Ireland?

Or an Indian child in Pakistan? Survival is survival in times of strife and hysteria and crisis. The world is now in a state of crisis.

Under the circumstances, teachers would consider such transfers of learning with pride. For instance, a child who learns to memorize the Latin declensions and then transfers his memorization skills to mathematical formulas is considered to have transferred his skills of learning from one subject to another. Yet, a child who learns the language and behavior of the streets in order to survive there, and who later transfers that learning to the classroom, is condemned, feared, and considered educationally deficient. The strength of the street child, the ability of the poor to transfer the learnings of poverty into the classroom, is not recognized as identical to the process of transferring the skills of memorization from Latin to mathematics. Instead, teachers decry the transferred skills of survival that the children have mastered, and maximize the learnings they wish to impose. Not only is the denial of the street the romanticization of their own morality, it is also an expression of their hostility. Punish the kids.

Thus we come full cycle. The romanticization of reality, both inner and outer, leads to a false sense of security and power. All is well with the world.

Except—is it? There are always nagging questions waiting to be asked. Are we really as moral as we try so hard to believe we are?

There are those who flip the coin to find the answer. They see the other side of romanticism—revolution.

9

The Rebels: The True and the Pseudo

If our ineffective schools are to change for the better, it is the teachers who will change them. They will have to assume the role of crusading rebel. Many teachers are already crusading rebels in the best sense of the word; some are in the process of becoming. They have moved inwardly to seek self-awareness, which often means to accomplish self-change, and they have freed themselves emotionally so that they can move outwardly to seek changes in our social structures. Since they are teachers, their outward movements toward change are naturally in the direction of the schools. They advocate and agitate for necessary reforms. It might be for a free lunch program, for the rights of students to teach themselves, for the rights of teachers to make their own decisions in a school. They are healthy rebels. They have accepted the responsibilities of their maturity and the opportunities of freedom to exploit those responsibilities. They are not afraid to be accountable to their students.

Yet, if one were to confront them with the concept that they were indeed rebels in a good cause, many would be surprised and some would undoubtedly deny it. They would assert that they were merely acting and teaching in the best interest of children. They are indeed crusading rebels, however, constructively fighting for constructive change. They are a force for good.

There are other teachers, however, who loudly proclaim their rebellions, who publicly cast themselves in the role of rebels, but who are not true rebels at all. They have not achieved inner expansion. They have not grown up, and their so-called rebellions are often nothing more than educational temper tantrums or games of sheer childish negativism, with no worthwhile purpose underlying their acting out.

They are seeking to establish their authority through emotion, but actually are uncommitted intellectually. Their rebellions often are expressions of petulance, very much like those of the child who always says no to parents in an effort to assert independence even when he would like to say yes. Since parents are perceived by most of us as progenitors of authority, the pseudorebels defy those in their schools who stand in lieu of parents—their principals, assistant principals, and others in authority.

Both groups of teachers, the true rebels and the pretenders, the constructive and destructive, come in all ages; maturity is not determined by chronological age. I have known young rebels who were mature and therefore constructive in their rebellion. I have known teachers close to retirement who were still rebelling against their own parents, even though they were totally unaware they were doing so, and were convinced that their pseudorebellions really were against social, economic, and educational injustice. The true rebel fights for personal freedom for self and others. The true rebel understands that personal freedom both reflects and produces political freedom.

Freedom starts with the inner ability to make one's decisions and the ability to use one's mind. Piri Thomas, author of *Down These Mean Streets*, told me that he first began to learn what freedom really meant when he was in prison. He could let his mind fly and bring him out of his body. Books became his passion and through them he began to realize that his brain was his greatest weapon of rebellion and freedom. He used that weapon and became a talented and successful writer.

Thomas F. Lee also understood the nature of freedom. He

taught it superbly. I met him when I was visiting a city high school in Michigan.

It was the first day of the new term, and although I knew it was not a good time to observe (first days are generally hectic), it was the only time I had before returning home.

When I arrived at the school both the principal and the assistant principal were cordial and gracious, but busy. It was understandable that they could not spend much time talking with me. Nevertheless, the assistant principal offered to give me a brief tour of the building. As we passed by the classrooms and as I peeked in through open doors or through the glass panes on closed doors, I saw teachers distributing books, pupils filling out forms, students greeting each other, teachers writing on blackboards. There was movement everywhere, both in the corridors and in the classrooms. The tone of the school was casual, pleasant, and busy.

When we arrived outside Mr. Lee's room, the bell had just rung for a change of period. Mr. Lee was standing in the corridor, talking to a student. I was introduced to him as we passed.

"My next class coming in is twelfth-grade history," he said to me after introductions were over. "Would you like to come in?"

The assistant principal turned to me. "Would you have time?" she asked. By the way she said it, I had the distinct feeling that she didn't want me to have the time. I was curious, however, so I said I would sit in. She left and I followed him into the room, while the second bell signaled the beginning of the new period.

Although it seemed to me that all the students knew him, he introduced himself to them with a flourish, stressing the f in his name. "I am Thomas F. Lee," he announced. It seemed to be some sort of school joke, because everybody laughed.

Later I found out that he always stressed the fact that although the surname was the same, he was no relation to Thomas E. Lee, and he didn't want anyone to confuse them, particularly as

Thomas E. Lee was white and he was black. When he introduced me, there were a few curious glances toward the back of the room, where I sat, and then attention turned fully toward him.

"Okay everybody," he said, "before we get started on today's work I want to give you the assignment for tomorrow."

The usual assortment of groans was heard, but nevertheless, assignment books were taken out and pencils were poised. The students were ready to write.

"I want you to go out on any street corner in your neighborhood for one hour this evening between five and six and count the number of red cars that go by. Bring in the information tomorrow."

The students busily wrote their assignment. Then there was silence.

"Isn't anyone going to ask me why I am giving such an assignment?" he asked suddenly.

Not a word was said.

"Doesn't anyone think it's a strange assignment?" he asked.

There was a giggle or two from the girls.

"Even a little bit stupid?" he parried.

There was more giggling.

"How many of you are going to do it?" he asked.

Everybody's hands went up.

"Well, I hope you're lying," he said.

There was a roar of laughter.

"Because it is a stupid assignment," he said. "It makes no sense.

"Well then, why do you want us to do it?" some boy called out.

"I don't," he answered. "I wanted to see how many of you would ask why I was giving it. No one did. Question—you must learn to question. Don't do things simply because a teacher tells you to. Ask why. Maybe there's a reason—maybe not—but ask, think. A teacher's word is not God's, and even printed words in a book can be wrong. Question!"

The questions came fast and furious. The discussion became heated, at times almost argumentative. It was almost as if a fuse had ignited those students. They talked about the necessity for inquiry. When does one question? When does one accept? They talked of the difference between faith and science, and the place of inquiry in both.

When the bell rang, indicating the period was over, we were all taken by surprise. We were deceived by time, it had gone so quickly. Another groan went up, this time out of reluctance to leave. Those students walked out of that room, still talking, some arguing, all stimulated by thought. No assignment had been given for the next day. None had to be given. Those students went home to think.

What Mr. Lee had taught those students was the beginning of constructive rebellion—the questioning of authority. He had used himself by making his own authority vulnerable to attack. Only a teacher who feels secure in his authority can invite a class to rebel constructively. Thus, he was the tool by which he taught.

When I left his room I congratulated him on his inspiring lesson.

"Well, you know," he said, "Watergate makes you think."

I returned to the principal's office to say good-bye, to extend my thanks, and to tell him how much I had enjoyed Mr. Lee's class.

"Oh, he's a good teacher, all right," Mr. Bromley agreed. I sensed a mild tone of disapproval in his voice.

I took a wild stab.

"Your assistant principal didn't seem to want me to observe him," I said.

He smiled. "Well, you never know what Tom is going to do—sometimes he's too radical for us."

This time it was I who smiled. I believed that Mr. Lee asked embarrassing questions—and that's what Mr. Bromley probably meant by radical.

"If only he'd stick to teaching," Mr. Bromley continued, "but he always has a cause. Two years ago he wanted us to start a black studies program, yet we don't have that many black students, but Mr. Lee insisted that white students needed to learn as much about the contributions of black people as black students did—in fact, more, and we compromised. Many white parents objected and so we instituted a humanities course, one that covers black history as well as the history of other minority groups, the Indians, the Mexicans, and so forth."

"That sounds wonderful," I interjected.

"It's good, very good," he agreed. "We had our problems with some parents, as I said. After all, this is a predominantly white area—but I agreed with Mr. Lee, he was basically right, white students need to learn about the history of minority groups, but now—"

"What?" I asked, expecting a further extension of the course, possibly the history of the Irish or the Jews or the Italians. I really didn't know what I expected. I almost laughed when he told me.

"He wants to make printing a vocational course for girls, but how many girls are going to get jobs as printers?"

I could feel his consternation.

"Apparently Mr. Lee doesn't believe in job discrimination," I answered.

"Yes, yes, I know," he interrupted, "I don't believe in job discrimination either—but let's be realistic—girls as printers?" He asked the question as if it were totally incredible.

I didn't have the time to answer that skills, including printing, are neither male nor female; they are merely skills. But we were interrupted by his secretary and he had to leave. Soon after, I had to go. I left happy, however, knowing that there are teachers like Thomas F. Lee in our schools, teachers who are constructive rebels.

The pseudorebels act as they do, however, not because they feel their own authority, but because they lack it entirely. Often they do a great deal of harm, because their actions may even stifle the true reform for which they so vehemently defend the cause of rebellion.

Jonathan Foster, for instance, was a teacher studying for his doctorate in psychology. He taught remedial reading in a poverty program in Detroit. I had met him originally at a psychology conference in which he had been a very vocal member of a group calling themselves the radical caucus. They were, he had explained to me, professional agitators for reform. At that meeting, for instance, they had been trying to prevent a psychologist from speaking because they were opposed to his point of view, which they claimed was racist.

Jonathan and I had disagreed entirely on the issue, because while I, too, did not believe in the speaker's thesis, I believed repression was far more dangerous than anything the speaker could possibly say.

We became friendly even though we were in basic disagreement, and when he invited me to visit his class when I came to Detroit, I accepted.

The day I visited him, however, it was almost like the first day we had met. He was vocal and angry. He had just been asked by the director of his program to hand in a statistical report regarding the children in his class who might be eligible for free lunch.

He began to grumble to me, almost as soon as he saw me, that he'd be damned if he would do it.

"But why?" I asked.

"Because I hand in those reports every damned year," he said. "And they take hours to do. I knew I should have saved a copy but damn it, somebody has them somewhere, if only they'd get off their rear ends and find them."

I knew how he felt. Sometimes it seems to me and to everyone else who works in a bureaucratic structure that it is someone's sole job to develop ways to ask teachers for complicated reports—reports that no one ever seems to look at and that no one can ever seem to find.

But I couldn't see the point of not sending in this particular report. Too much was at stake. Refusing to send in that report meant that the children in his class wouldn't receive free lunches. What kind of battle was that for Mr. Foster to fight? It was merely his frustration and his anger against authority that prompted him to rebel. It served no purpose otherwise and did a good deal of harm. While he talked humane reform, his actions reinforced inhumanity.

When I suggested this idea to him he became annoyed with me.

"Well, I didn't agree with you before, and I don't agree with you now," he said. "If I don't send in that report, and I won't, we'll still get those kids free lunch."

I didn't see how and I didn't see the point. It seemed to me that Jonathan had not learned how to pick his fight. He was frustrated and angry and ready to rebel against any authority. In a sense, he really was self-indulgent, thinking of himself and his own feelings rather than the issues at stake.

Teachers like Jonathan, who rebel mainly out of frustration and the need to express their own individuality, often defy minor school regulations, such as refusing to sign in in the time book or not handing in reports punctually. They are absent frequently without real cause and often they are excessively late. Lateness, of course, can be tolerated in some jobs, but not in teaching, where children often have to wait outside a class-room for a teacher to appear. Lateness, absences, petty defiances, are often misconstrued by immature teachers as symbols of freedom, much as they are by rebellious adoles-cents, who, with guidance, can grow out of their need for this kind of defiance.

In adolescence young people are struggling to find their own independence, so it naturally is a period of revolt against paren-tal views. But it is also a period of integration and growth. Adolescents who become mature adults learn that one can love one's parents, value their love, return their love, and still be capable of making decisions that might be in conflict with some parental values. Values between parents and children may and do differ, but love can remain constant if the values of each are respected. The mature teacher is able to see this distinction and also able to realize that student values will differ from teacher values in much the same way that teacher values differ from the values of parents.

The mature teacher, however, caught in the middle between parent and student, does not sell out to either. Maturity means the ability to develop and keep a value system *of one's own*.

Unfortunately, however, some people seem to feel that love and values are the same; that is, if one loves someone, one adopts her or his values. This simply is not true. A parent can love a child or a child a parent and still develop her or his own value systems. Values do not and cannot remain constant. Of necessity, the values of each succeeding generation change as values in political, moral, and social ethics change. This is as it should be. Slavery was once a desired value by a large segment of our population. It no longer is. The value of freedom has superseded it. Segregation of races in schools and housing also was once a desired value. Now by fiat, if not by morality, it no longer is. Those who continue to cling to the morality and values of their own time of growing up cannot move with the times of their children, and a hiatus is created. When either parents or the children assume moral superiority for their particular position, the gap widens and the conflict becomes bitter.

Immature teachers, still struggling for independence, cannot accept the probability that student values may differ from their own. Identifying with their students, many such teachers seem to think that in order to be effective, they must mimic the values of their students, even to assuming their dress, language, and behavior. It is as if they skip their own generation and try to become their own children. It is, of course, a wishful statement of their need to remain forever young and another form of rebellion against their own parents. In that rebellion the school aligns with home. The school system that theoretically has nurtured them the way their own parents have nurtured them becomes a substitute target for their hostility.

They see themselves as waging important battles against issues of educational injustice, but in actuality the battles they wage are against the authority of home.

Mary Lennox is a good example. When I first met her I was very impressed. She told me that she wanted to leave the school in which she was teaching because she was too hampered by the school organization.

"They worry when you have paper on the floor," she laughed, "and I really believe that children cannot be repressed, cannot be confined the way they are."

She was a woman in her early forties and had been teaching several years. She was seeking a transfer from that school, she said, because she wanted to work in a school where the prime function of the teacher was to teach students how to guide their own lives.

I loved the things she said and I hired her, not bothering to call her principal; after all, what could a repressive principal tell me, I thought. I was certain I had made the right decision. I could not have been more wrong.

It took only a few weeks for me to realize that to her freedom meant a complete lack of organization in the classroom. Clothes were strewn all over desks and chairs even though a clothes closet was available. As a result, garments were lost or misplaced and fights erupted over them. Books were also strewn all over; many were torn or defaced by angry and frustrated students who were looking for guidance and found only chaos. It would have been impossible to locate a particular book in that room even if someone were foolish enough to try to read there. It was impossible for learning to take place in that room. As a result, her students learned little. They did whatever they pleased. They gossiped frequently. Sometimes they played games. Occasionally they slept. Most often they fought.

When I tried to explain to her that students needed to learn how to regulate themselves, and that they could not learn to do so if she didn't help set the tone or regulate herself, she cried angrily, "Well, they're doing their own thing, isn't that what you want?"

I told her that I heartily believed in the philosophy of "doing your own thing." The whole program at Livingston is one of making decisions. Students should and can decide for themselves what it is they need to learn. Students should and can learn how to make a decision and how to follow through on those decisions, how to accept the consequences of a decision and how to be accountable to others for these decisions. If that isn't "doing your own thing," what is?

Miss Lennox, however, interpreted "doing your own thing" as doing nothing. It was an interpretation that led to a total lack of responsibility. Moreover, it was an excuse for self-indulgence. Taken to its ultimate conclusion, of course, such self-indulgence leads only to nihilism.

Miss Lennox resisted conferences with more experienced teachers who could have helped her. She seemed to feel that she knew all the answers and could solve every girl's problem by herself. She did not need to rely on anyone else's knowledge or experience, even when things obviously were going very wrong. She talked with vehemence about freedom as if it depended mostly upon a total rejection of all experience before hers.

"The girls are really too disturbed to understand freedom," she stated with exasperation at one point when she was in my office.

"Perhaps they're disturbed in the first place," I answered, "because they haven't ever really had or understood freedom. Freedom is self-regulation and self-determination. These girls have been repressed all their lives and told what to do. Repression hasn't worked for them. Neither will anarchy. They want to find order in their lives. They need to be taught how to create it."

"I am teaching it," she answered.

"Freedom means taking it upon oneself to be accountable to others," I said.

Suddenly, she became very angry. "Are you telling me I'm not responsible?" she asked. Before I could answer, she cried, "And I thought you'd be different!"

She stormed out of my office.

Within minutes, five students burst into my office, calling me all kinds of names. Isabel was particularly vocal.

"What you got against Miss Lennox?"

"What makes you think I have anything against Miss Lennox?" I asked.

"Cause she told us," Isabel answered, "she told us you don't go for her because she believes in freedom, and you, you want her to be strict with us and shit like that."

I assured them that Miss Lennox had misunderstood what I had said, that we had had a conference because teachers and principals do have conferences, and that we had been talking about what freedom was. "I probably didn't make myself clear to her," I told them.

They accepted my explanation and we began to speak of other things, but inwardly I was seething. Miss Lennox had selfishly projected her anger upon the students. She had also projected her need to rebel. They, of course, had their own problems and conflicts to resolve. They didn't need hers. Eventually we agreed that she should leave, and she transferred to another school. When she left it was amazing how quickly those very same girls whom she had diagnosed as too "disturbed" to understand freedom suddenly became cured of their "disturbance." They became, under the guidance of a good teacher, able to organize themselves and their own classroom learning.

Teachers like Miss Lennox often confuse authority with autocracy, not recognizing that an authority is someone who creates a system of thought, while an autocrat imposes thought or order on others. Teachers who feel their own authority do not need an autocratic environment. They do not need bells to tell them they must silence a class and proceed with a lesson. They do not need curriculums to follow that were ordained by others. They can do it for themselves. Moreover, teachers who feel their own authority can accept it in others.

Teachers who lack authority fear it in others and are constantly rebelling against it. Teachers who lack authority reject the authority that is found in books and in history. They reject the authority of knowledge. In this way, change becomes impossible, because these tenuous rebels will not learn from the experience of others. They do not move on. They stand still, and their provincialism solidifies during those very moments in which they are convinced of their radicalism. Thus, not accepting the research or the knowledge of others, because they cannot accept the authority of history, they remain rooted to the status quo. They can never move on to new experimentation because they are so suspicious of accepting the work of any so-called authority. After all, authority is anathema.

I watched one first-grade teacher try to teach a little girl to write her letters. The teacher struggled to get the child to hold the pencil correctly. The pencil was extremely thin. The little girl's hand kept overreaching. She could not write. I knew, as everyone who teaches primary grades has learned, that small children can grasp chunky pencils or large crayons better than thin pencils. It makes coordination easier. It therefore makes learning easier. I wondered why that teacher didn't know it also. Almost any book that discusses the psychomotor development of children will make that point.

When I asked her about it later, she admitted that she had heard it mentioned before, probably in one of her education or child psychology courses, but she really didn't quite believe it.

Meanwhile, children were struggling with that puny pencil because their teacher had chosen to ignore forty years of research.

All I could think of was a surgeon operating without anesthesia because he did not believe in the research on anesthesia. Some facts of history and science, after all, have to be accepted.

We can redesign the wheel, but we don't always have to rediscover it.

Now, I certainly don't want to go on record as indicating teachers should believe everything that they are taught, that they should accept as gospel everything they read. In the words of Thomas F. Lee, they should question. They should have the right to experiment. They should have the right to fail. Creativity must not be stifled.

Questioning the work of others, however, and experimenting with it is quite different from merely ignoring the work of others or from refusing to learn from the work of others. Some truths, after all, have been established beyond doubt. Thus, in their revolt against authority, many teachers become anti-intellectual, and what better way to prove it than by pretending to give up middle-class comforts and adopting the ascetic pose of poverty?

In order to give up middle-class comforts, however, one first must be middle class, which is why pseudorebels are predominantly middle class and white. Black people *as a group* are not ready to give up a status that as a group they never had. Many blacks are trying to move into the middle class economically, not out of it. Having known poverty personally or seen it in its historical context as a social concomitant to being black, they know it is not amusing to be poor, nor is there any status in it. White teachers of the middle class, however, having no such understanding, often try to imbue poverty with excitement and status. What better way to demonstrate one's rebellion, what better way to hurt the sensibilities of one's middle-class parents? Living a life of pseudopoverty becomes synonymous with righteousness and beauty.

Generally, middle-class school communities won't have these teachers. Ghetto schools, on the other hand, often have no choice. Teachers who *talk* a good game of revolution find jobs with the poor in periods of affluence. These pseudorebels, in fact, flourish in affluence, because only in affluence can poverty be a desired affectation.

There are many truly dedicated teachers, however, who choose to teach in poverty areas. They come out of conviction, dedication, and enjoyment. They do not believe they have to pretend to be poorer than they are, or other than their true selves to feel the problems of the poor and work toward solutions. One teacher I know helped parents organize a food cooperative in New York City. Another teacher in Chicago helped organize a day-care center. A third teacher in California gave of his spare time freely to organize adult classes in remedial reading. Not one of these three thought of themselves as unusual, or even as rebels. They did, however, believe in action.

Teachers struggling to relate to students, struggling to teach, wanting desperately to help their students, however, cannot always accomplish the impossible. There are some problems that have no solutions. There are some situations a teacher, or anyone else for that matter, can't control. A teacher can't bring back a deserting parent. A teacher sometimes can't stop a child from engaging in behavior or a course of action that is disastrous. The best teacher, under the best of circumstances, cannot change the reality of the child. He/she/they cannot will an intolerable situation into a story with a happy ending. There are many problems so insoluble, many situations so intractable, that the teacher simply cannot really help a child. Such teachers fight not only for reform, they often fight against their own feelings of defeat. They will not be defeated.

One teacher, trying desperately to soothe a child whose father was an addict and whose mother went from one boyfriend to another, cried to me, "I can't be what Rachel wants me to be—her family!"

No, she couldn't. But she could be and she was a supportive, loving, and caring person. She helped Rachel feel important. She helped Rachel to believe in herself.

Yet, I knew what she suffered. She bore part of Rachel's pain; she also bore the pain of not being able to change Rachel's life. She did not permit herself to be incapacitated by that pain and by guilt—pain for not being able to change Rachel's life—guilt for a society that permitted her own child to have so much and Rachel to have so little. Her concerns with the realities of the lives of her students made of her a wonderful teacher.

"Look," she said to me once, "I don't believe in deserts. We can make things grow in them."

She was a true rebel.

The true rebel acts. The pseudo ones talk. The true rebels are committed to a specific time, a specific place, and specific children. The pretenders are only ephemeral in their commitment. They teach for a day or a month or a term. A trip to Europe may intervene, a year hiking across the United States, a week in Puerto Rico, or merely a return to suburbia. They do not work with diligence at love or commitment or responsibility. They merely talk about it.

One group of teachers I knew, for instance, decided to bring teaching to a ghetto area in New Jersey. They laid their plans with gusto and an eye for publicity. Laden with flowers and a television crew, they staged a teach-in. They gave a flower to every child, played a few reading games with the children, had their pictures taken, and left.

When it was all over, one parent asked despondently, "Well, how did that help? Our children still can't read, and we still live in the slums."

When I talked with one of these itinerant revolutionaries, she talked of her love for the children: "Something I really never understood before," she said, "love."

She still didn't. Her act of love was an act of self-glorification. It was also an act of hostility. It brought a promise to some children and their families. And it killed that promise immediately.

"My father was an academic stud going from college to college every few years teaching philosophy," she told me. "What he didn't know about life was pathetic. And my mother is a butch. She doesn't know it, but I do—"

As she spoke, her angers against her parents became apparent. As a child, she had always felt that her parents had resented her. She was an only child, and all her life, from childhood and continuing into adulthood, she felt unwanted. She was angry. She wanted to hurt them back. I had no idea of course if what she said about her parents was true. It really didn't matter, however. It was her perception of them that was true for her. It was her reality. She hated her parents because she felt unloved. As an adult she tried to do everything that could displease them in order to hurt them—always, however, under the slogan of love.

She fit herself into her perception of the heroic mold. She talked of love but was consumed with hatred. She told me she was off for another town, another teach-in. She was committed to no time, no child.

Pseudorebels often preach a false honesty. "Get in touch with your feelings," is a favorite piece of advice to themselves as well as to students. They are undoubtedly right. One should be honest with oneself. But then, they go one step further. "Get in touch with your feelings and then tell everyone how you feel."

What a disservice to children. What a disservice to the self.

One cannot always be honest to others about one's feelings, especially when honesty serves only the purpose of hurting someone's feelings. Honesty of feelings or honesty in expressing one's perceptions does not make those perceptions true or real. The perceptions are true or the feelings real only for the person perceiving or feeling them, and that does not necessarily make them true or real for others.

It is not a virtue, even though it may be honest, to say, as children are wont to, "I think you're ugly" to another person, without reason other than that one may think it.

Children must be taught not to lie to themselves, but they also should be taught that blurting out everything they may think or feel to others, without considering that *other* person's feelings as well, is not always desirable.

There are times when judgment should intervene and should prevent an impulsive expression of feelings. Living together requires that certain amenities be upheld—amenities that make it tenable for all of us to live together. A "thank you," a "please," make living together more pleasant. A child should learn to say these words without always loving or even liking the person to whom the words are said.

In other words, total honesty is many times only a vindication of aggression and hostility, and in preaching this kind of honesty, teachers often are only expending their own hostilities and indulging their own rebelliousness. This is particularly so when teachers, for no real reason at all, confide their sexual experiences to their students. It sometimes becomes somewhat a badge of honor and a sign of supposed freedom to tell their students they are living with their boyfriend or girlfriend.

"But why?" I asked one young woman whom I had in my class at college, "why must you announce your private life to your students? Do you think they care or really need to know?"

"Why not?" Miss Donins answered. "I'm not ashamed, why should I keep it a secret?"

I really had no answer for her at first. My initial reaction, when she told me of her admission to her young class, had been one of disapproval. Then I began to question myself. Why was I opposed to her honesty?

Our values were different—mine may be right for me; hers right for her. I had no intention of trying to convince her to adopt my values any more than she could convince me to adopt hers. Why then did her honesty offend me? Then I knew. What offended me was her need to tell her young students of her sex life. It was she who needed to tell them, rather than they needing to know. Her need to rebel carried with it a need to exploit that rebellion, and to find an audience to whom she could dramatize it. The compulsion to tell was really the teacher's.

If a discussion of marriage had been pertinent in the classroom, if in discussing the sexual revolution in the world today there was a reason for such a discussion and such a disclosure, I could conclude that it was justifiable, just as I would assume it justifiable to talk about any issue of sexual liberation. But to discuss one's sex life merely because it is an "in" thing to do and a rebellion against one's middle-class background designed to line one up closer to students, to be one of the crowd, is not the function of the teacher.

Some white teachers with the need to rebel often become very antiwhite. In their need to repudiate the values of their upbringing, they in effect repudiate themselves. In repudiation of themselves they repudiate their race. White is bad. Minority, particularly black, is always beautiful, always good. It is always right. White reformist teachers, in repudiation of all parental values, take the ultimate stand in defiance of parents. These teachers become racists. It is the very accusation they often make against their parents, when in their liberal stance of love, equality, and justice for all, they often accuse their parents of being prejudiced. They are, of course, equally prejudiced, only with a different bias.

I remember one conference of child-care workers that I attended in New York City. A white teacher decried all the prejudice she saw around her. Black children were definitely discriminated against. There were fewer services and resources for them than for any other group. She was quite right. Compelled to espouse her cause even further, to speak well of the black population, she stated, "After all, all black mothers love their children."

A black psychiatrist immediately became angry.

"Would you say," he asked, "that all white mothers love their children?"

She saw her mistake and began to retract her statement. He didn't give her a chance.

"Then don't say all black mothers love their children. Some do, some don't, just like white mothers. The black society is not a monolithic society any more than the white society is; yet, do you notice that at meetings like this when a black person is introduced, he is invariably introduced as a representative of the black community. Have you ever heard of any white person being introduced as a representative of the white community?''

He was a rebel—a constructive one. He gave us a question.

10

Black Is to Black as White Is to White

The majority of teachers in our schools are from the white middle class. As the number of teachers from the minority groups is increasing, the tensions that already exist in the schools become heightened by new tensions. Since the largest number of minority teachers are black, the tensions are greatest between black and white teachers in schools where there are a substantial number of both black and white teachers. These tensions run high, therefore, in racially integrated schools.

In most racially integrated schools, both white and black teachers distrust and fear each other. Both groups feel threatened that at any turn of a conversation or event, they will be accused, by look if not by word, of being prejudiced. Thus, black and white teachers often do not dare disagree with each other openly. In order to keep disagreement at a minimum, communication has to be kept at a minimum. That is, communication has to be superficial in order for everyone to be polite. In this superfluity, politeness is a barrier. Feelings are avoided.

The avoidance mechanisms are self-protective, or so we would like to believe. In actuality, they are self-destructive. Chief among these protective-destructive mechanisms is our so-called tact. Tact prevents teachers from speaking out in disagreement against anyone's point of view. Tact mandates silent listening—even when one hears a remark to which one is totally opposed. Tact, therefore, is a mechanism that prevents communication. We will not recognize, for instance, that it is tact that often prevents people from speaking out against injustice. Listening without rebuttal is acquiescence to prejudice. Thus, tact is often merely an excuse for acquiescing to someone else's prejudice when one hears it. Both black and white teachers try hard to develop their tact. They do not recognize that underneath their so-called tact is fear—fear of disagreement, fear of being rejected, fear of being disliked, fear of having to fight. Fear immobilizes us.

White teachers who fear communication are afraid of confrontation. The tendency then becomes for white teachers to interpret everything or anything that a black teacher says as militant. If a black teacher disagrees with them or questions them, they find it easy to tell themselves that the teacher is a militant. The word releases their own anger. It's a bad word for a bad person. It demands nothing of them and exonerates them of all blame or guilt, particularly when the black teacher is young. The white teacher at these times often forms a syllogism. Young black teachers are all militants. Militancy is bad. Therefore, all young black teachers are bad. All the fears of the white teachers in the face of youth and black militancy become entrenched.

The black teachers, on the other hand, also often avoid communication. They in their turn do not want to be considered prejudiced either. Yet, when a white person disagrees with them, there is always the disquieting question, not always asked, of whether the disagreement is not really a matter of prejudice.

For instance, as a psychologist and in my role as principal of a special school, I have seen many black children as well as many white children whom I would diagnose as severely emotionally disturbed. Yet, I have found many black teachers who would take issue with me as far as the black children are concerned. They cannot accept the concept of mental illness or emotional disturbance for a black person, particularly when it is a white person making the diagnosis. They do not believe that individual pathology in black people exists. They believe only in the social pathology of poverty and slum living. Eliminate that and mental illness will disappear.

To a large extent, of course, they are right. Social injustice is a breeding ground for mental illness or emotional disturbance. Eliminate social inequalities and we would have a society far healthier than it is. And certainly they are right in condemning the institutionalizing of black dissidents and the labeling of them as disturbed or emotionally ill when in fact they are not disturbed or mentally ill but are reacting to the injustices of their lives. Yet, mental illness does exist among black people. Being black offers no immunity. Many black teachers, however, do not see individual pathology—only the social pathology that may produce it.

I have had bitter arguments with some black teachers, black paraprofessionals, and black community workers over their inability to accept the concept of emotional disturbance in black people. One was with Jerome Smith, a black teacher from Baltimore who visited Livingston. He was shocked at the language the girls used. He was particularly shocked at Marie, who was extremely explosive that particular day. Her vocabulary was a string of curses alternated by a string of threats.

Marie was a fifteen-year-old who had been referred to Livingston because of her assaults on others and her uncontrollable rages. She was a sweet girl, always willing to try to please teachers. She desperately wanted to learn and could spend hours doing academic work. She was retarded in reading and arithmetic, but she had a great love of both subjects and could cling to them compulsively at times. There were other times, however, that Marie was extremely volatile. Sometimes she came to school with explosion written all over her. One had only to say good morning and she would become enraged. She did not calm down easily. Her rage fed upon itself, becoming a self-excitatory process of complete loss of control.

Marie had exceedingly poor body coordination. She had a malfunctioning heart and she suffered from severe headaches. Her performance in psychological tests pointed to the possibility that Marie's lack of control was related to some organic difficulty. It was probable that her uncontrollable rages, often for no determinable reason at all, were similar to an epileptic attack. Marie's mother, however, refused to take her to the clinic for a detailed physical work-up. As Marie was a minor, no hospital or clinic would treat her or give the necessary diagnostic tests without the mother's signed permission. The mother refused to sign.

When Marie had been very young, a neglect petition had been brought against the mother by the Bureau of Child Welfare because of the mother's refusal to give her adequate physical care. I turned to them again to get medical help for Marie. Neither they nor I, however, could get Marie the treatment she needed. I knew without doubt that Marie was a damaged child both physically and mentally. Yet, all Mr. Smith saw was a child who needed to be punished.

I explained that Marie was a master at accepting punishment, that her mother beat her frequently, to the point where, on at least two occasions, she had to be sent to the hospital, and that the beatings probably were significant factors in causing Marie to behave the way she did in the first place.

But Mr. Smith disapproved. It was people like me, he told me, who didn't care enough to make girls like Marie stop temper outbursts.

"But Mr. Smith," I felt myself almost pleading for him to understand, "don't you realize that beatings don't work, that punishment doesn't work, I can't make her stop? All we can do is help Marie to see herself as a better person. When she feels better about herself, she will act better. The most important thing we can teach Marie now is that she doesn't have to act this way, and to believe in herself."

In our final discussion, however, he told me that white people used permissive techniques—and he spat the word *permissive* at me—because we really did not care about black kids. He believed in imposing rigid discipline.

I am always amazed how many teachers, black and white,

strongly believe in punishment. I cannot understand how they do not see that punishment is a heritage of slavery. Not only were slaves punished by their white masters but they were of necessity punished by their own parents to be good. Being bad meant being sold or whipped. Punishment by a parent was a sign of love. It taught the children how to survive.

Punishment is an anachronism today, especially when it is the black teacher, so eagerly striving for independence, who uses the weapons and cultural remnants of slavery.

In the past, punishment and repression have led to revolution. They still do. Repression will not lead black children to learn, any more than it will lead white children to learn. It only makes them revolt against learning.

To discuss these issues openly is extremely difficult, because blacks and whites generally are suspicious of each other. We ascribe motives to each other that may not be true. Out of fear, we become separate even in schools that are integrated. White teachers generally flock together. So do blacks. Walk into any teacher lounge and the polarity becomes visually evident. This intensifies and rationalizes our divisiveness. We say that black teachers really understand black students better than do white teachers. It then follows that white teachers understand white students better than do black teachers. It becomes a matter of common agreement between blacks and whites, an agreement based on fear—one that is totally untrue—that the values of the black and white communities are different. Therefore, teachers must teach children of their own racial group.

But I ask—don't all parents, black and white, want for their children the same things: education, good health, and happiness?

Yet, many black and white teachers talk of values in much the same breath as they talk of lifestyles. Certainly lifestyles between black and white people may be different, not necessarily from choice but from imposition of injustices. The patterns of slavery created different lifestyles. Differences, of course, need to be explored, but they need not be divisive. The black teacher who insists that blacks are totally different from whites is therefore as much a racist as the white teacher who deplores black culture or denies its existence. Very often, black teachers who consider themselves "different," as having more "soul," are reacting to the hundreds of years of slavery in which they had been deemed to have had no soul. They have to convince themselves as much as the whites of their own inner beauty. This is no different a mechanism than the Jewish people's considering themselves "chosen" above all other groups. They considered themselves "chosen" to deny the years of slavery, suppression, and persecution. Both blacks and Jews, as victims of suppression and persecution, have to defend themselves against believing the lies of the persecutors. Jews become "chosen," blacks have more "soul"—both spiritual concepts. Underneath the spirituality have been years of self-hatred and self-doubt. The self-hatred and self-doubt eventually erode, but the "chosenness" and the "soul" remain, compensation for the years of suffering. Group identities emerge, and along with them the concept that one group is superior to another.

Now that blacks in their rightful search for equality are expressing their belief in themselves, the threatened whites unleash their fears, often in the form of prejudice. What we need is more time to find each other. Eventually, I am certain, we will. At present, however, teachers of both races are apprehensive.

Black teachers, moreover, do not have an easy time functioning in what is essentially a white structure. Whether they are militant or not, when they disagree with that white power they are often accused by the whites of racism and militancy.

It becomes easier, therefore, for both groups to rationalize their fears and cling to the comfort of teaching children of their own race. By doing so, they are limiting their own experiences and denying themselves the enrichment of knowing children of diverse races and backgrounds. They are denying themselves the satisfactions of reaching the human emotion, which, after all, transcends cultures.

Black men as well as black women are sorely needed in our schools. They are needed not only for our black students but for our white students and for our white teachers as well. Unfortunately, black teachers are as poorly trained as white teachers. Unfortunately, too, some black teachers, like some white teachers, come to teaching out of the wrong motivations. When there is no true understanding of motivation, neither teacher, black or white, can be of value to any child, black or white.

11

The Incestuous Supervisor

Education would not be in its present bankrupt state if supervisors did their jobs more often, such as firing teachers who were not good. Isn't it amazing, for instance, that in New York City less than a handful of teachers are ever fired in any given year for being poor teachers? Could it possibly be that out of sixty thousand teachers or more, every teacher except for five or six is a good teacher? When teachers are fired because of budget cuts, they are fired on the basis of seniority, not teaching performance.

No, supervisors do not rock their respective boats. They do not call for change. They are the power and they like the power. No supervisor gets to a position of power without playing every power game in the system. No supervisor gets to a position of power without agreeing with everyone already in power and stepping on those who aren't. No supervisor gets to a position of power without shaping himself or herself to reflect the image of the person in power.

The promotional supervisory route goes from teacher to chairman of a department to dean to assistant principal to principal to assistant superintendent. It is an incestuous route, which produces the flawed offspring of inbreeding.

The breeding pond of the supervisor is not unlike that of the amoeba. In fact, I used to believe that supervisors originated from a one-celled animal or an amoebalike form. Each individual cell splits from itself to form a new whole and then goes off to swim in its own supervisory pond. This process of asexual reproduction produces many amoebae but little fun. Supervisors, after all, are serious people.

Then I developed a second theory—supervisors are really robots. They are spun off an assembly line in bolts and nuts and are screwed together by a master robot in its own mechanized image. Here, too, there is reproduction but little fun. But then, supervisors are serious people.

I vacillated between these two theories for quite some time as I observed supervisors on the genealogical make and in the incestuous climb. Then one day, I was separating two girls who were fighting in a school corridor, a silly thing for me to do, because I am a bad separator, when, suddenly stepping backward, I lost my balance and fell. My ankle immediately began to swell.

The fight settled, the two girls contrite, I dialed my supervisor at the Board of Education, spoke to a supervisory underling but a supervisor nevertheless, and told him that I had been hurt and was leaving to go to the hospital.

His first question was not "How did it happen?" or "How badly are you hurt?" but "Who are you leaving in charge?"

I told him.

"Have a nice weekend," he said, and that was the entire content of our conversation.

It was obvious that if he really was a robot, he was programmed for Friday. On the other hand, if his heritage was that of an amoeba, it was equally obvious he had been masturbating with his nucleus.

Then—insight! He was neither. My supervisor was an ostrich. He had his head in the kindergarten sandbox and in that inverted anatomical position—which is not easy when one is sitting at a desk—said sand had gotten into his mouth, preventing the air from reaching his brain. In other words, he had been thinking.

I have no doubt now that supervisors are ostrichlike creatures who stick their heads in the sand, put their tails to the wind, and strut with their underfeathers up. What better way to be licked? What easier way to lay an egg?

Actually, amoeba, robot, ostrich, it really makes no difference. It's personality that counts. The prime characteristic of a supervisor, for instance, is the possession of an undeveloped ego pretending to be developed. Often this trait reflects itself in an extraordinary ability to use words as a method of uncommunication. It is known as the emetic method. One word from the supervisor and everybody regurgitates.

For instance, one superintendent spent an entire conference talking to sixty principals who earned a combined annual salary of over a quarter of a million dollars a year about "the dog as a therapist." "Animals have provided tremendous interest to children," he said, "and are readily used for both their intrinsic scientific relevance as well as for motivational kicking off into the prime areas of knowledge which are pertinent to today's relevancies."

All he meant was kids like pets.

The principals mentally counted their money as he talked.

It was better than regurgitating.

The second characteristic of supervisors is protective coloration. This is a defense mechanism also known to chameleons and frogs. Supervisors melt into the walls of their offices so that in moments of urgency they cannot be found. The custodian's office, which often is the most luxurious office in the building, usually provides the best camouflage.

The third and last characteristic of supervisors is that they be men. As they reproduce themselves unilaterally anyway, women are really superfluous.

There are approximately three million teachers in this country and three hundred thousand supervisors. Of that three hundred thousand, less than 10 percent of elementary school principals are women. Moreover, only 1 percent of high school principals are women and less than $1/2$ of 1 percent of superintendents are women.

It is common belief that the women who do become supervisors are not women at all. They are really men at heart. Their prime function appears to be to castrate men down to their own clitoral size. I speak with some conviction as I am one of these women and have been accused of the same.

Most teachers in the classroom, in fact over 80 percent, are women. Of that percentage, over 90 percent become kindergarten, nursery, elementary school teachers. Men become high school teachers. Woe befall the very few men who dare to become nursery school or kindergarten teachers. They immediately label themselves as effeminate; they, of course, rarely become supervisors.

Every person in every school system throughout the country knows, for instance, that men who want to be primary teachers really don't want to be supervisors at all, they want to be mothers. Why no one considers the possibility that they may want to be fathers, I don't know. Apparently there is no fathering motivation at all. Or, if there is, it really is mothering. That's why we speak of alma mater but never of alma pater. At any rate, we all know that mothering is very primary in teaching, but fathers do become the bosses.

In pursuit of New York City's statistics for the ratio of men supervisors to women teachers, I was told at the Board of Education that such information was not available, but that it was available in the New York State Department of Education in Albany. Upon calling Albany and asking how many women were supervisors in New York State, I was told that they couldn't give me the answer because the information was locked in their Bank of Educational Data, which they fondly called BED. I thought it quite appropriate for women to lie there, because how else could they keep us in our place?

Now, I am not saying that women will change the state of education at once when they get the power. After all, there are probably as many stupid women as there are stupid men—as many confused women as there are confused men, as many power-driven women as there are power-driven men. I just think women should have equal opportunity to be as inefficient as men.

I remember meeting one woman superintendent who snorted, sniffed, and snickered and who told me that married women with obligations to a family belonged in a classroom, not in a principal's office. I also remember another superintendent who told me that the only way to become a superintendent was to buy a mink coat and attend the "right" synagogue.

I disavowed the advice of both and cried MEOWE.

Several years ago, I called together a group of ten women and we organized Making Equal Opportunities for Women in Education, or MEOWE. We thought the name particularly apt. Unfortunately, in calling for our general membership meeting, we could not get the New York City United Federation of Teachers' newspaper to accept our ad. Neither, of course, would they give us an outright refusal. Apparently they did not take our views seriously. There was just no problem with women, they thought, why were we griping? Our ad simply was never printed. The union, of course, was keeping its male-centered power unto itself.

MEOWE was aborted.

I should have wept, I suppose. I didn't.

I should weep now, I suppose. I can't.

Instead, I have learned from some very wonderful children that I can thumb my nose, figuratively speaking, and laugh.

The droppings of tears can't crumble a monolith.

Perhaps the exploration of laughter can.

12

Teacher Training and the Fortress Mentality

Like ancient and discarded fortresses, the teacher-training colleges and universities are highly visible, beautiful to tour, but totally anachronistic. Teachers seeking protection from the hordes of problems that are increasingly encroaching upon them turn to them for sanctuary. They are not helped, however, because the fortress is empty, the sanctuary an illusion.

The teachers, like the children, are merely surviving. Like London Bridge, our schools are tumbling down and it is our teacher-training institutions that are giving them a mighty shove. Their concern has been with physical expansion and fund raising to meet the costs of that expansion. Thus, they have built bigger and better walls, and succeeded in keeping the teachers in and shutting the children out. In this misshapen policy, the teachers are training to become warriors, the children are designated the enemy.

The separation is not only by physical space, it is also by mentality. Teachers are trained to protect themselves against the natural vicissitudes of children, namely, their natural aggressions. They are also trained to stifle their own. Thus, the trouble with teacher training is that teachers are trained.

To train, according to *The Oxford English Dictionary*, is "to discipline and instruct (an animal) so as to make it obedient to orders or capable of performing tasks."

Is it accident that most educators speak of teacher *training* and not of teacher *education*? I think not.

The phrase *teacher training* speaks for itself. It reflects the very real feelings and attitudes that the teacher trainers—the college instructors and college professors—bear toward teaching, toward teachers, toward children. It is apparent that the stated philosophy and the function of the teacher trainers is to train teachers to obey orders and to perform tricks. Once having been trained, the teachers, in their turn, train their students to obey orders and to perform tricks.

The skeleton of education is laid before us.

Obey the instructor and receive credit for a course. Pass an examination, a trick if ever there was one, and receive a grade. A task is set, a reward is given, and the student supposedly learns. These are methods of conditioning; it is not insightful learning, and while conditioning does have a place in education, in that one should leave a building when the fire alarm sounds, conditioning should not replace thought.

Obedience and trick-performing, however, are the two main ingredients of college conditioning, which we call teacher training. Ask any teacher who has ever taken an education course. The courses are training grounds in obedience. The performing of tricks usually comes at the end of the term.

I saw the phenomenon of obedience very clearly one day when I sat in on an education course at a small college in New Jersey. As soon as the class started, Dr. Aulen, the instructor, took attendance by reading the roll. On four different occasions he reminded students that they had been absent the previous week—as if they didn't know. It was not a very subtle indication that he resented their absences on a personal level, especially when at the completion of the roll call he delivered a two- or three-minute lecture on the number of absences permitted by regulation per term. It was clear that Dr. Aulen was going to stick rigidly to those regulations even though the course was a graduate one and his students were teachers, social workers, and probation officers.

That business over, Dr. Aulen insisted that everyone arrange his or her chair in a circle. He sat at his desk, which immediately became the nominal head of the circle—should a circle have a head? Then the class started in earnest. He asked a question, called on someone to answer the question; then he asked another question and called upon someone else to answer. There was no crosscurrent of discussion, no thought—just question-answer, question-answer. Dr. Aulen might just as well have been giving a test; those students might just as well have been sitting in straight rows, separated by empty seats, so that they could not cheat on that test.

During question-answer time a few students came in late. No matter who was talking, he interrupted with "Join the circle please." Twice, he even interrupted himself. His request was command.

Each late student was then obliged to get a chair from the back of the room, drag it to the front of the room, and insert it into that enchanted circle. That meant everyone already in the circle had to move. During the ceremony all talking stopped spontaneously, which was not particularly a disservice to the group. Dr. Aulen, of course, believed he was being very avant-garde. After all, didn't children in the best progressive elementary schools in the country, and according to the best educational theory, sit in a circle?

A circle should stimulate discussion. This circle, however, strangulated discussion, because Dr. Aulen treated his adult students the way he thought children should be treated—in the way of the ring master, with the authority of a whip. Yet, whenever I had spoken personally to Dr. Aulen, he seemed to have believed totally in the principles of psychology and mental health that should be inherent in all instruction. It was not clear to me, however, whether Dr. Aulen had ever truly understood those principles or whether, once having understood them, he had given them up. Whichever it was, it was unfortunate that the principles he had so liberally espoused had become mere educational clichés. That enforced circle into which his students were shackled was but another cliché.

Dr. Aulen was not a hypocrite. He was merely an obedient child grown. So are most college instructors. That is how they proceed through the system themselves. That is how they become college instructors in the first place—by obeying—suppressing individuality, suppressing aggressions, suppressing personal decisions.

Obedience becomes the route to education, to success, to happiness.

Teachers, in obedient reaction to their college instructors, uphold their part of the process in unspoken agreement. They act the way they expect children to act, they obey their college instructors just as they expect their pupils to obey themselves. Instructors lecture. They take notes. Instructors test, they regurgitate those notes. Instructors give grades, they accept those grades. Instructors pass or fail them. They accept the judgments as indication of whether or not they have learned. They measure their own stupidity or wisdom, not on what they feel they have learned or not learned, but on what the college instructor tells them they have learned or not learned. Thus, they cannot even make the very personal decision of determining whether they are smart or dumb, knowledgeable or unknowledgeable, competent or incompetent. They are able to measure themselves only by the way their instructors grade them, and grades are based not on learning or knowledge but on obedience to the instructor and the performance of tricks.

The syllogism then becomes obedient students receive good grades. Good grades mean good learning. Obedient students therefore learn.

Is this what education should be? Are we forgetting that our rebels have been our greatest teachers? Jesus? Moses? Socrates? Mohammed? Gandhi?

The patterns of obedience are patterns of dependency. Obedience fosters dependency. Should not teachers think? Apparently not, not when one considers that teacher-training institutions are masters at keeping teachers in a state of dependency.

Their prime purpose, it appears, is keeping in the business of keeping in the business. What better way than by making teachers obediently dependent upon them?

Teachers, in their turn, present themselves as offerings to the colleges. In justification of their self-deception that it is indeed the children who are upsetting the teachers' applecarts, they willingly stay longer and longer in college, taking graduate courses, matriculating for master's degrees and doctorates in education. Masters of what? Doctors of what? Often nothing more than longevity and the ability to sit through education courses. Add the fact that the more courses a teacher takes, the higher is that teacher's salary, and the economic value of dependency is clearly demonstrated. But the process of dependency does not stop there. It is passed down to the students, who are also forced to remain in school to be dependent upon their teachers. The tragedy is that so many teachers accept their roles of dependency. Many even demand them. They are like people dying, who in fear of being abandoned by their doctors and nurses, become helpless and dependent upon them, and refuse to speak up for their right to die with dignity.

"How many pages must a term paper be?"

"How many books do we need to read?"

"How many cuts are we allowed?"

I have had these questions asked of me almost every time I have ever taught at a college. I have always refused to give direct answers. Instead, I throw the question back at the student: "How much do you need to read?" "How much do you want to read?" "How many times will you need to be absent, want to be absent?"

I also refuse to assign grades. Instead, I ask students what grades they need, what grades mean to them. I ask students to grade themselves.

"What if I cheat?" one teacher laughingly asked me once. "What if I give myself an A but I haven't learned a thing?"

"Then I can only assume," I answered, "that the A is the most important thing to you and more important than learning, and I will respect your need and give you that A. So you make the decision.''

That student received an A, but he also learned. Another student, however, was critical of me.

"When are you going to teach us something?'' she complained at the end of the second session of the course.

"Don't you think you're learning?'' I asked.

"I haven't taken one single note,'' she answered.

"Is that how you judge learning?'' I asked her.

"I really feel I should be taking notes,'' she said coldly.

"Why do you feel like that?'' I asked. "Would you tell me the purpose of notes?''

She became exasperated.

"There you go again,'' she said, "you never give an answer. How can I take notes when you're always asking questions?''

I tried to explain that note taking is often only a ritual; it is form rather than substance, but she looked at me as if I had lost my mind. Then she muttered something and left.

I didn't see her the following session and then I learned she had dropped the course. It was obvious she could not take the path I offered to learning.

I was sorry, because I knew she was sincere. I also knew she wanted to learn. Most students do, even those who are going through the perfunctory motions of taking a course for salary increment. They do not want merely to pay for a grade, sit in a course without learning, get a degree for doing educational time. They are honest and sincere and they want to be good teachers. Unfortunately, they have become so concerned with note taking and with asking each other in stage whispers, "What did he say?'' and "How do you spell that?'' that thought is sacrificed to the ritual task.

Notes, of course, may be important at such times when a student may want to remember a specific thought or speculate on a specific idea. A note in these cases is a stimulus to thinking. Occasionally a note might even consist of a significant fact, one that might not readily be found in a book, or one that may be needed for immediate reference. But notes that consist only of a series of facts are almost always superfluous. One can go to a book for that.

The function of a college instructor, therefore, is not to give facts via note taking but to point to the meaning of facts and to question the facts themselves. After all, that the moon is inaccessible to man was once a fact.

Fact is not thought.

Unfortunately, most teacher trainers are themselves so fearful of thinking, so fearful of emotion, and so fearful of children that they tend to lecture rather than to teach. Not only do they lecture, but they lecture from books that they themselves have written. Not only do they lecture from books that they themselves have written, but they read aloud to their classes from the books that they themselves have written. In this process of lecturing, which they call teaching, the trainers assume many poses: superiority, boredom, indifference, laziness, even commitment. All are character defenses. It is their way of protecting the conceit that they are omniscient, that they know everything there is to know, and that it is their job to tell it.

I know one professor at a well-known university in New York whose practice it is to tell his graduate students that he will give them an A at the end of the term if they can replicate his notes perfectly from memory. He also tells them that he will give out B's if they prefer not to take the examination but write in their test booklet the words "mental rehearsal has taken place." This means, he explained, that they have studied.

How blatantly absurd! How tragically criminal that this professor is training teachers to teach *handicapped* children—children who need the best teachers, not the least prepared and therefore the most frustrated.

College instructors, however, are not usually selected on the basis of proven teaching performance but on the basis of their "vita" sheets or life experiences. The vita is a resumé of one's professional life. It lists experience, publications, and membership in organizations. A vita stating that one belongs to a civic group, is a member of four education societies, is the author of several letters to the editor of a local newspaper, and has served on a mayoral committee to study the disposal system of garbage can be very impressive, particularly if the vita covers more than three pages.

Moving up the promotional ranks also depends on the vita. It must grow longer each year. One cannot add to one's past; therefore, it is the present that must increase. Publications therefore become an important part of the vita. A college teacher must publish frequently, preferably once a year, if promotion is the goal. Many instructors therefore spend more time worrying about what to write and how to get published than they spend time teaching—which of course may not be the gross loss it at first appears to be.

Promotion also depends upon charm, politics, and ignorance. In the college circuit, charm is the ability to be ingratiating, politics is knowing when to use the charm, and ignorance is being cunning enough never to appear more knowledgeable than those in power. A full professor, after all, does not want to be shown up by an assistant professor, much less by a mere instructor. That is why so many top college administrators surround themselves with inadequate people. Anyone who is smarter or more competent rarely makes it to the top.

Thus, I have seen college programs in teacher training initiated by professors who had charm, knew the right people and played the right politics, but who knew nothing about the children they supposedly were training teachers to teach.

For instance, I have seen courses in guidance given by professors who never guided a student in their lives, or at the most spent six months at it.

How often I have seen courses in teaching the problems of youth in an urban society taught by a professor whose only experience was teaching in a small town in Massachusetts. Or in the most prestigious boarding school in Maine.

How often I have seen courses in teaching disturbed children taught by professors who never taught a disturbed child.

I learned my lesson in this regard many years ago when I was asked to teach a class of eight disturbed young children in a summer session at a university in New York.

At that time, the university had just received a grant to start a program of teacher training for those teachers who wanted to work with emotionally disturbed children. The proposal for the grant called for a professor to train the teachers and for a class of children to be used as a demonstration class.

I was a teacher at Bellevue Hospital at the time and I was wildly excited to be asked to be the teacher of the demonstration class. I expected to learn from the head of the program, who was widely proclaimed as an expert in special education.

When I went for the interview she told me that the children who would be in the demonstration class went to an outpatient clinic in a nearby psychiatric hospital. They would be selected by the clinic staff, and provision would be made for them to travel to the university every day for a six-week summer session. Each session was to last three hours.

I asked if I might participate in selecting the children. She thought there would be no objection. She then went on to tell me that I would be given a room in the university and would I please see to it that the children did not run through the halls, cause a disturbance, or be too noisy.

I was extremely surprised at her naïveté.

She then told me that what she would like to see demonstrated was group activities in academics. She didn't expect the children to stay seated all day, of course, and it was quite all right if I had ten-minute intervals of song and movement, that would take care of their restlessness, but she was concerned about the noise, and would I please remember to keep them as quiet as I could.

I was becoming uneasy.

"But they're disturbed," I stated rather stupidly.

"Yes, of course," she agreed.

"Well, you know, disturbed children sometimes have temper tantrums," I explained, annoyed that I had to explain it.

She looked at me nervously, I thought.

"You mean, you think they might get out of hand?" she asked.

I could only repeat, "But disturbed children sometimes do have temper tantrums."

"Of course," she agreed, but I knew she really wasn't agreeing at all, "but we will be in a college building. They have to be quiet."

"You want them disturbed," I asked, "but quietly disturbed—is that it?"

I didn't get the job.

A few weeks later she sent me a polite note telling me that she would start her new program of training teachers to teach disturbed children without a demonstration class. I learned later, although I had already guessed it, that she had never taught a disturbed child in her life.

College teachers are generally driven to the college campuses not because they have been proven to be the best teachers of children but because too often they have been the most fearful, and therefore the worst. They could not wait to get out of the classroom far away from the children. I have known teacher trainers who had taught less than a year in schools. I have known some who never taught children at all. Yet, they become the experts on how to teach children. The irony is that for the rest of their professional lives—that is, the longer they remain at college—the more distant they are from children. Tenure and security, then, do not give us better teacher trainers. They give us only older teacher trainers.

In their desire to be rid of children, college instructors are not unlike supervisors. It is no wonder, therefore, that many supervisors, who are also out of the classroom, are part-time instructors at teacher-training institutions. Nor is it any surprise that, after retirement from a school system, many supervisors become full-time college instructors.

Teachers looking for knowledge about children, about themselves, and about teaching, are continually being cheated by the universities. They look with desperation toward the colleges for tools with which to work. The college instructors cannot tell them that the tools lie within themselves. Having little understanding that teacher education must center not on method and not on courses but on finding the truths of humanity that lie within each of us, college instructors have not found the truths for themselves. Therefore, they cannot teach it.

Instead, they concentrate on the inadequacies of children and on methodology to overcome these inadequacies. The latest innovation in teacher training, for instance, is "competency-based education." I don't know, of course, when education was considered not to be based on competency. I do know, however, that educators in hushed tones talk about competency as if they were in prayer. Whatever happened, I wonder, to the religions of former years: "cores of interests," "units of work," "the contract plan"? Desanctified, I suppose.

Yet, courses proliferate. A favorite is Human Relations. I am always amused when this course is mandated by teacher-training colleges, as if ordering teachers to take a course called Human Relations is good human relations.

It really matters little, however, what courses are called. It is the professors who can make the difference between a good course or a poor one, no matter what the title of the course is. As long as college instructors teach within the barren space of a college classroom in which emotions and thought are as alien as the children, teacher-training will continue to be at best uninformed, at worst destructive and inhibiting to truly creative teachers.

It is true, of course, that teacher trainers make concessions to the inevitability of children by assigning student teachers to schools. Many teacher-training colleges assign student teachers to the local public schools. Others have their own "laboratory" schools, which are often housed on the college campus and which service mainly the children of the college faculty, interspersed with some neighborhood children. The laboratory schools, therefore, are often extremely selective in their choice of students and hardly representative of the public schools in which the student teachers will eventually find themselves. Moreover, the laboratory schools are not really run by the college departments of education. They are run by the principal of the school, who often is not even represented on the college faculty.

Whether student teachers are assigned to college laboratory schools or the neighborhood schools makes little difference, as there is a sharp cleavage between the staffs of the schools and the college staff of teacher trainers. Teacher trainers are adept at removing themselves from the realities of the classrooms, good or bad.

I have never yet seen a college teacher-trainer, for instance, successfully take over a class of children and demonstrate a good lesson. I have never even seen one try.

What I have seen, however, is the great number of student teachers who are placed in classrooms with teachers so damaging that the student teachers learn only the methods of emotional assault, if not in fact physical violence.

Can we be surprised, therefore, when our student teachers believe that there is no other way?

Where are the teacher trainers in all of this?

Generally, biting their nails and moaning that they do not agree, but what can they do? After all, they are not running the schools, and student teachers, after all, have to be trained in schools.

They are quite right. Student teachers have to be in schools, not to be trained there but to be educated there. The remedy therefore lies in abolishing our teacher-training programs as they now exist. We must create a program of teacher education in which the education of teachers is carried out primarily by master teachers, who are successfully teaching, and by their students, who will act as consultants.

This means that teacher training cannot be isolated in buildings called colleges; they cannot continue being readied for the conflict called teaching. The war trainers must go. Teachers must be taught by teachers who are successfully teaching. They must be taught by master teachers in the classroom, who will help them sort out those elements in themselves that are healthy for teaching.

Who, after all, are better potential educators of teachers than teachers who are still successfully teaching? Who are better educators of teachers than the children being educated? Who is more knowledgeable about what the consumer needs than the consumer?

Classroom teachers who are successful teachers of children are our master teachers. They should be given college status and allowed to educate teachers. By demonstration of classroom techniques, by discussion, and by utilizing methods of self-exploration, they can lead teachers to examine their motivations in teaching. They can educate teachers, however, only while they are in the classrooms teaching children. If ever they are tempted to leave the classroom and become full-time teacher educators, they succeed in becoming only teacher trainers. Of course, it is conceivable that a master teacher-educator may wish to take an occasional leave from the classroom and devote full time to research or to teacher education. Such a leave can be well spent, but the teacher who wants to educate teachers must always return to the classroom. Teacher educators or master teachers, as indeed they are, should never totally remove themselves from classroom teaching. A part of their program must always be devoted to the children. Teacher educators need the stimulus of the children to keep them riveted to reality. The children, therefore, must play an active role in educating teachers. They should be used not only as consumers but as consultants as well.

As consultants the children could serve an admirable purpose. They could help the teacher look into the self.

"Why do you yell so much, Miss Lewis?" I once heard a child ask a teacher. "Didn't your mother listen to you when you were a child?"

Miss Lewis was not wise enough to listen. She reported the child to the principal.

A teacher who has learned to look into the self, however, would not have been as frightened or as angry. That teacher would have given that question serious consideration. A teacher who has learned to look inward, who is free enough to respect the opinions of children, should be able to learn from children. Children consultants can be the most potent resource teachers have.

How valuable for a teacher to listen to the problem as it is analyzed by children. How important for that teacher to view the problem from the vantage point of children.

Surely children can explain children's points of view, particularly to teachers who are having difficulties with a child, a class, a lesson. Surely children can help teachers understand in what way teachers contribute to the problems of the classroom.

I once listened to a teacher listening to a student while I was attending a principals' conference in New York City. I was seated at a long table in the school cafeteria, waiting for another teacher, when a woman brought her tray over to the table and sat a few seats away. A boy was with her.

"Aw listen, Mrs. Rosenberg," the boy pleaded, "he don't mean nothin' by it, I know, he's my friend."

"He sure has a big mouth," Mrs. Rosenberg answered.

"Aw, it starts out big but it comes down to a dribble," the boy explained again.

"You mean he doesn't mean it?" she asked.

"He's just trying to be funny."

"Well, he's not," Mrs. Rosenberg answered, "pretending he couldn't read that math problem. He can read very well, it's just damned annoying—I haven't time for such nonsense."

"Haven't you got time to laugh?" the boy asked seriously.

Mrs. Rosenberg looked up sharply.

"What did you say?" she asked.

"He likes to clown around," the boy said. "Maybe if you

laughed once in a while instead of getting mad, he'd stop.''

At that point my friend came over to join me and I didn't hear the rest of the conversation, but it seemed to me that that boy had the makings of a consultant.

Children know much more about education than teacher trainers are likely to admit. It is time we used their knowledge.

I can envision a corps of student consultants in every school being educated by other students and their teachers to act as consultants, being paid to act as consultants. They would be learners and teachers.

The power of students has not yet begun to be tapped. It is time to recognize one truth—when the fortress is down and the children let in, teachers may find there is no battle after all.

13

Sugar-coated Unionism

Unionism has not come easily to teachers. They have resisted it much longer than have other groups, mainly for two reasons: They are not generally activists, and they have barricaded themselves behind professionalism. Professional people are not workers, and unions are for workers.

Only very recently have teachers begun to see the necessity for teacher unions, and certainly they are necessary. Unfortunately in their late conversion to unionism, teachers have over-reacted. They seem to have forgotten that unlike other unions, the product involved is not automobiles or clothing, but children.

It is incumbent upon teacher unions to remember the children, to consider their welfare equally with the welfare of teachers. Unfortunately, they do not, although they say they do. In the way of the teacher, that is, in the way of self-delusion, they sugar-coat their self-interest with the claim that what is good for teachers is good for students. Thus, in striving for their own benefits, they claim that they are really benefiting their students. If this contention were true, then every time teachers received higher salaries the educational system would become better. Yet, I don't know of any teacher who became a better teacher or who worked harder because of a raise. A good teacher with or without a raise still remains a good teacher. On the other hand, there are thousands of poor teachers who have remained poor teachers despite wage increases.

I certainly am not opposed to good wages. What I am opposed to is the myth that better wages will produce better teachers, or that higher wages will attract better people. Assuming that better means better qualified, I can only state that most teachers are overqualified now in the sense that they are over-trained and overschooled, which caused the difficulty in the first place. The longer they have remained in school and in college, the longer have they been subjected to the system, the longer have they endured the processing into conformity, the longer they ask such questions as, "If you can't punish, how can you control?" They do not see that discipline must be inside a person and that discipline should *not* be a synonym for punishment. Being better qualified, therefore, generally means spending more time perpetuating these follies. The unions, in calling for better qualified teachers—meaning that teachers should stay longer in college and get more and more degrees—are unwittingly in league with the colleges.

The unions, like the colleges, although their motives may differ, also try hard to keep teachers away from their students. The colleges do it out of fear, the unions out of concern for the teacher's welfare. Everyone, it seems, works toward the separation of teachers and students.

Unions claim, for instance, that it is necessary for teachers to be given time in school away from the children in which they can do their clerical work, prepare lesson plans or confer with other school personnel. These "free time" activities, or "preparation time periods," as they sometimes are called, will supposedly benefit the children because the teachers by these activities become better teachers.

The delusion is that the time spent on behalf of the children will ultimately benefit the children. Yet, while most teachers are off "benefiting" the children and undoubtedly, many are, some merely nap or chat or take a coffee break, and the children aren't benefiting at all. They are being squeezed into somebody else's class in order to be "covered." The activities they are squeezed into often are irrelevant to what the children are learning in their own classes and therefore a waste of educational time. These periods of coverage frequently are a great stimulus to misbehavior. Thus, what starts out to be a benefit to teachers ends up with other teachers baby-sitting with the classes of those teachers who have free time. Ultimately, of course, teachers then take turns having free periods. They relax when they are free and sweat it out when they are covering.

How this becomes a benefit to teachers is a moot question. It certainly is no benefit to children, no matter how well a good teacher may spend that free period or preparation time.

Then there is the question of tenure. Unions claim that tenured teachers generally are better teachers than substitutes. I would assume they are correct in that tenured are generally more experienced. Yet, tenure has also kept thousands of teachers in the classroom who should not be teaching. Tenure, in effect, has put teachers in the position of holding on to their jobs for life. There are thousands of teachers who have developed emotional problems after tenure was granted. Thus, they have become damaging to children. Should they be permitted to continue to teach? After all, people do change. The teacher who took an examination ten or twenty years ago may not be the same person today. Should that person who has become unfit to teach be wedded to that job until retirement do them part?

I have seen teachers defended by their unions who should not be defended—a teacher who for years regularly came to school drunk, a teacher who was absent forty Mondays of each school year, a teacher who was excessively late almost every day of the term, a teacher who frequently lost control in his classes and became violent, a teacher who actively hallucinated.

In speaking to one union official about these cases, I was told that a union has the obligation to defend any member who asks for a defense. "Our heart may not be in it," he said, "but we'll do it."

"Even when you know the person is damaging to children?" I asked.

He shrugged. "Every person is entitled to a defense," he said.

I agreed that every person has the right to be defended by a lawyer in court. Is this right analogous to the right of every teacher to be defended by a union? I think not. What about the rights of children to have mentally healthy teachers? Who will speak for the children?

The time has come for unions to examine this issue carefully, just as the time has come for them to examine the issue of incompetent teachers.

The school system itself cannot be trusted to do so. At present it is up to the supervisory staff in each school to weed out incompetent ones. They do so with reluctance, incompetence, and fear. Mostly, they shove the problem into the supervisory closet: Keep these teachers out of sight as much as possible, give them the least troublesome classes, or give them no classes at all. Thus, these incompetents become our closet teachers, sequestered and protected. Ironically, because they are our poorest teachers and our most inadequate, they get the best classes—the children who can cope with them or learn despite them. What an injustice to children who need the best teachers but who get only the most tenured ones.

Supervisors do not tackle the issue squarely because they fear the union. The last thing in the world they want is a union grievance, a union confrontation. They use the excuse that it is extremely difficult to prove incompetence. And of course it is true.

I have seen teachers with excellent plans, with good order in the class, with children learning, yet who were full of hatred and contempt for the children and who showed that hatred in attitude, rather than deed. How can one prove attitude? Because proof is burdensome, supervisors are prone to avoid these issues. They run from confrontation. They play the transfer game. Give the teacher a good recommendation and let someone else worry. Sometimes, when principals do want to take a stand, their superintendents won't let them.

I know of one principal who not only wanted to fire a teacher but bring charges against that teacher for hitting a child with a lead pipe. The superintendent refused to back the principal. The teacher was transferred. The superintendent was promoted.

Teacher unions must have more courage than the educators who run the schools. It is the teachers joining the unions who can make things change.

There are thousands of mentally ill, severely disturbed, and incompetent teachers in our schools who should not be teaching children. I am not suggesting that they be fired without their rights protected. I am suggesting that teacher unions take a forward position of working out their own regulatory mechanisms by which these teachers are removed from the classroom.

All other professions have begun to see the moral necessity for establishing their own ethical codes, regulating their own professions in order to protect the public. Among them are physicians, lawyers, psychologists, dentists, optometrists, nurses, pharmacists. Even the police in many cities have their own internal mechanisms of discipline. Why not teachers?

I suggest that unions in demonstration of their concern for the welfare of children set up systems whereby they can remove teachers from schools when these teachers are incompetent or ill, and when the supervisory staffs in the schools have failed to do so.

I also suggest that unions take another revolutionary step forward—that they be in the forefront of organizing community groups, parent groups, and student groups, together or individually, who would act as ombudsmen for students. Ombudsmen are advocates—they would speak for the rights and welfare of students in schools. No such organized group does so now. Yet, such groups are desperately needed. Students are our most powerless group. Often, so are parents, who are intimidated by the school structure. A walk into a principal's office turns everyone into a frightened child again—even the most irate parent. An organized ombudsman group could speak for those parents and those students who bear grievances against the schools or against individual teachers.

It would take courage for unions to help organize such groups, for in a sense, they might at any given time be setting up groups that might in a specific instance be in opposition to them. An ombudsman group, for instance, might bring charges against a teacher a union might be defending.

Yet, what greater evidence of authority than the ability to invite disagreement, even dispute? By advocating the organization of ombudsman groups, unions might well be demonstrating their own authority and integrity as well as their real concern for the welfare of children.

14

Teaching Is the Pursuit of Aggression

If teachers were to accept their own aggression, to explore and exploit it, they would be able to tap their own wells of strength and to accept both themselves and their students. The acceptance of their aggression would release them from their inhibitions and would free them from self-imposed moralistic judgments that are false to the nature of being human. They would then teach not out of aggression that is internalized and turned back on themselves, that is, out of masochism, but out of self-power, out of self-authority, which is aggression utilized constructively.

The need for aggression in both teachers and children must not be denied as it now is. It must be accepted and used. Releasing aggression can lead and will lead to aggressive teaching, to teaching that reaches outward and that gives power to children. In teaching students how to make decisions, teachers are teaching the skills of self-power and demonstrating their own. Teachers can give power to children, can help them learn to feel power, only when they have a true sense of their own, only when they feel their own authority, only when they stop being afraid of their own emotions.

Thus, when teachers accept their own feelings and their own needs—that is, their own needs to love and be loved, their own needs for immortality and youth, their own needs for power—they will be able to make of education what it could and should

255

be, a leading forth process, as the Latin root *educare* "to lead forth," indicates.

Education would then be a process whereby all feelings are accepted because they are deemed acceptable. All behavior is not. Behavior that is not acceptable is simply not acceptable. Both students and teachers would make themselves aware of the difference and would analyze unacceptable behavior not in terms of its unacceptability but in terms of unidentified needs. The questions to be asked are: What is this child saying by the behavior expressed? What are the child's needs? How is that unacceptable behavior meeting those needs? How can those needs be gratified another way—a more acceptable way? How can we teach that way to the child? Behavior of course includes learning behavior. A child who learns well is saying one thing; a child who is not learning says another.

In this process of need identification, violence becomes almost impossible, because violence cannot occur where needs are identified and recognized. Violence occurs only where needs are unfulfilled and behavior is repressed. Only then, out of frustration and its resultant tensions, do people lash out. Demanding silence for long periods of time, for instance, makes noise inevitable. It is a demand contrary to the needs of children.

I once heard a swimming teacher give a lesson to a child who was struggling to stay afloat in a pool. The teacher was becoming increasingly annoyed at the child's difficulties.

"Child, pretend you are dead," she finally ordered.

Kerplunk. The child sank.

She dived in after her and came up angrier than before.

The child cried. It was a moment of emotional violence for both.

That teacher had no idea of the fears she had generated in that child. She had no idea of her own hostility to that child. She had no idea that she had just created trauma, which made learning impossible.

Teachers often make learning traumatic for children out of

ignorance of needs. They feel that by virtue of having once been a child they are now authorities on children. The trouble is they have forgotten what is was like to have been a child and often they do not want to remember. The pain is too great. Yet, they must. They must tease out of their own memories their own real feelings. Only when teachers are able to identify their own feelings as well as the needs and feelings of their students will they be able to teach well.

The artist Jacques Lipchitz said that sculpture had to be stated, restated, teased, and displayed. He might well have been speaking of education. Education should be an aggressive process in which everyone learns how to state, restate, think, rethink, and utilize one's learning. Movement is the key word.

Education, like the neurons of the brain, would then be an expressively aggressive process, dynamic and explosive. It would then be the leading forth of an individual from the nucleus of the self through the unfolding of needs to self-gratification. It would be a union of mutual gratification whereby teachers in gratifying their own needs would also be gratifying the needs of their students, and students in gratifying their needs would be gratifying the needs of the teachers. Education would thus be a process of mutual aggression and mutual power jointly identified and jointly expressed.

In this process of mutuality, where the needs of students and teachers would be recognized and matched, everyone together, students and teachers, administrators and parents, parents and teachers, parents and students, students and administrators, would test the components of reality. They would all free themselves from their own fears and their fears of each other so that they could then trust themselves as well as each other.

In this process of trust, testing the components of reality means that everyone would accept the idea that conflict is a universal element in human experience. With the acceptance of conflict in the self and in others, schools become the place of internal resolution, which makes learning possible. One can learn best when one is emotionally free.

In this process of education, the school as it now exists has no place at all. We must discard the concept of the school as we know it, along with the word *school*, because it is not feasible to build reforms on old structures. We have to build anew.

Toward this end, I would suggest that we build Educare centers, centers truly concerned with a leading-out process for both teachers and students, the word *students* meaning teachers and learners of all ages, from kindergarten through adulthood. The school structure as we now know it is a barrier to the intermingling of students of all ages.

Education in the Educare Center would be pyramidally based—education for the staff, both professional and non-professional, which means that master teachers would be teaching teachers and teacher aides; education for the members of the adult community, which means that grandparents could bring their grandchildren to school and learn alongside them in the same classes, because there is no reason why art or literature or music or creative writing cannot be jointly taught and jointly learned; and education for the children themselves, from nursery school through high school and preparatory to college. Through the Educare Center, the parents and the communities would be partners in learning. So would the colleges, but not the teacher-training components of these colleges as they now exist. The education of teachers must take place in Educare centers, with the master teachers as instructors of both the children and student teachers. The flow between Educare and the colleges, therefore, would go both ways; teachers would be given college status while they taught both children and teachers, and students enrolled in the colleges would be going to the Educare centers to learn directly from the children and their teachers.

The Educare Center would consist of a building or of several buildings, even a discarded school building would do. The program of Educare would be based on six major premises:

Education must center on teaching children *how* to learn rather than teaching them *what* to learn.

Learning is a lifelong, continuous process; it is not finite, ending upon reaching adulthood.

Individuals learn in many different ways. What is most effective for one individual may be least effective for another. For instance, some people learn best when they read, while others learn best while listening.

An individual's potential is many times greater than what testing reveals. That is, most people can learn much more than they actually do.

Environments can be created that are particularly conducive to learning. Thus, the setting in which one learns can aid and increase learning.

Individuals must master the basic tools of reading, writing, listening, and speaking in order that they may effectively explore the world about them and find their place in the scheme of society. Thus, everyone must learn how to inquire, observe, classify, make tentative judgments, experiment, analyze, and evaluate.

In this process of inquiry, which is the process of education, emphasis will be placed on the structure of the subject rather than on the content of the subject. That is, children will not learn by rote that two and two are four. They will, however, examine the process that leads to the conclusion that two and two are four, and they will learn how to apply the process to other situations in which the same or similar conclusions may then be drawn. Similarly, no program in science can give a child all the facts of a science. What the program can do is to teach the child the processes of science so that the child then has the equipment to pursue the facts.

In other words, the Educare Center will teach children *how to learn*. Children will be able to learn from their own concrete experiences, both external and internal, to observe and study the experiences in order to make and test judgments. Decision making, resolution, and judgment toward action will be essential learning steps.

Within Educare centers children will learn how to examine

and how to exercise freedom. They will be permitted to make decisions. Thus, they will be allowed to make wrong decisions —to experience failure, as it were. Experimentation, research, and learning are based on freedom of choice and on the right to fail. Children learn when they are permitted to examine their failures, to study their wrong choices and wrong judgments, and to retest new judgments and choices that grew out of their previous failures.

Within this framework I envision a new concept of secondary education. The dual system of vocational high schools versus academic high schools has already proven a failure. One in every twenty of the nation's youth who has the potential to graduate never does. The high school as it now exists must therefore be abolished.

Secondary education in Educare must serve all students: the intellectually gifted, the creative, the handicapped, the college-oriented, the vocationally oriented, and those who are still undecided. It would consist of a series of seven faculties: mathematics, art, science and technology, physical and health education, home economics, social sciences and language arts. Each faculty would present in depth the subject matter for which it is responsible. Moreover, the same content would be offered at many levels of difficulty. For example, every student in a literature class would be able to appreciate the poetry of Chaucer through different skill levels, some in the original Middle English, some in modern English, and some in a simplified version.

The faculties themselves would be comprehensive. They would not be departments offering merely a series of distinct and separate courses. In fact, the word *course* would be discarded and the phrase *study area* substituted. Study areas infringe one upon another. Stenography, for instance, involves spelling and formal grammar. Students would be taught to see these relationships within a faculty and to view a study area in its totality. Educational emphasis would be placed upon the interrelationships and interdependencies of one faculty upon another. For instance, the vocation of printing is generally taught today in a vocational high school. In the faculties, however, printing would be taught in the language arts faculty. In this way, students of printing would meet with students of language. Segregation by trade would give way to integration of study area. Thus, students would not only see the interrelationships among science, technology, and the arts, but they would also realize their own dependencies upon each other. Different vocational fields would be so allied that it would no longer be possible for students to be isolated by an artificially imposed track system.

A basic philosophy of the faculties would then state that students would not be trained to work in or for a specific industry. Skills, however, would be taught which could be applied to an industry. For example, students studying electronics and electricity could combine basic knowledges and skills that would be necessary for a comprehensive understanding of the field. Application to a career or a trade would come upon graduation, when a student might decide to go to college to study electrical engineering or work as a television repairman.

The faculties, however, would not train the student to be a repairman, although repairing a television might be part of a study area. Neither would the faculties prepare students for any specific industry, such as welding, cabinet making, or food trades. First, it is incumbent upon industry to do on-the-job training to suit their own specific purposes. Second, schools cannot be held responsible for industrial training when constantly changing technologies and increasing automation are quickly making current jobs obsolete. Too often, schools are teaching for jobs that no longer exist, while they are not teaching the skills necessary for many newly created jobs.

The educational philosophy that children must be taught how to think rather than what to think will permeate all levels of the Educare Center and will be in evidence in every classroom and play and recreation area. The content of what is taught cannot be considered as a conveyor belt contrivance whereby students reach out for bits of knowledge labeled for specific grades. Rather, opportunities for learning will be offered everywhere, in the laboratories and classrooms and lounges as well as in the play and recreation fields.

Unfortunately, many educators, parents, and children still believe that learning and play are separate, and that learning is always a completely conscious act; that is, that an individual is always aware of what he is learning and when he is learning. Research in learning, however, does not bear this out. Both children and adults *do* learn without always knowing that they are learning. Learning *does* take place many times through play; in fact, in the primary schools particularly, learning and play are actually synonymous.

The concept that teaching and learning take place only in a laboratory, lecture, or classroom, must be discarded. Toward this end, the words *cocurricular* and *extracurricular* will become obsolete, as will the word *curriculum*. All activities will become an integral part of the school program, thereby becoming a part of the organic structure of the Center. No educational activity should be relegated to the lesser status of being "extra" and therefore less significant. In most school systems, journalism, creative writing, drama, orchestra, choral singing or speaking, debating, sports, are now designated as "extra." A very limited number of students participates because the activities are usually not given full credit for graduation and because they are offered after the hours of the regular school session, when students have other obligations or interests.

In the Educare centers, all such activities and many more will be an integral part of the regular school day and made available to all students at several times of the day and week so that students can incorporate them into their programs. In order to accomplish this goal, both the school year and the school day will of necessity be lengthened, offering students the opportunity to attend during all hours of the day and evening as well as during the summer. And because work opportunities will also be offered during all hours of the day to those students in need of them, students will not find it a financial hardship to remain at the Center for as many hours as it becomes necessary to pursue all their interests. In the Educare classrooms, furniture will not be rooted to space, and space will not be rigidly designed, so that classrooms can expand or contract at the design and need of children.

Children can and will learn that they can alter, modify, affect, interact with each other and their environment, and hopefully control their individual and group destinies. Toward this end, the physical environment of the school has important implications for the learning process. Children who, from the tenderest age, can modify their classroom environment by changing the textures of walls, altering the size of a room, changing color schemes, modifying furniture or a playground, are learning that people can control their physical environment. Extending this learning into other areas, children later learn that they can control their own political, social, and economic world. Teaching children this immensely significant fact—that they do have a certain measure of control over their social, emotional, as well as physical environments—can be the single most important learning experience of their lives. It is the learning that gives them the skills of power.

An Educare Center will grow the way a person grows, assuming through the process an identity of its own. Each Educare Center, therefore, will be more than the sum of its parts, more than the sum of a collection of assistant teachers and their students; it will become a unity, a set, an extension of the personalities of the teachers and the children. Like the creation of an artistic endeavor that grows within the brain of its creator and is shaped into form, the Educare Center will develop its own paths, its own artistry, and its own forms. When it becomes an institution, when it has fully diagnosed itself and society, neither it nor society will be the same and, like the present schools, it will no longer serve a purpose. Educare centers therefore cannot replicate themselves. They should never reach the status of the status quo. If they do, they no longer will serve the purpose of meeting the needs of the current generation. If they do, they will only achieve the status of education as it is currently defined, "the systematic instruction, schooling or training given to the young in preparation for the work of life." How sad.

I was talking to a very good teacher at Livingston, Marcia Bernfeld, who reminded me of how teachers used to struggle endlessly to teach their children how to tell time. Teachers are still struggling, of course, but soon the struggle will become obsolete, because the skill will become obsolete.

"Have you looked lately?" she asked. "Everyone has a digital watch."

She was right, and if any traditionalist will argue, as undoubtedly they will, "But children have to learn to tell time," I would be compelled to ask, "When was the last time you had to read a sundial?"

In other words, replication of a model is not education, because education must center on meeting the needs and goals of a specific group of individuals at a specific time. Individuals divided by time and space, the time of history, the space of geography, are of necessity different. Their education must, therefore, be different.

Within Educare almost anyone can teach. Anyone, that is, who has something worthwhile to teach and who is human enough to accept human feelings and brave enough to explore them.

A world-renowned painter I know was not permitted to teach art in a public high school because he had not gone to college, did not have a college degree, and had not taken a teaching test. What a loss to students. This could not happen in an Educare Center.

Within Educare, teachers would say to students, "We will explore with you whatever you want to know. There will be no subjects that are restricted, no subjects deemed too insignificant or too profound. The students will determine for themselves what they want to know and what they need to know. There is a sharp distinction between the two. A part of learning will be devoted to making that distinction. Children have the capacity to make these decisions for themselves if they are taught how.''

The ''Teaching How'' is the teachers' role.

The concept of Educare, to lead forth, puts the teacher in the aggressive role of guiding students into finding their own values and making their own decisions. This does not mean that teachers must be devoid of their own values. They cannot. They must not. Even in sleep, our censoring mechanisms indicate we have values. Our nightmares are examples. We reprove ourselves and punish ourselves for that which we may truly desire and of which we are ashamed.

Teachers who believe that teachers must be objective are asking the impossible. There is no such thing. The fact that we work in schools indicates that we place a value on education. The job of the teacher, therefore, is to help students find their own values, not to impose her or his own or pretend objectivity. Unfortunately, teachers have generally shifted in two directions. There are those who believe that they have the key to righteousness. They preach ''thou shalt'' and ''thou shalt not.'' They have no doubt that their values are the correct ones. They may be. For them. They may not be for their students. Times and values are changing. Yet, they try to impose their morality on their students. On the other hand, there are those teachers who say that their only value is objectivity. They merely say ''Uh-huh'' to their students, neither approving nor disapproving of anything. They mold themselves on what they believe is the luxurious isolationism of Freud. As a result, their students do not see them as thinking, feeling people with viewpoints and values of their own. Thus, in trying to remain totally objective and keeping their values away from their students, they have succeeded only in becoming the nondescript transmitters of factual knowledge—which too often has been the only role, a colorless role, that teachers have assumed.

Teachers, however, have an obligation to their students to present themselves as people who have developed their own value systems. Thus, teachers should have the right to define their own values when such definitions are called for. They should have the right to discuss their political orientation and to give their views on modern-day moralities. These rights, however, do not give them the right to proselytize their values. The classroom is the appropriate place for a discussion of values in which the teacher's value is only one. The teacher's job, therefore, is to present all viewpoints, to permit discussion, and to give to students the right to their own decisions.

I call for the ideal. It is not easy, because in the presentation of values even the way the teacher asks a question may be a statement. We cannot escape values. We should not try. We should know they exist and always be alert to the dangers of unconscious proselytizing to one's viewpoint. Yet, why do we fear saying who we are? Children are not as delicate as we pretend they are. They can often tolerate intellectual and emotional differences better than their parents can. Parents often do not give their children credit for their perspicacity and parents often become upset at viewpoints expressed by teachers that are contrary to their own. Yet, if they had faith in their children and in their teaching of their own values, they would not so fear a dissenting viewpoint. Neither should teachers fear dissension.

Dissent is essential in education. It creates an environment of feeling and thinking. It creates an environment where everyone—teachers, students, and parents—are willing to define those elements in themselves that resent change. With a definition of the elements of dissension, education would be anything but dull. Educare centers would then be places for the conscious and the subconscious to be worked with and on.

They would be places of feelings and words, not suppressions and silences. They would be places where students are not only learners but consultants to teachers, teachers to other students, and workers. For their work, students must be paid. Work is not only economically desirable but educationally and psychologically desirable. Educare centers therefore are places of *thinking*, where decisions are made daily and where children are taught how. In a world where we all feel vulnerable, we want to be able to make personal decisions that will affect us, decisions that will show us that we really do have power over our own lives even though we do not have power over war, famine, disease, and politics.

We need to learn how to control our own destinies. And we can.

The answer to our problems lies then not in more money or in better educational theory or in better behaved children but in ourselves—in our ability to guide ourselves and to guide our children into making their own decisions, forming their own values.

Yet, we are plagued with pessimism. We feel defeated and so we let ourselves be defeated. The problem is that we do not know we are defeating ourselves.

Until we become aware of ourselves as possessing human, not superhuman, qualities, until we are alert to the dangers inherent in gratifying our needs at the expense of children, and until we lose our shame of our humanness, we will continue to destroy ourselves and the children we teach.

The teacher-idealist will emerge in the classroom as a practicing teacher only when the surface motivations are unfolded and the real nature of feelings, drives, and motivations is permitted to emerge. Only when teachers can admit to hating children as well as loving them, to needing power, to using the classroom as a means of getting that power, to fearing old age and needing the chronic presence of youth, will there be self-understanding, and only then will the destructive defensiveness of teachers disappear. Only then, when aggression, love, and power are used constructively in the classroom as potent forces, can education really succeed.

It is this undercover teacher whose needs must be explored, whose needs must be met without using the children, and whose security is not threatened by this digging process of self-examination who can change education.

The reformer is in every teacher somewhere below the surface.